Jung and Shamanism in Dialogue

Other Books in the Jung and Spirituality Series

C. Michael Smith

Jung and Shamanism in Dialogue

RETRIEVING THE SOUL/ RETRIEVING THE SACRED

Paulist Press
New York ✧ Mahwah, N.J.

Cover design by Kathy McKeen

Library of Congress Cataloging-in-Publication Data

Smith, C. Michael.
    Jung and shamanism in dialogue : retrieving the soul / retrieving the sacred / C. Michael Smith.
        p.   cm. — (Jung and spirituality series)
    Includes bibliographical references.
    ISBN 0-8091-3667-8 (alk. paper)
    1. Psychoanalysis and religion. 2. Jung, C. G. (Carl Gustav), 1875–1961. 3. Shamanism—Psychology. 4. Jungian psychology. 5. Psychotherapy. I. Title. II. Series: Jung and spirituality.
BF175.4.R44S64   1997
291.1'44–dc21   97-25336
                                                                          CIP

Published by Paulist Press
997 Macarthur Boulevard
Mahwah, New Jersey 07430

Printed and bound in the
United States of America

Contents

PART THREE
SOME IMPLICATIONS AND APPLICATIONS

ACKNOWLEDGEMENTS

A book such as this is indebted to many individuals, institutions, and disciplines, too numerous to mention all here. There are certain individuals who have played a special role in bringing this book to birth and I would like to mention them here. Special thanks to Robert L. Moore, the Jung and Spirituality series editor, who formerly as my teacher and doctoral advisor inspired a number of the insights, including the methodology, employed in this book. It was he who inspired the dialogic topic and encouraged me through the process of writing it. I must also extend an enormous "thank you" to my wife, Toni Smith, who read portions of the manuscript, gave helpful advice, and endured my absence for long periods of time while I was working on this project. It is she who is my most loyal source of encouragement and inspiration. Then there are those friends who contributed to this book in a variety of ways, either through numerous unofficial dialogues and supportive encouragement, or through editorial revisions: my Jungian analyst friends David J. Dalrymple, John R. Haule, Tess Castleman, Thomas Kapacinskas, E. C. Whitmont and Sylvia Brinton Perea, and my co-workers in practice Marc T. Milhander, Dennis Waite, Krista Matthews, and my manuscript secretary Lee Ann Parm, who resolved many technical difficulties for me. I wish to thank my students at the Chicago Theological Seminary and University of Chicago Hospitals, and wish also to thank Dani, Joe, Josh, Katie, Jason, and Eric for their enthusiastic cooperation. I must finally thank the staff at Paulist Press for their advice, patience, and help and express deepest gratitude to Bill Kelley, who provided his cottage at Lake Chapin so that I might enjoy the solitude necessary to produce such a work.

C. Michael Smith
Nub Lake
Summer, 1996

SERIES FOREWORD

The Jung and Spirituality series provides a forum for the critical interaction between Jungian psychology and living spiritual traditions. The series serves two important goals.

The first goal is: *To enhance a creative exploration of the contributions and criticisms that Jung's psychology can offer to spirituality.* Jungian thought has far-reaching implications for the understanding and practice of spirituality. Interest in these implications continues to expand in both Christian and non-Christian religious communities. People are increasingly aware of the depth and insight that a Jungian perspective adds to the human experiences of the sacred. And yet, the use of Jungian psychoanalysis clearly does not eliminate the need for careful philosophical, theological, and ethical reflection or for maintaining one's centeredness in a spiritual tradition.

The second goal is: *To bring the creative insights and critical tools of religious studies and practice to bear on Jungian thought.* Many volumes in the Jung and Spirituality series work to define the borders of the Jungian and spiritual traditions, to bring the spiritual dimensions of Jung's work into relief, and to deepen those dimensions. We believe that an important outcome of the Jung-Spirituality dialogue is greater cooperation of psychology and spirituality. Such cooperation will move us ahead in the formation of a postmodern spirituality, equal to the challenges of the twenty-first century.

Robert L. Moore
Series Editor

Introduction

This book attempts to present a cross-disciplinary dialogue between ancient and contemporary forms of shamanism and the analytical psychology of C.G. Jung, including post-Jungian theory and practice of Jungian analysts. The reasons for such a dialogue are several. Books on both shamanism and on Jungian psychology are currently receiving a growing readership, suggesting an interest in the underlying spiritual issues involved in psychopathology and various problems in human living. There is also a growing interest in the value of spiritual resources in psychotherapy and healing, and in living a healthful and balanced life. The 1990s have brought with them a renewed interest in living in ecological integrity with the planetary environment, recognizing the vital balances required to sustain life on the planet now and in the future. There are a plethora of books on spirituality, the paranormal, near-death and out-of-body experiences, aura reading, and various forms of spiritual and natural healing. Many of these areas of focus seem new to many people living in modern western society, but one who is familiar with the history of religions on the planet knows that these phenomena are not something new, but something known, experienced, and assumed in the great religions, and in the earlier forms of religious experience that preceded them. In the archaic past of human evolution, it was the shamans who first emerged on the scene as mediators of the sacred for their people and for purposes of survival and healing. The shamans developed the first technologies of the sacred and learned how to use it for healing and healthful living. For those of us living in the culture of modernity, the sacred has not been broadly assumed to be a fundamental resource for healing of physical and mental problems for a long time. Rather, most individuals have become accustomed to seeking help from the

1

secular and scientific health care professionals. Many who profess
a faith or who have developed a spiritual practice in modern western society have not seen a connection between their spiritual
practice and their mental and emotional problems. Western culture has kept spirituality and health problems in separate
domains. Perhaps this has been largely due to the kind of dichoto-
mous assumptions exemplified in Descartes' philosophy, in which
the mental and spiritual domains are separate and unrelated to
the natural and physical domains. People living in western societies tend to think troubled individuals who suffer from schizophrenia, bi-polar disorder, from addictions and depression, are
suffering from syndromes that are genetically inherited or are
caused solely by organic factors such as chemical imbalances.
While not rejecting the importance of physical factors in the origins of sickness, one of the reasons for this book is to demonstrate another way of thinking of them that respects their natural
organic and psycho-spiritual basis. Both the psychology of C.G.
Jung and the view of traditional shamanism have affirmed both
components of sickness, even though they both give priority to
the psycho-spiritual pole of experience. Both systems of healing
address the bodily components of illness through the importance
of ritual, dance, movement, expressiveness, image, aromatic
scent, and medicines although they do not place their emphasis
in equal degree. Both address the human soul as a reality that
interfaces with the body and so is partly dependent upon it, and
partly independent of it. Both Jung and shamanism view the soul
as being partly directed by organic and social influences, and
partly free to direct such processes. As technologies of healing,
both disciplines speak to the soul and body, and draw upon the
sacred as the ultimate therapeutic resource. For the shaman this
resource is often directed through power animals, spirit guides,
and other familiars. In Jungian therapeutics, this resource is typically understood in terms of the deep center of the psyche, a
numinous centering point of meaning and direction, and the
totality of psychological contents at the same time. For Jung, the
real therapy, as he conceived it, was the approach to the numinous. Jung designated the deep and numinous center of the psyche the archetypal Self. It may be viewed as the manifestation of

the divine presence within the psyche, or of the "image of God" within the psyche. It typically manifests itself in a variety of forms and personifications, some of them bearing close resemblance to the shaman's spirit guides and familiars.

One reason why Jungian psychology is becoming so popular is that it offers a way of understanding oneself and one's problems in living that is as much spiritual as it is psychological. Jungian psychology offers a way of self-understanding that gives a place to the sacred (and the numinous) in grounding and directing one's life from a center of meaning and knowledge greater than the individual's ego can provide. Perhaps the emergence of interest in shamanism within modern western culture has also arisen as an alternative way to meet the same needs for meaning and for healing and healthful living in a cosmos that is ultimately experienced as sacred and friendly. If both Jungian psychology and shamanism are increasingly appealing to more and more people living within modern western society, then it may be worth taking a closer look at both disciplines to examine more carefully what forms of self-understanding and healing they are offering, and to see if they can be brought together in some intentional and collaborative way that may increase the place of their insights and methods in the diagnosis and treatment of modern western forms of illness. Perhaps the most salient common feature of shamanism and Jungian psychology is that they both offer a way of soulful living that takes its direction from spirit, a transcendent dimension of wisdom and power. For Jungians this transcendent dimension within the psyche, referred to as the archetypal Self, may be conceived as including whatever the individual considers to be ultimate reality, or as somehow being included in the divine life: a kind of "Atman" presence. For shamanism, the transcendent source of wisdom and power has typically manifested itself in some type of spirit guide or power animal, although this may yet be a manifestation of whatever the shaman considers as ultimate reality. Both Jung and shamanism offer considerable possibilities for helping the modern western health care profession understand how to draw upon the sacred for healing purposes. Both can be transformed through a mutually respectful encounter between their wisdoms, experiences, and technologies for healing. Perhaps we may receive an expanded view of the possibilities in psychotherapy, and perhaps shamanism may become more psychologically knowledgeable in a way that expands its own therapeutic repertoire. Perhaps such an encounter can lead to a spiritually more resourceful understanding of how to help individuals experiencing serious problems in living in a way that may gain increasing public legitimation. These are some of the questions, and hopes, that motivate the following study.

PLAN AND ORGANIZATION

In approaching our subject matter we shall be engaging in a method of relating the two disciplines that can be considered a dialogue. In a true dialogue (conversation) each partner must listen well to the other, paying attention to what is articulated and unarticulated (but perhaps implied) in the other's position. This is followed by a critical response based upon careful and sympathetic listening. We will be using such a method, in the pages which follow, for bringing the two disciplines into cross-disciplinary relationship with each other. Each fundamental aspect of shamanism will be reviewed and will be compared and contrasted with corresponding and differing fundamentals of Jungian psychology, and vice versa. Some resulting implications and/or problems will be noted.

The discussion is divided into three parts. In Part One, the basic elements of classic shamanism are reviewed in some detail. In Chapter One the operational definition of shamanism is given, followed by discussions of fundamental elements of such shamanic phenomena as the call and initiation, shamanic cosmology, and the importance of image and myth in sickness and healing, shamanic paraphernalia, and use of percussion. Chapter One also discusses the basic diagnostic and therapeutic conceptions of shamanism, of soul loss and retrieval, and of extraction. North and South American variants are distinguished from Eurasian variants. The question of the mental health of the shaman is also reviewed. In Chapter Two, "Technician of the Sacred", the importance of the sacred and of ritual structure and leadership in shamanic healing is explored. This discussion reviews phenomenological understandings of the sacred as it manifests itself across cultures, and insofar as it is employed in shamanic healing. The work of Rudolf Otto, Gerhardus Van der Leeuw, and Mircea Eliade provides a set of compatible frameworks for understanding the experience of the sacred, and its healing power. The work of anthropologist Victor Turner on ritual process, and of Jungian analyst and theorist Robert L. Moore on ritual structure and leadership, helps us to understand the transformative power of shamanic ritual and psychotherapeutic process. This discussion is intended not only to inform us of the nature and power of shamanic rituals, but also to make more apparent the possibilities of good ritual process and leadership in psychotherapeutic treatment. It can also serve as a lens through which the therapeutic process may be observed in a cross-disciplinary way.

Part Two, entitled "Jung and Shamanism", explores the life and work of C.G. Jung, and draws comparisons and contrasts with shamanism. This discussion is kicked off by first examining the basis of Jung's work in his own life experience. Thus Chapter Three, "Jung the Wounded Healer," examines Jung's life as it would that of a shaman. It explores some of the fundamental shamanic elements in his life, giving attention to his early childhood formation and to his midlife crisis, and offers a kind of shamanic pattern of wounding, call, and initiation as parallels— but also giving attention to the differences. Special attention is given to Jung's break with Sigmund Freud and the resulting loss of identity and breakdown in which he made his *nekyia*, a descent into the unconscious, in which Jung encountered the spirits, developed a relation with a spirit guide, and had extraordinary visions, some of which were prophetic of his future life, mission, and work. Jung described his midlife crisis as a condition of soul loss and recovery. Out of his recovery he obtained a vision for his life's work, and a new sense of purpose which he committed himself to for the benefit of himself, but also for his tribe (western culture).

Chapter Four is entitled "Jung's Theory of the Soul". In this chapter the fundamentals of Jung's theory are discussed and the basic elements of Jung's mature psychology are given, followed by comparisons and contrasts with shamanism. The layers of the collective unconscious, the role of the archetypes, the importance of the *numina* and spirits in healing, and the importance of image and symbol are brought into dialogue with the corresponding elements in classic shamanism. The role of complexes, the "little devils," in illness and therapeutics is discussed and then compared and contrasted with shamanism. The central role of the archetypal Self, the sacred center of Jungian psychology, is identified as the basis for healthful living, and the role it plays in illness and healing is explored. This is compared with the role of the sacred in shamanic therapeutics. Chapter Five, "Jung's Interpretation of Shamanism," reviews what Jung specifically had to say about shamanism, as found in his collected works. Jung's view of shamanism as an archaic individuation process is surrounded by parallels from alchemy, in which Jung looks at certain shamanic phenomena such as sacred stones, the world tree, and the celestial bride as manifestations of the archetypal Self. Various aspects of shamanic psychology and functioning, such as the shaman as trickster, shape-shifter, and epistemological mediator, are explored. Jung's own statements about soul loss, possession, and exorcistic rites are compared and contrasted with the perspective of classic shamanism. From Jung's perspective, this chapter sums up the underlying archetypal structure of shamanism and shamanic ritual process.

Part Three, "Some Implications and Applications," consists of three chapters which explore several contemporary theoretical implications and potential applications resulting from these discussions. Chapter Six, "Dissociation, Possession, and Soul Loss," gives extensive discussion of the similarities of modern dissociation theory with shamanic theories of soul loss. Tracing a history of dissociation and comparing and contrasting the experiences of shamans and individuals suffering from multiple personality, the author seeks to show one area where the dialogue between classic shamanic resources and Jungian psychology and therapeutics can be most beneficial. Two examples of the use of shamanic resources in dissociative and other mental disorders today are given. One example reviews the treatment methods of psychiatrist Colin A. Ross, M.D., who interfaces hypnotherapeutic methods with shamanic metaphor in his treatment of dissociative disorders. The second example explores the soul retrieval work of Sandra

Ingerman, a contemporary white urban shaman and former psychotherapist. Ingerman also relates her understandings of soul loss to psychological dissociation, and sees soul loss as widespread in modern culture. Not only does she see shamanic soul retrieval as helpful in the dissociative disorders, but sees it as effective in treating a wide variety of disorders related to trauma, shock, accident, and injury. She includes addictive disorders, co-dependency, and depression amongst the examples of troubles which classic soul retrieval is effective with. Although practicing purely as a shaman today, Ingerman is careful to acknowledge the importance of counseling and psychotherapy in helping patients integrate the retrieved souls and soul-parts. Both Ross and Ingerman have provided examples of how the resources of shamanism may be useful in treating various forms of mental disorder and psychopathology in contemporary western society. The examination of their work is then followed by Jungian reflection upon their work in an effort to understand these hybrid forms of contemporary shamanism from the perspective of Jungian and post-Jungian theory. The chapter ends with a discussion of a problematic and intractable form of pathologic dissociation associated with demonic possession and noxious alters. The insights of anthropologist Felicitas Goodman and Jungian psychology are used to provide additional understanding of how well-formed therapeutic ritual can be especially effective in treating such serious and potentially life-threatening forms of disorder, which are often refractory to the more conventional psychiatric and psychotherapeutic methods.

How well-formed therapeutic ritual can be so effective is the subject matter of Chapter Seven. "The Power of Ritual, Image, and Archetype" takes up this problem by drawing attention once again to the importance of image as a potential cause or cure of illness, and correlates these understandings with data from neurobiology and post-Jungian theory of archetypal structures and processes. These discussions necessitate a broadening into a multi-disciplinary discussion that includes perspectives from medical anthropology, neuroanatomy, psychophysiology, cancer research, and neuro-linguistic programming in an effort to further understand the illness-causing and health-promoting powers of image and ritual. Post-Jungian theorists and researchers such as Anthony Stevens, Ernst Rossi, Douglas Gillette, and Robert L. Moore are examined for additional insight into the relation between archetypes and brain structure, with special attention to the implications of image and ritual in shamanic healing and psychotherapy. The chapter is concluded with a review of the work of Robert L. Moore and Douglas Gillette on the relation between the shaman as ritual elder and the magus archetype.

Chapter Eight, "Implications for the Future", moves beyond the focus on classic soul loss/retrieval and dissociation to a more fundamental problem in western society: loss of the sacred from the assumptive world. This chapter seeks to argue that soul retrieval in itself is insufficient and incomplete when the underlying view of the world is profane and secular. Shamanic soul retrieval is a psycho-spiritual form of healing that only makes sense if the sacred is presupposed in the assumptive world of both patient and healer. The importance of the assumptive world is explored from a Jungian perspective, and the argument is advanced that retrieving the sacred is necessary in western culture generally, and in the health care culture of western society specifically. Retrieving the sacred is an important part of retrieving the soul in post-modern western society.

Part One
SHAMANISM

Chapter One

Overview of Classic Shamanism

DEFINITIONS

The term *shamanism* is commonly used to refer to a complex of practices of a magico-religious character concerned primarily with what may be called, in our modern western idiom, psychospiritual and psychosomatic healing. The word *shaman* has been derived from the Russian language through Siberian Tungisic *s'aman;* its precise and original meaning is uncertain. But there are corresponding terms in other cultures, for example the Yakut *ojuna,* the Mongolian *buga* (*boga*), the Turko-Tartar *kam,* and Vedic *sram.* The latter Vedic term may give us a clue to its meaning, *sram* = to heat oneself or practice austerities.[1] Although its ultimate root may turn out not to be Siberian, it refers to a complex of related practices indigenous to Siberia and Central Asia, with cognate words denoting specific magico-religious practices in which malignant spirit powers are overcome with the aid of more powerful helping or tutelary spirits.

Whatever its etymological derivation, the word *shaman* has been broadly used to denote a specific group of healers in diverse tribal cultures and traditional societies who have been also previously referred to by names such as medicine man, medicine woman, witch doctor, sorcerer, magician, and, in some cases, seer, prophet, witch, and priest or priestess. It was customary, until the major study of historian of religions Mircea Eliade on shamanism,[2] to confuse these various conceptions and practices with shamanism. Eliade sought a more limited or restrictive definition by which to distinguish shamanism from other forms of healing presupposing the sacred. Since Eliade's monumental work on shamanism, many scholars in the fields of cultural anthropology and cultural psychology have adopted Eliade's more restricted, if complex, definition. Eliade's first definition is that shamanism = technique of ecstasy. This is to say that a distinguishing feature of the shaman is that he or she practices by means of ecstasy or trance. But Eliade is careful to point out that ecstasy is employed by other healers, magicians, seers, mystics, and witches. The shamanic ecstasy is distinguished further by a specific ecstatic method which belongs to the shaman, and to the shaman alone. This is the trance state by which the shaman's soul is believed to leave his or her body and travel or ascend to the upperworld or descend to the lowerworld. There it encounters spirits (malignant and benign), souls of the dead (e.g., ghosts of human and animal creatures), and lost souls which have wandered away or been stolen. There the shaman encounters helping spirits as well. A further distinction is made, however, between the shaman's relation to the spirits, and those of other individuals who may be possessed by them, or call upon them. Eliade notes that in both the primitive and modern world there are individuals who profess to have a relation to the spirits, to call upon them, to become a medium, a channeler, whether they are possessed by them or control them.[3] In defining the shaman's relation to the helping spirits he notes that the shaman differs from a possessed person in that he or she controls his or her spirits, and in that the shaman is a human being who "is able to communicate with the dead, demons, and nature spirits, without thereby becoming their instrument."[4] With respect to healing also, the shaman employs a unique ecstatic method, although there are other medicine men and women and healers who employ the sacred for healing purposes. Thus, not every ecstatic or every healer can be considered a shaman, although the shaman may be considered a medicine man/woman or ecstatic.

There are other anthropologists and psychologists who have taken a broader definition of shamanism, referring more to the fact that the shaman is a healer or ecstatic who enters into altered states of consciousness at will, and this without Eliade's distinguishing features of the descent or ascent to the lower and upper worlds, or the commanding of spirits.[5] This broader definition permits the including of any ecstatic practitioners who enter controlled altered states of consciousness, and may be more applicable to the complex forms of shamanism found in many native North American ritual healers or medicine men and women, particularly in the Southwest, Plains, and Eastern and Southeastern Woodlands. One of the major distinctions between Siberian and southern Asian forms of shamanism, and North American shamanism, rides, to some extent, upon Eliade's more restricted definition. But it should be noted that certain North American groups among the Eskimo, Northwest Coast Indians, and Ojibway fit very precisely Eliade's limited criteria.

CLASSIC SHAMANISM

Given Eliade's restricted definition, many scholars consider shamanism to be preeminently a phenomenon of Siberia and Inner Asia. There are other reasons for this attributed preeminence. Although shamanism may be central or peripheral to various societies, throughout the regions of northern and southern Asia the life of local societies has centered upon shamanism. This does not mean that the shaman is the one and only manipulator of the sacred for religious or healing purposes, nor does it mean that he or she completely usurps these fields, for often other religious, medical, herbal, and mystical functionaries exist alongside shamanism. In many tribes, for example, a sacrificing priest (sometimes a priestess) co-exists alongside the shaman. The Asian shaman may even be an officiary of a religious or monastic tradition in some cultures (e.g., a Bon Po shaman). Among the Buddhist lamaseries of Tibet, for example, are certain lamas who are known also as shamanic healers. Sudhir Kakar, the psychoanalyst and cultural psychologist, documents the case of a Buddhist monastic leader (the Lama of Macleodgani) who is also a shaman known for his ability to heal various mental disorders through shamanic methods. The idiom of this healer is part shamanistic and part Buddhist; the methods of diagnosis and treatment employing this mixed idiom are shamanic.[6] At any rate, the shaman remains a dominating figure, and it is he or she alone who, throughout Asia, is master of ecstatic experience *par excellence.*

METHODS OF RECRUITMENT

The chief methods of recruitment of shamans are two: 1) hereditary transmission, and 2) spontaneous vocation (or call). There are also various individuals who seek to become shamans by their own free will (questing), or by the will of the clan (often when no other candidates are available). These self-made shamans, in Asia at least, are generally considered to be less powerful than those who have been called or who have inherited the profession.[7] However the shaman may be selected, he or she must receive two types of instruction before he or she will be recognized or legitimated as a shaman. The first type of instruction may be termed ecstatic, coming primarily though dreams and trances. In addition to this there must be instruction in traditional shamanic methods (ecstatic techniques, healing methods and techniques, ritual formulas, chants, amulets, etc.,) of relevance to the culture, the names and functions of the spirits, the genealogy and mythology of the tribe, and the "secret language". This two-fold instruction by the spirits and the master shamans is considered an initiation, which may be public or which may occur totally in the neophyte's ecstatic experience. Thus the absence of a public confirmatory initiation ritual does not imply the absence of initiation, for "the latter can perfectly well occur in a dream".[8] This latter type is found, for example, among the Rocky Mountain tribes of North America, where shamanic power can be inherited, but then the transmission "always takes place through an ecstatic experience".[9]

SHAMANISM: COSMOLOGY AND RELIGION

Shamanism is not itself a religion, although it constitutes an original form of religious experience. It is more accurate to say that shamanism is a set of techniques and an ideology which becomes attached to a religion (or tribal mythology) and which has its own history and system of beliefs. As such, shamanism must always be considered within the context of the religion and the society which it serves. Shamanism is a very ancient and archaic form of religious experience and a healing profession with elements discernible the world over from Paleolithic times to the present. As societies and cultures have evolved into more complex groupings or civilizations adopting the cosmologies of the great religions (e.g., Buddhism, Islam, Christianity), shamanic elements are still discernible, sometimes in strikingly complete form; at other times just fragments of shamanic imagery, belief, or practice remain. However, in the more restricted form of the shaman as one who enters an ecstatic trance in which the soul leaves the body and journeys to the underworld or upperworld, there are certain forms of cosmology (as well as religion and society) which correspond to such belief and practice.

The shamanic flight presupposes a sacred cosmology, often objectified in tribal myths and beliefs which envision the sacred or ultimate reality as structured in what might be called an archetypally ordered, three-storied cosmology. This cosmology entails the concept of the earth, which is our world and for the shaman a plane of non-ordinary reality. There is also the upperworld (sky world) as the abode of helping spirits, angelic beings, and the like, and the underworld below, with its ghosts, ancestral and malignant spirits, and various mysterious places.[10] The vocation of the shaman as one who breaks through the various planes in consciousness presupposes the ability to move between these realms at will, discovering and reporting their structure and nature, and drawing upon their resources for healing and restoring order for the people. Often these realms are objectified in art, song, myth, or ideograms which illustrate these other dimensions. The shaman's vocation is to break through these planes for the purpose of establishing effective communication between the three cosmic zones. There are a variety of symbolic expressions used to indicate or thematize the path, access, or channel of communication with the spirit realms.

IMAGINAL COSMOLOGY: INVERTING MYTH AS MAP AND GUIDE

For most members of tribal society, there is belief in these dimensions, but there is little personal experience of them, except in the dramatic forms enacted in public ritual and ceremony. Belief in upper and lower worlds may be literal, but something not explored in ecstasy. For the average member of a traditional society, the mythic three-storied cosmology serves as a "sacred canopy" (Peter Berger) to be believed in and lived in accord with. It is the source of collective and social origins, of their ethical foundations, and serves to guide lives through the life-cycle. However, for the shaman, it is much more; it is a private and personal, rather than mere public, experience. The shaman typically takes the mythic cosmology of his or her culture and "inverts it" (Eliade), that is, turns it into an inward geography, using it as an itinerary and guide in his or her journeys to the upper and lower regions of non-ordinary reality. There are two psychologically related reasons for this:

1) The shaman's journey employs the imagination, and the use of myth as inner map gives the shaman a way of imagining non-ordinary reality, so that he or she may move about intentionally in it.

2) In trance, the mind tends to be subject to distractions and wanderings. By having an inner map, the shaman has a rich and complex guide which helps him or her keep focused upon the task, and prevents aimless mental wandering. The shaman's use of ecstatic trance is always controlled and intentional. This does not mean it is over-controlled or lacks spontaneity. If the shaman enters a tunnel and travels down into the lower world to find an illness-causing spirit, he or she does not know what sort of spirit he or she will find, nor in what context.

MAGICAL TREE AND AXIS MUNDI

Eliade notes that some variation of an *axis mundi,* a central axis which links the upper and lower worlds with our world, and supports it, is often symbolized by a cosmic tree, a sacred mountain, or a ritual pillar.[11] These representations are given ritual expression in shamanic rites (especially in public shamanic initiation rites). For example, among the Ojibway of northern Michigan and southern Canada, the *Tcisaki* diviner shaman constructs a very small conjuring lodge out of three pine tree poles. One tree with its branches is extended higher than the others, symbolizing the cosmic axis, the path by which the *manitou* (sacred spirits) may enter the conjurer's lodge.[12] Sometimes the world tree is mounted in public initiatory rituals permitting the initiate to demonstrate shamanic prowess. As an interior psychological aid (or tool), the shaman's magical tree is imaginally seen, being used in trance for climbing up to the hole in the sky, where the shaman can pull himself or herself up into the sky world, or for descending into the lower world through its roots.

HOW THE SHAMAN IMAGINES DISEASE

The shaman's conception of the cause of illness is imagined in terms of spirits and deities, which, existing in the upper and lower worlds, can affect human beings on earth (our world) for good or ill. Shamanic therapeutics begins with a two-fold process, that of imaging the cause, and that of actively imaging the cure. That is, it begins with a diagnosis (determining the nature and cause of the illness imaged as pathogenic spirit or object), followed by a corresponding curative image (rectification, restoration, or cure by a helping spirit). Typically the shaman will go into ecstatic trance to determine whether or not the soul is impaired by intrusion of pathogenic objects or spirits projected into the body by sorcerers (black shaman), or by offended spirits. Once the cause has been determined, the therapeutic method is imaged and employed. According to anthropologist and shamanic scholar Michael Harner, there are two main or primary methods of shamanic healing: 1) restoring something which is lacking in the person who is ill, or 2) removing something that does not belong. The latter therapeutic does not require the shamanic journey, and is usually employed for a more localized illness. That is, it consists in working here in the middleworld, typically using divination techniques and moving back and forth from what Harner calls "ordinary" and "non ordinary reality" in order to see the illness and remove it by specific methods.[13] Typically the shamanic efforts are focused on locating the foreign or pathogenic object in the body of the afflicted, and then extracting it, usually by the technique of sucking.

The restoring method does typically involve the shamanic journey to retrieve the lost soul. According to Harner the individual who has lost his/her soul is at death's door, comatose, or in a suicidal state of despair or severe depression; that is, he or she has lost a vital principle or power. The shaman then typically journeys into the other world to retrieve the lost soul or power and restore it to the person.[14] Henri F. Ellenberger, in a more detailed effort, has listed five types of shamanic disease theory and their corresponding therapeutics. They are as follows: 1) "disease object intrusion", the therapy for which is "extraction of the disease"; 2) "loss of soul", the therapy for which is finding and restoring it; 3) "spirit intrusion", the therapy for which may be exorcism (depossession) if it be by a spirit entity, mechanical extraction if it be an object, or transference of the foreign spirit somewhere else; 4) "breach of taboo", the therapy for which consists typically of confessions and ritual propitiation; and 5) "sorcery", which requires a counter-magic therapeutic.[15]

IMAGINATION AS CAUSE AND CURE OF SICKNESS

Viewed in terms indigenous to shamanism, illness is most frequently caused by invading spirits. Viewed in the language of psychology, spirits are perceived inwardly as images. The image, according to Jeanne Achterberg, may be viewed as both the cause and cure of sickness in shamanism.[16] This is true whether the sickness manifests itself physically or psychologically and spiritually. The shaman, in trance, diagnoses by entering an imaginal geography intensified vividly by ritual sonic and rhythmic driving, often through percussion (drums, rattles, monotonous chants, etc.). There, pathogenic spirits/objects are depicted, that is, imaged, and therapeutic action taken by means of images. Anthropologist Janet Siskind gives an example of the way Sharanahua shamans employ therapeutics on the patient's belief system by means of shamanically constructed images related to tribal mythic figures and themes. Siskind notes that Sharanahua patients typically report dreams that, interestingly enough, overlap with the diagnostic/healing categories of the shaman's songs. The shaman evidently selects from among the patient's reported dreams those images that fit his or her classification. Typically only one or two dream images are reported by the patient to the shaman. According to Siskind's analyses, most of the images or symbols in the patient's dreams echo the myths and stories of the culture. Siskind reports the case of Tomuha, treated by the shaman Ndaishiwaka, the patient's brother-in-law. The case illustrates the Sharanahua shaman's way of working with the imagination, of the patient and himself, to effect a cure.

> Ndaishiwaka's sister-in-law, Tomuha, was vomiting; her liver hurt, and she strongly wanted to die. Her father-in-law went to bring Ndaishiwaka (he was working away from the village at the time). The next morning he arrived at the village. He asked Tomuha what she had dreamed, and she described seeing a high bank of the river. In her dreams she climbed up and sat there alone. The shaman sang about a high bank of the river. Tomuha was slightly better the next day but still very ill, so he went to get ayahuasca, cooked it, and drank it that night. He saw the high bank and Tomuha sitting alone. A *Culina* is coming near her and he says, "You will die, Tomuha", and throws a magical substance into her so that she vomits and cries out. "But I am there", says the shaman, "and I am shaking my spear, and the *Culina* is frightened and runs away. And you will not die, Tomuha". Then the shaman sang about *dori*, the magical substance. He saw Tomuha coming up the river, alone in a canoe. She was cured.[17]

Suskind points out that Peruvian images underlie a piece of Sharanahua belief, that strangers are dangerous. The *Culina* thus represents the image of direct and pathogenic malice. The shaman speaks to and works with the patient in the language of the imagination, evoked through the curing song. We may conjecture, from a psychological standpoint, that by acting upon pathogenic images produced by the patient, the shaman is able to evoke a healing response at the neurophysiological and unconscious psychological levels of experience. As we shall later see, one of the major areas of convergence between shamanism and Jungian psychology has to do with the value of images. Jung placed a great importance upon images ("Image is psyche"). The therapeutics of the soul, for Jung, involves listening to the psyche speak through images, and responding to the psyche in terms of images.[18]

Like the shaman, modern psychotherapists often work with imagery to effect healing responses. The employment of imagery in psychotherapy has been part of the history of depth psychology. There is great affinity between the uses of imagery suggested in clinical hypnosis today, and that employed by shamans traditionally. Another good example of the importance of images in shamanic therapeutics can be observed in traditional Southeastern Cherokee shamanism. The Cherokee shaman traditionally employed a color imagery symbol system for what may be psychologically understood as hypnotically altering the patient's experience. In order to gain a better sense of the interplay of cultural, shamanic, and personal imagery in shamanism, we shall look at the Cherokee system of imagery used in diagnosis and healing.

CHEROKEE USE OF IMAGERY IN CONCEIVING ILLNESS AND CURE

Traditionally, for Southeastern Cherokee Indians, the most common forms of illness were conceived as being caused by animal spirits retaliating against humans for their disrespect. The depiction of the causes and methods of curing illness in imaginal terms was systematic. For example, if a hunter forgot to show respect by making appropriate prayers and petitions to an animal whose life he took by asking its permission and explaining his reasons, then the animal spirit of that species, for example, Bear, would seek after him and afflict him with illness. The ritual formulae (chants/songs) of the Cherokee shaman addressed these diseases and the offended spirits believed to cause them in a language of images designed to effectively attack the pathogenic images. The Southeastern Cherokee myth which recounts the origins of sickness and cure illustrates the role which images played in shamanic therapeutic conceptions.

> In the old days the members of the brute creation were gifted with speech, and dwelt in amity with the human race. The increase of humanity, however, crowded the animals into the

forests and desert places of the earth, and upon the inven-
tion of lethal weapons, man commenced the wholesale
slaughter of the beasts for the sake of their flesh and skins,
and trod upon the lesser animals with contempt. The animals, driven to despair, resolved upon retributive measure.
The first to meet were the bears, headed by old White Bear,
their chief. After several speakers had denounced mankind
for the bloodthirsty behavior, war was unanimously decided
upon, and the nature of human weapons was discussed. It
was discovered that the bow and arrow were the principal
human weapons, and it was resolved to fashion a specimen to
see if they could not turn man's weapons against himself. A
piece of wood suitable for the purpose was procured, and
one of the bears sacrificed himself to provide them with gut
for the bowstring. After the bow was completed it was discovered that the claws of the bears spoiled their shooting. One
of the bears, however, cut his claws, and succeeded in hitting
the mark. But the chief, the old White Bear, interposed with
the remark that the claws were necessary to climb trees with,
and that all would have to starve were they to cut them off.

The next council was held by the deer, under their
chief, Little Deer. They resolved to inflict rheumatism upon
every hunter who should slay one of them unless he asked a
pardon in a suitable manner. They gave notice of this decision to the nearest settlement of Indians, and instructed them
on how to make propitiation when forced by necessity to kill
one of the deer folk. So when a deer is slain by the hunter, the
Little Deer runs to the spot, and bending over the blood
stains, asks the spirit of the deer if it has heard the prayer of
the hunter for pardon. If the reply be "yes", all is well, and the
Little Deer departs; but if the answer is in the negative, he
tracks the hunter until he is in his cabin and strikes him with
rheumatism, so that he becomes a helpless cripple. Sometimes the hunters who have not learned the proper formula
for pardon attempt to turn aside the Little Deer from his pursuit by building fire behind them in the trail.

The fishes and reptiles then held a joint council, and
arranged to haunt those human beings who tormented
them, with hideous dreams of serpents twining around
them, and of eating fish which had become decayed.[19]

Lastly, the birds and insects, with the smaller animals,
gathered together for a similar purpose, the grubworm pre-

siding over the meeting. Each in turn expressed an opinion, and the consensus was against mankind. They devised and named various diseases.

When the plants, which were friendly to man, heard what had been arranged by the animals, they determined to frustrate their evil designs. Each tree, shrub, herb, down even to the grasses and mosses, agreed to furnish a remedy for some one of the diseases named. Thus did medicine come into being, and thus the plants came to furnish the antidote to counteract the evil wrought by the revengeful animals. When the shaman is in doubt as to what treatment to apply for the relief of a patient, the spirit of the plant suggests a fitting remedy.[20]

The rationale for Cherokee shamanism rests upon this myth of the origins of sickness and healing. The cause of illness is imaged in terms of offended animal spirits, and cure is imaged in terms of sympathetic animal and vegetation spirits. The symbolism of the colors and the four directions added another component to the mythic imagery. For example, if one offended an animal spirit, then the shaman will call upon the right counteracting spirit from the four directions with their respective colors. That is, a greater healing image is called upon to destroy a pathogenic image. Cherokee therapeutics presupposes a kind of sympathetic magic, which operated by association. A piece of rope, for example, could symbolize a snake because of the similarities of shape and length. When it comes to illness, the pathogenic color and animal spirit type then indicate the type of therapeutic spirit and its color which must be called upon to extract, obliterate, or counter the destructive spirit. In some cases all colors and directions were used in rituals which look remarkably like modern hypnosis in their suggestiveness and strategic thoroughness. For example, to remove a rheumatism the shaman diagnoses its cause, in this case the intrusion caused by Little Deer, an archetypal deer god; then the shaman calls upon the agency of some powerful animal spirit which is the enemy of the deer—this is usually the dog or wolf. Lewis describes one such ritual:

The shaman thus invokes Red War Dog, who begs him to come to the assistance of the sick man (chants). This spirit is supposed to arrive and carry off with him a portion of the disease in his mouth. The Blue, Black, and White Dogs of the other lands [directions] situated at the remaining cardinal points are also successively invoked, and lastly, the White Terrapin of Wahala is prayed to remove what the dogs have left. He is supposed to do so and the shaman declares that a cure has been accomplished.[21]

We could say that the shamanic conception of cause and cure of illness, as illustrated in this Cherokee example, presupposes the notion of images as being either potential slayers or healers. The importance of images in shamanic healing, as in medical and psychotherapeutic healing today, can hardly be underestimated. The tools of the medical profession also have an image aspect. A pill, whatever its biochemical properties, is psychologically experienced as an image of something that will heal, help, or bring relief. Placebo studies have confirmed that something that looks like medicine can be therapeutically effective, and patients who report that their medications are working before they've had time to be medically effective suggest that therapeutic images can have a dramatic beneficial effect upon mind, brain, and body.[22] As we continue with our discussion of other basic features of shamanism, of shamanic tools, methods, and ritual, it is important to remain mindful of the primacy of images in these other features.

SHAMANIC SPECIALIZATION

In many tribal and traditional cultures there are distinctions and classifications of shamans, according to their gifts and specialized functions. There are what are called "white" (benevolent) shamans, and "black" (malevolent) shamans, although the latter type are now more commonly called sorcerers, and appear to be an aberration. There are shamans who diagnose and treat illness, and there are those who are specialized as diviners or conjurors, and weather controllers, and who do not perform curing rituals. Often, however, the shaman encompasses all of these roles and functions.

Although the imagination plays an abundant role in shamanic experience and practice, few shamans would want to say that they were dealing with images. This would be a modern psychological way of speaking. Certainly if spirits are viewed from a psychological disciplinary angle they manifest themselves as images. The traditional shaman prefers to speak of these manifestations in their own sacred/animistic idiom as spirits and other numinous entities. Traditional shamans would also not accept an understanding that they were merely projecting mental contents and images of their own psyches, although there is often awareness of such projection. Michael Harner asserts that shamans believe that the mind is used to pass through itself into that which is not-mind, not personal psyche, into something which is beyond the personal mind.[23] The cosmos is viewed as something far greater than the personal mind, something which can be assessed through the mind, through images.

ARE SHAMANS CRAZY? SHAMANISM AND PSYCHOPATHOLOGY

Anthropologists, psychoanalysts, and other scholars studying the strange behavior of shamanism have debated whether or not the shaman is psychopathological. Certainly illness is often associated with the shamanic call and initiation. Until more recent years many scholars believed that the shaman was always psychopathologically ill, perhaps suffering from nervous disorders such as hysteria, epilepsy, or even from a psychosis. According to Eliade the problem was wrongly formulated. First he argues that it is not always true that shamans are, or always have to be, neuropathics. Second, those among them who were ill became shamans precisely because they were able to effect a cure of themselves. Finally, Eliade claims, "To obtain the gift of shamanizing presupposes precisely the solution of the psychic crisis brought on by the first symptoms of election or call."[24] Most scholars sympathetic to Eliade's views now agree that the shaman, if he or she undergoes a psychic illness, is constitutionally stronger than the neuropath precisely because he or she can heal himself/herself.

Eliade does not deny the sometimes severe nature of the illness. He even goes so far as to claim that the shamanic illness is often of crisis proportions sometimes bordering on madness.[25]

However, since the youth or initiant cannot become a shaman until after this crisis is resolved, it clearly must play a role in his or her initiation:

> The shock provoked in the future shaman by the discovery that he has been chosen by the gods or spirits is by that very fact valuated as an "initiatory illness". His sufferings are exactly like the tortures of initiation. Just as, in puberty rites or rites of entrance into a secret society, the novice is "killed" by semidivine beings, so the future shaman sees in dreams his own body dismembered by demons. The initiatory rituals peculiar to Siberian and Inner Asian shamanism include a symbolic ascent to Heaven up a tree or pole; in a dream or a series of waking dreams, the sick man chosen by the gods or spirits undertakes his celestial journey to the World Tree. The psychopathology of the shamanic vocation is not profane; it does not belong to ordinary symptomology. It has an initiatory structure and significance; in short, it reproduces a traditional mystical pattern.[26]

Once healed of the initiatory psychopathology, the new shaman displays a strong and healthy constitution, which cannot be called psychopathological.[27] This view has been somewhat confirmed by psychological research. Psychoanalyst and research psychologist Bruce L. Boyer, M.D., conducted a study of Apache and Mescalero shamans in 1962. He conducted in-depth clinical interviews and administered the Rorschach (inkblot) test to the socially confirmed shamans as well as to a number of non-shamanic (ordinary) and pseudo-shamanic (not socially legitimated) tribal members. Amongst the true shamans, Boyer did find some evidence of hysteria, but not the more major forms of psychopathology (psychosis). The fact that he found some hysteria did not mean that this condition was pathological on Apache and Mescalero terms. It may be that such hysteria responses were more symptomatic of the shamanic psycho-physical constitution than of pathology. Boyer did observe some preoccupation with sex, bodily reactions, and excitability, all important psycho-physical aspects of shamanism. He concluded that shamans were "healthier than their societal co-members."[28]

INITIATORY ORDEALS

As has already been suggested above, the shamanic initiatory pattern involves an ordeal where there is a death and dismemberment, and then a reconstitution or rebirth of the shaman. Siberian shamanic initiatory ordeals are considered to be paradigmatic in their death/rebirth imagery. Siberian shamans claim to die and lie dead (inanimate) for three to seven days in their yurts (solitary spaces). During this period of death, demons or ancestral spirits come and cut them up into pieces. Their bones are stripped of their flesh and cleaned; their bodily fluids are thrown away and their eyes ripped out of their sockets:

> According to a Yakut informant, the spirits carry the future shaman's soul to the Underworld and shut him in a house for three years. Here he undergoes initiation; the spirits cut off his head (which they set to one side, for the novice must watch his own dismemberment with his own eyes) and hack his body to bits, which are later distributed among the spirits of various sicknesses. It is only on this condition that the future shaman will obtain the power of healing. His bones are then covered with new flesh, and in some cases he is given new blood.[29]

The images of these initiatory experiences are remarkably similar wherever they are found. In addition to this death/dismemberment experience, the initiatory ordeal frequently includes journeying to the upperworld or underworld and the acquisition of helping spirits, or power animals, upon whom the shaman may call in the future for divination, healing, and other activities. Through these initiatory ordeals the shaman-elect transcends ordinary human constraints and limitations, gaining access to, and knowledge of, the gods and spirits, often animal helping spirits, and a language with which he or she may communicate with them.

RELATIONS WITH SPIRITS AND SHAMANIC CONTROL

Numerous individuals in traditional societies may claim to have helping or guardian spirits. The shaman is only distinguished from these in that he or she commands these spirits, and does so for specific purposes, usually to restore individual, social, or climatic order and health, or for divination purposes. The shaman, however, controls only a limited number of such spirits, and these will be the ones with whom he or she maintains an active and respectful relationship. Again, the shaman does not typically become possessed by a spirit, but transforms himself or herself into the spirit via his or her ecstatic technique. This aspect of control is essential in understanding the shamanic task. The shaman, by contrast with ordinary members of his society, is master of many psychological states/conditions, including ecstasy and trance depth, imagery vivification, and dissociative capacities. Even those South American shamans who use hallucinogenic substances (sacred drugs) for the purpose of evoking ecstatic states, typically use low enough doses so as to maintain control of their trance depth, and remain intentionally focused on their healing, divinatory, or other shamanic task. An exception to this is found in some *ayahuasca* rituals. Hallucinogenic substances in high doses prevent the control of trance depth, and thus make unpredictable the amount of intentional control the subject may have. One can get lost in hallucinogen-induced trance states. Thus, it is essential to underscore that the shaman remains intentional (purposive), and by necessity controls his or her psychic states.

FUNCTIONS AND TECHNIQUES OF ECSTASY

Shamans typically enter into ecstatic trance for four reasons: 1) as mediator for the community, taking an offering to the celestial deity; 2) to seek, find, and restore the lost power or soul of a sick person that has been stolen or wandered away; 3) to guide the souls of the dead (psychopomp); and 4) to increase knowledge of the other worlds and their spirit beings. The shaman may be able to divine the future, control weather, and do other remarkable things, but he or she is indispensable in any situation which concerns transformations and disorders of the human soul. The most commonly associated function of the shaman is that of doctor or healer. However, while he or she may be concerned with herbal or medical treatments (e.g., surgery,

setting a broken bone), or with rites of passage and other cere-
monies, they are not his or her primary concern. Other healers
and ritual leaders can and do perform those functions. According to Eliade, it is the soul and its disorders which is the special
province of the shaman:

> Everything that concerns the soul and its adventure, here on
> earth and in the beyond, is the exclusive province of the
> shamans. Through his own pre-initiatory and initiatory
> experiences, he knows the drama of the human soul, its
> instability, its precariousness; in addition, he knows the
> forces that threaten it and the regions to which it can be car-
> ried away....If shamanic cure involves ecstasy, it is precisely
> because illness is regarded as a corruption or alienation of
> the soul.[30]

As a doctor of the soul, the shaman is, we might say, counterpart to the psychoanalyst or psychotherapist, only working in
a sacred idiom, and with techniques of ecstasy, helping spirits,
and well-formed shamanic rituals complete with familial and/or
community support as resources. Since the soul can be affected
malevolently or stolen away by malevolent spirits (ghosts, ancestor spirits, demons, deities, animal spirits, or sorcerers), the
shaman must enter into ecstatic trance for the diagnosis and spiritual resources to effect a cure (extract or exorcise malevolent
influence, retrieve lost soul).

MINOR SHAMANIC FUNCTION

If healing is the primary shamanic function, there are minor
ones we should briefly mention. Divination and clairvoyance are
often used in conjunction with healing, but may also be used to
control weather, determine the whereabouts of a person, recover
objects which have become lost, and to perform ceremonial and
other tasks related to the community which the shaman serves.
Shamans sometimes become involved in fakir-like demonstra-
tions, handle hot coals, cut themselves (and become immediately
healed), exercise psychokinesis, and the like. These demonstra-
tions may be for the purpose of practicing (exercising) of

shamanic methods and abilities, but may also be for the purpose of attaining or maintaining community support and legitimation of the shaman's potency, at least when performed publicly.

SHAMANIC PARAPHERNALIA

Shamanic paraphernalia often reveal an abundance of suggestive imagery which speaks from and to the imagination of shaman, patient, and community. Among the most important items of paraphernalia are costume, drum, rattle, medicine bundle, and other equipment. Special costumes are not a universal feature of shamanism; however, they appear frequently enough to mention that they often are adorned with talismans and other symbolic objects and designs which may reflect not only the shamanic cosmology but also the power animals or tutelary spirits of the shaman. Because of the importance of shamanic flight, bird symbolism is often a prominent feature in shamanism, and birds, especially the Thunder Bird and Eagle, are considered powerful helping spirits. Hence the shamanic costume and other equipment will frequently enough be adorned with feathers. The costume also often involves symbolism representing the shaman's initiatory experience, including skeleton symbolism and symbols of the helping spirits of the shaman.

The drum typically comes from the scared tree which stands at the central axis of the world and supports the three-storied cosmos. The drum, especially helpful in inducing the shamanic trance, is often something of a representation of the shamanic cosmology, often representing the world tree by which the shaman mounts up or descends into the spirit world. Shamanic masks serve to announce the incarnation of a spirit, rather than function as a disguise. In short, the shamanic paraphernalia (costume, rattle, drum, mask, etc.) can hardly be understood apart from shamanic cosmology and initiation in general, nor apart from the specific meanings of the shaman and his or her culture.

The shaman's paraphernalia and tools mark the shaman and his or her therapeutic seance with a special importance, a sacred value, and, by virtue of their colorful and provocative imagery, serve to heighten the sense of drama and expectancy that something important and significant will happen. This imagery, along with the other imagery employed in the shamanic ritual, may serve to overload the ordinary conscious viewpoint and provoke a sense of sacred time and space, a non-ordinary consciousness, in which the healing work is to be done.

NORTH AMERICAN SHAMANISM

According to Eliade, the North American shaman is more difficult to distinguish from other ritual elders, priests, magicians, and medical specialists who employ the sacred in their rituals and craft.[31] Past anthropological literature on North American shamanism has, for example, considered every variety of healer, religious specialist, priest, and sorcerer a shaman. This is in part due to the tendencies of nineteenth- and early twentieth-century anthropologists to consider any type of primitive religious specialist a shaman. But there are other reasons for a broader conception of shamanism in North America than those limited criteria used to define Siberian and Asian shamanism. Michael Abram, M.D., a physician and Tsalagi (Cherokee) scholar on a reservation in North Carolina, distinguishes between Cherokee priesthood and shamanism.[32] He claims that it was the "White Man" who "cut things up into separate classes", but for the Tsalagi people, a "shaman may also be a priest, or sometimes be a priest, a chief, a clan elder, or other public officiary; there are no clearcut distinctions". One might suspect that this has been true of many other North American tribes. In fact, scholars like Ake Hultkrantz and Sam Gill have also drawn attention to this situation.[33] Shamanism in North America appears to be a very complex and diverse phenomenon. Gill appears to take the broader view of shamanism with respect to North America. He argues that the central element of North American shamanism is spiritual power, "its nature, acquisition, accession, use, and loss".[34] The North American spiritual concepts are often difficult for those who have been shaped by modern Western culture to understand. Spiritual forms show wide variance in North America. Among the Cherokee of the Southeastern Woodlands, there were a multitude of spirits, human spirits, animal spirits, inanimate and vegetable spirits, animal and human ghosts, fairy-like creatures called "the little people," and sorcerers (malicious spirit beings disguised as humans who steal souls and "spoil the saliva"). All of these possessed power and could become involved in human illness and spirituality.[35] Typically, throughout North America one will find spirit forms identified with animals and other natural forms (rocks, plants, lakes and streams, etc.) and other spirit forms with mythic forms and deities. Ancestral souls and spirits of other living creatures (Bear, Wildcat, Eagle, etc.) may become the shaman's spirit helper or power animal.

Access to spiritual powers, or shamanic selection methods, comes in a variety of forms. There is inheritance, personal (vision) quest, election or selection by a spirit power or by the clan or tribe, and through an extraordinary affliction usually psychic in nature. Unlike South American shamanism, quests of power usually do not require use of hallucinogens in North America (Yak, Tarahumara, and Huichol shamanism of Mexico are some exceptions), but more commonly involve use of fasting, sweat lodge, isolation, and other non-pharmacological means (e.g., as among the Iroquois, Cherokee, Sioux, Potowatami, Ojibway, and many others of the Plains and Southwest and Northwest coasts).

One of the confounding features in native North American cultures is that, unlike the Siberian and Asian forms, anyone (not just the shaman) can access spirit powers, go on vision quests, and seek for a guardian spirit or power animal. Hence the shamanic quest for power and the quest for a spirit guardian often seem indistinguishable.

The shaman may only be distinguished by the power of his or her helping spirits, and his or her mastery of ecstatic trances for healing and visionary purposes. North American shamanic initiatory experiences may be very brief or quite long. In contrast to the classic Siberian/Asian forms, images of death, skeletization, rebirth, and magical flight may occur, but, according to Gill, this is relatively rare, and they usually do not occur in North American forms.[36]

Acquisition of spirit power is typically accompanied by the revelation of a power object by spirit helpers. The variety of power objects is considerable. Feathers, sacred stones, bear claws, shells, beads, arrows, and other charms and amulets are examples of some of the more common power objects. Disease is felt to be a loss of power, whether that loss be caused by spirit or pathogenic object intrusion, by sorcerers or offended spirits, or by soul loss. Therapeutic response requires reinvesting the patient with power, often in the form of application of power objects ritually applied along with chant, songs, and sacred formulas (which also contain healing power).

According to Eliade, throughout North America the main forms of disease are construed along the lines of a two-fold distinction: pathogenic object intrusion, and soul loss.[37] Hultkrantz distinguishes between object and spirit intrusion in native North America.[38] The North American shaman may do other things, but healing is his chief function. Eliade notes that while other healing specialists may be able to extract pathogenic objects, the shaman is necessary to retrieve and restore a lost soul.[39]

OBJECT INTRUSION AND SPIRIT INTRUSION

An object or pathogenic spiritual being (of minor dimensions) may cause physical or psychosomatic symptoms upon entering the patient's body. For example, there may be tissue swelling, soreness, itching, pains, and other psychosomatic problems. Sometimes the distinction between the object and intruding spirit is sharply drawn, while in other cases they are synonymous. Cases of object intrusion have been well documented in North America, whereas spirit intrusion is less frequent, or has been less frequently documented (occurring in such areas as western Alaska, the Northwest Coast, amongst the Central Algonquins, Southeast Indians, and the Navajo of the Southwest).[40] There is typically a spiritual agent responsible for these intrusions, often a sorcerer. Object intrusion is most often believed to be caused by malevolent intent by sorcerers; or when an offended spirit has caused the disease, it is often the result of a taboo violation. The intrusion diagnosis is not to be identified with possession, which is a psychological concept. There are cases in Europe and Asia where demon possession has been documented, with effects upon the psyche and body which are often catastrophic and which require the offices of shaman or ritual exorcist;[41] but these are not a part of what we are terming North American spirit or object intrusion. According to Gill, object intrusion also sometimes appears to be a symbolic objectification of the illness.[42] The corresponding treatment is usually extraction by sucking techniques, in which the healer, whether in trance or not, and whether in light or heavy trance, directly places his or her mouth (or uses a tube, e.g., a piece of horn) where the pathogenic object is diagnosed to be, and then sucks it from the body. The pathogenic object may be displayed in some material form to show the success of the treatment. It was once believed that this was a charlatan trick, but recent researchers suggest that the demonstration of a material object can have a placebo effect, which helps convince the patient and the family or community that success is assured.[43] Increased expectancy enhances therapeutic responsiveness.

SOUL LOSS: DIAGNOSIS AND CURE

The other major form of disease theory is soul loss; it is largely psychological, or psycho-spiritual in nature, and is based upon a variety of complex theories of the soul. According to Hultkrantz, the soul, or one or more souls (sometimes this is envisioned in North America as a power animal or helping spirit), becomes lost, stolen, or wanders away, resulting in a withering away. This belief presupposes a view of the person as typically having a separable soul or vital principle, often known as the "free soul", that in states of psycho-physical weakness or unconsciousness and comatose conditions distances itself from the body. Alternatively this withering away may be caused by a sorcerer who wants to destroy the person, or the soul may be enticed or snatched away by a ghost or spirit being. Shocks and sudden injuries (i.e., trauma) can dislodge the soul, causing it to leave the body and wander off. Hultkrantz argues that in order to understand this Native American psychology one must understand that there are typically two soul complexes in human beings:

One covering the several souls or potencies that sustain individuals when they are in a lucid consciousness, the other
consisting of just one soul that is the image of the person
and is active when one sleeps or is entranced or unconscious—in other words, an extracorporeal soul, representing
a person in his or her entirety. The first set of souls com-
prises the body souls that rule the heart movements, pulses,
emotions, and will power of the waking individual, while the
image soul is the so-called free soul, which can detach itself
from the person and is then the carrier of the ego. There is
an interchange of functions between the two soul concepts,
which alternate in representing human beings.[44]

Typically in a case of soul loss the soul leaves the body for
the realm of the dead. The person does not biologically die as
long as some body souls remain with the body.

However, if the free soul crosses the boundary and moves
into the land of the dead (i.e., the condition becomes life threatening), the other body souls will depart, breath will cease, heart
beat will stop, and the patient dies. It is typically paramount for
the North American shaman to retrieve the soul before the bodily souls depart, which means before the soul reaches the land of
the dead. Hultkrantz claims that it is only very rarely that a
shaman can rescue the free soul from the land of the dead, thus
restoring the patient's life and preventing biological death.[45] It is
only recently, with the publication of the *Diagnostic and Statistical
Manual of Mental Disorders–Fourth Edition* (DSM-IV),[46] that the
modern mental health profession has given recognition of soul
loss as a culturally determined or shaped mental syndrome.

The diagnosis for soul loss is made when the afflicted person
suffers from fever, or when there is a reduction in mental capacities (a reduction in vitality or conscious lucidity), and the patient
appears to be withering or languishing away. In our modern Western psychiatric idiom we might interpret the patient as being in a
trance state, or a dissociative state, ranging from various degrees
of dissociation, derealization, or unconsciousness to a comatose
condition. We shall discuss the modern understanding more
extensively in Part Three. According to Hultkrantz, it is the
patient's state of mind which principally determines the diagnosis,
even though physical ailments may sometimes be explained in the

soul loss idiom.[47] Cures for soul loss may involve the shamanic seance in which the shaman, in trance, dispatches his own free soul or power animal toward the land of the dead (in which the patient's free soul is moving) to retrieve the lost soul. The shaman must interfere with the lost soul before it reaches the land of the dead and bring it back, restoring it to the patient's body. Occasionally, as we have suggested, great shamans can enter the realm of the dead and convince the lost soul to return, or can snatch it away from the realm of the dead. Among the Coast Salish Indians it is believed that it is a guardian spirit or guardian soul that has been captured by the ghosts of the dead and carried to their land in the west. There are similar views among the Cherokee, who traditionally believed the lonely souls of the dead sought to enchant and entice souls of the living to come west into the realm of the dead beyond the mountains, to keep them company. Souls and power appear to be identified in such cases. Loss of soul is loss of vital power. Elsewhere the shaman sends out his or her own guardian spirit or power animal to retrieve the lost soul (or guardian or power spirit). Sometimes the soul is believed to stray, but hang around the village. The shaman must sneak up on it and capture it, carrying it back in his or her cupped hands and replacing it into the heart area and fontanel at the top of the head (entrance and exit points for the soul). Often there are dangers for the shamanic journey, such as dangerous spirits or spirit animals (gnomes, teeth-showing creatures, monsters, etc.), and temptations which may ensnare or destroy the shaman's free soul. Where shamanism has become weakened (diluted), soul loss may be cured as if it were a case of intrusion. In some cases it may be that object or spirit intrusion becomes responsible for the symptoms formerly attributed to soul loss.[48]

OTHER ASPECTS OF NORTH AMERICAN SHAMANISM

There are some North American tribes that heal by medicine societies rather than by individual shamanic performance. The Zuni Pueblo medicine society, for example, is composed of previously afflicted persons who were healed by that society. They are a society of wounded healers. The cosmologies and healing techniques correspond often quite closely with those of the shaman, including sucking rituals for intrusions, and cases of soul loss and restoration have been reported, although it is not certain how these soul recovery rituals were performed.

Among North American shamans there are several other functions which are important in addition to healing. These are primarily such functions as weather control, divining, and clairvoyant practices, especially those related to hunting, war, foretelling the future, and finding lost persons or objects. These functions according to Gill are usually secondary to healing but in cases of specialization, this would not be the case.[49] Shamanic practices sometimes include the use of esoteric languages by which the shaman communicates with the spirits (they are usually animal languages, as the helping spirits are often animal spirits). In North American tribal societies the shaman's role fluctuates from being marginal to being central to the life of the community.

Chapter Two

===

Technician of the Sacred

SHAMANISM AND THE SACRED

The shaman is a technician of the sacred. It is impossible to understand the richness of shamanism without some understanding of the importance of the sacred and of the shaman's relations with the sacred. This is so because the shaman's calling is to a sacred vocation and because the shaman is the ritual master of the sacred, being able to effectively locate, guard, and utilize the creative but dangerous energies of the sacred for therapeutic or other socially beneficial purposes. Any understanding of the religious and spiritual components of shamanic practice requires an understanding of the nature of the sacred, and of its importance to the shaman's way of life, therapeutic practice, and social function.

In this chapter we shall review the concept of the sacred as it has been illumined by three seminal scholars, Rudolf Otto, Gerhardus Van der Leeuw, and Mircea Eliade. Our discussion will involve a review of those aspects of the sacred most relevant to shamanic/animistic world view, but will also involve discussion of the sacred in other cultural contexts, including those of our familiar western civilization. That is, we shall follow the historical/phenomenological method of Otto, Van der Leeuw, and Eliade in order to clarify the phenomenology of the sacred by providing parallels from our own western cultural experience. Our discussion of the sacred in this chapter will set the stage for exploring the ritual role of the shaman, and will provide various key concepts upon which to focus the dialogue between Jungian psychology and shamanism in the remaining parts of the book.

ANIMISM

Shamanic relations with the sacred rest upon a pre-theologi-
cal and pre-political spiritual vision and experience. Having probably arisen in the Paleolithic-hunter period of cultural evolution,
when small tribal groupings had not given rise to priesthoods and
credal dogma, shamanic authority rested upon the sacred power
and efficacy which shamans could command for the benefit of
their people. That is to say, the shamanic vision of reality and the
shamanic authority rest upon levels of experience rather than
upon priestly ordination or institutional hierarchy. Although
shamanism is not a religion, but a method of experience which
can be called spiritual, it is often associated with a primal form of
religious experience called animism (from the Latin *anima*, soul,
suggesting nature ensouled, enspirited, or animated). Animism is
a view of the world as ensouled, or enspirited. Like the view of
many theoretical physicists today, nature is alive, everything is
alive with spirits. In the animistic world, there are ancestral spirits, plant and animal spirits, benevolent and dangerous spirits,
and numerous others. Proper concourse with the spirits is necessary for harmonious and healthy living. Violation of the spirits
results in discord, chaos, and famine, or sickness. The shamanic
view of ultimate reality presupposes this type of animistic vision
of the world. Mysterious power and energy seem to be the ultimate reality implicit in animism, in its rituals of worship, propitiation, atonement, in its interdictions against taboo violations, and
in its methods of restoring health and order. This mysterious
power and energy has been variously called *mana, orenda, wakan,*
and other names, and has been given a cross-cultural designation
by phenomenologists of religion as the sacred, or the holy.

RUDOLF OTTO: THE SACRED IN ITS
NON-RATIONAL ASPECTS

Western conceptions of ultimate reality (i.e., of deity) have
typically emphasized attributes of God as moral law giver, as good
will, and as spirit. But, according to Rudolf Otto, these conceptions have typically ignored the non-rational aspects of ultimate

reality. Shamanism, indebted as it is to an animistic conceptuality, has experienced the ultimate reality as mysterious, fascinating, potentially dangerous, and powerful. Animism emphasizes the non-rational aspects of the sacred. According to Rudolf Otto, the neglect of the non-rational aspects has been the weakness of western conceptualizations of ultimate reality.

Otto, in his description of the sacred/holy, was more concerned to describe the feeling reaction to something experienced as mysterious and ineffable, something which, phenomenologically speaking, seems to appear universally in religious experience. Otto coined the term *numen* (adjectival form: numinous, from the Latin meaning god) to express the non-rational feeling reaction to that universally appearing object of experience. The numen is an irreducible concept. It refers to a universally appearing object, a *sui generis,* which can not be reduced merely by the explanatory concepts of sociology, psychology, anthropology, or of any other discipline. This mystery is beyond the power of words to sufficiently describe. It can be sensed by a faculty of feeling or intuition, but it still remains beyond the range of words to adequately express. In terms of our own Western cultural heritage, the Hebrew *q'adosh,* the Greek *hagios,* the Latin *sanctus,* and the German *heilig* evoke the sense of that ultimate reality which is beyond our rational and linguistic capacities to grasp or describe. In Native American shamanism, such terms as *orenda* and *wakan* have served the purpose of denoting this ineffable reality. Typically such words are considered sacred, and if they are said at all, must be said in a ritually prescribed or respectful way. It is blasphemy to utter them in a profane manner.

MYSTERY

Otto also characterized the numen as being wholly other, discontinuous with everything else in everyday experience. His analysis of the holy into three contrasting aspects has been summed up under the Latin phrase: *mysterium tremendum et fascinans.* As *mysterium,* the ineffable and inexhaustible character of the holy is experienced as a power that strikes one dumb, and mute. It is experienced more as a mood similar to that of stupor, dumb astonishment, amazement, awe, and wonder. Certain experiences which are strange, sublime, and overpowering, like confronting the mighty waterfall at Niagara, evoke a sense of astonishment and amazement. In experiencing the mysterious aspect of the holy we "come upon something whose kind and character are incommensurable with our own".[1]

FASCINATION

The holy is also described as *fascinosum,* that is, as having an intoxicating and attracting component. The shamans, as have sages, mystics, witches, and saints, possess a deep longing for the sacred, which can be described as an ontological thirst. The shaman frequently begins as a wounded youth who is irresistibly attracted (called) to the strange, mysterious, and the powerful, in a way which his or her ordinary tribal peers seem not to be. The *fascinans* aspect of the holy has an enticing and alluring effect upon the imagination. It may become a great object of desire, of obsession, or mystical and ascetical pursuit. As the source of religious longing, it can bestow a feeling of beatitude beyond compare.

Otto believed that the obsession with the fascinosum was the result of either a magical identification of the self with the numen, in magical and devotional transaction by means of conjuration, consecration, formula, and exorcism, or by the shamanic procedure of "possession, indwelling, and self-fulfillment in exaltation and ecstasy".[2] Otto believed that these modes originated in animistic magic, but soon evolved into the pursuit of the numen as an end in itself, in the higher religions. The culmination of numinal pursuit is to be found in the worshipful encounter with what "eye hath not seen, nor ear heard."[3] For the shaman, the purpose of the pursuit was to access helping power, to learn about the sacred, and to chart its mysterious geography. But beyond any practical function, it was a mystical pursuit which called upon the shaman, with an allure and power which evoked an obsession with it, and which could be refused or denied only at risk or peril to the shaman's soul.

TREMENDUM: THE REPELLING/HORRIFIC COMPONENT

The holy is not only mysterious, alluring, and enticing, it also has a threatening and horrific component to the experience of it. This component is evoked in the sense of over-powering might, majesty, and urgency, reflected in the mood of Jacob: "How dreadful is this place/This is none other than the house of Elohim".[4] It may be described as an uncanny feeling which penetrates to the core of one's being. It is evoked in the experience of nothingness before the holy, of being nothing but dust and ashes. This aspect is the source of ritual respect for the sacred, and the imperative to not pollute it with profane impurity.

THE AMBIVALENT NATURE OF THE HOLY

The experience of the holy, as Otto delineates it, is an ambivalent experience, since it consists of an attracting and alluring component, and a dangerous and repelling component. The feeling of the numinous may come suddenly, like a volcanic explosion, or gently and progressively like the gentle waves of the sea. Additionally, one pole of the experience may occur before the other, or both poles may occur simultaneously. The attracting and intoxicating component culminates in the sense of rapture, the impulse towards worship, and the desire to surrender to and indwell the numen. The repelling or horrific component evokes a sense of unworthiness in the presence of the holy. It results in feelings of moral or ontological guilt, and evokes a sense of the need for atonement or expiation. It tends to result in the impulse to set things right (e.g., ritual purification, propitiation, salvation, or reconciliation). Not only has this bipolar experience of the holy given rise to the religious need to worship, it has given rise to the impulse to restore relations with the ultimate, to restore order, to atone for sins and taboo violations, and thus has a teleological aspect. The dual aspect is evident in all religious forms, from the animistic/shamanic form, to the so-called civilized religions (Judaism, Christianity, Islam, Hinduism, Buddhism). Shamanism has sought the causes of illness in taboo violations which upset the ultimate spiritual order and the tribal order willed by the gods, ancestors, and other symbols of the sacred.

EXPRESSION OF THE NUMEN

Since the numinous is experienced as wholly other, expressing it is problematic. Ordinary language and rational concepts fail to do it justice, as it eludes them with its mystery. It can be evoked or aroused through the symbolic use of language, but it requires a natural sense of the numinous to be able to be conscious of it. Indirect means are typically used to invoke or evoke awareness of it, because it can not be taught or communicated through tradition. The shaman may be taught much about practical healing methods, techniques, rituals, and medicines by his or her shamanic peers and elders, but the experience of the numen is of an exclusively personal nature. The experience itself can only be invoked, incited, or aroused.

Direct means of expression involve the use of language, but in a way which stretches words to their breaking point, through symbolic images, or through words which have no literal meaning at all (the Hindu *om,* the Hebraic *halleluiah,* the Sioux *wakan*). Often sacred words must be passed over in silence, or must be said or chanted in a special way. Direct means only work if they rely on non-verbal means, such as an attitude of reverence/respect, attunement of mood, respectful tones, etc. Indirect means typically involve aesthetic and environmental conditions which arouse numinal feeling. Any atmosphere which can evoke a sense of extraordinary potency, beauty, awe, and elevation of mood or lofty aspiration, or perhaps a sense of the sublime, may become an indirect means for evoking a feeling of the numen. Places, events, or objects which seem strangely different, unique, miraculous, or powerful seem to hold a greater potential for numinal response. Otto draws attention to the ancient Stonehenge as having a power and grace which was numinal. He believed it may have originally been used to store up numen in a solid place by magical means.[5] Natural objects, for example, stones, bodies of water, mountains, the sun and moon, all may arouse the feeling of the numen. Sacred art has typically been able to arouse the numen, often through the use of impersonal and austere looks (Byzantine Madonnas), blackness (black Madonnas), and destructive personae (Kali Durga) because they suggest not only the alluring aspect but the *tremendum* or horrific aspect of the holy. The use of negative space in Oriental art, as well as in Gothic architecture, as well as the use of light and shadow (Gothic vaults), also arouse similar responses. The shaman's love of darkness, of graveyards, of the nocturnal, may be understood as a need for environmental contexts which are evocative of the ambivalent experience of the sacred.

VAN DER LEEUW'S CONCEPT OF THE SACRED

Van der Leeuw's descriptions and formulations of the sacred are very close to Otto's. Thus we want to mention mainly the areas where he extends the concept beyond Otto. Van der Leeuw's emphasis is upon the ambivalent experience of the sacred as power and dread. Like Otto he discerns an otherness in the object of religious experience: the first affirmation we can make about the object of religion is that it is a highly exceptional and extremely impressive other.[6] Like Otto he also emphasizes the affective experience of the holy, but characterizes it more as dread. In dread, there is both an attracting and a repelling element. Thus, the experience of the sacred is also an ambivalent experience. Positively, the attracting element is experienced in feelings of reverence, awe, trust, and love. Negatively, the repelling element is experienced as feelings of terror, horror, and fear.

THE SACRED AS POWER

The most important aspect of Van der Leeuw's analysis, for our consideration of shamanism, is his descriptions of the sacred in its aspect of power. Van der Leeuw associates the primal experience of sacred power with the Melanesian *mana,* with the Iroquois *orenda,* and the Sioux *wakan.* For Van der Leeuw, natural phenomena associated with the power of life or death were manifestations and effects of this power: sun, rain, thunderstorms, rocks, stars, mountains, trees, streams, etc. Exceptional qualities

such as strength, fame, influence, majesty, intelligence, authority, and the like were associated by primitive man with the
sacred. Effectiveness of shamanic healing is associated with the
numinous power harnessed by the shaman. Power and life force
are also associated, so that the greater one's strength, vigor, or
health, the greater the *mana*. Remembering that *mana* is the
Melanesian word for numinal or sacred power, Van der Leeuw
describes its significance for world creation, for the warrior, and
for the chieftain or king:

> Now *mana* actually has this significance; the warrior's *mana*,
> for instance, is demonstrated by his continual success in
> combat, while repeated defeat shows that his *mana* has
> deserted him. Power...is authenticated...empirically: in all
> cases whenever anything unusual or great, effective or suc-
> cessful is manifested, people speak of *mana*....The creation
> of the earth is the effect of divine *mana*, but so is all capacity;
> the chief's power, the happiness of the country, depend on
> *mana*.[7]

SHAMANISM, HEALING, AND POWER

The association of the sacred with power also is illustrated
in relation to evil (destructive or malevolent force). Evil force, in
the primal world view, is also powerful, but its effects are
destructive. If the sacred = potency, evil effects (illness, destruction, defeat) = accumulated impotence. Evil may cause a diminution of life force, or may destroy it altogether by draining away or
destroying its potency. Hence the shamanic healer is one who
has access to great power, and who, through commanding his or
her spirits, has the power to restore power to the afflicted. In
exorcism or extraction, for example, this principle is discernible
when a counterposing creative spirit is invoked to drive out or
extract an evil or destructive spirit. The potency of the helping
spirit must be greater than the potency of the evil or pathogenic
spirit (a principle, we might add, which is presupposed today in
Alcoholics Anonymous and other 12-step programs for addictions and compulsions).

THINGS, POWER, AND SHAMANISM

Shamanic amulets and talismans are believed to be saturated with power; they are storehouses of numen. The shaman,
for example, may give his or her patient an amulet to restore
power and/or keep the forces of danger and chaos at bay. Van
der Leeuw informs us that modernity has accustomed us to look
at things as "mere dead objects". He notes that the poet is one
who knows better, as well as does the animistic mind: "On the
contrary, the thing is the bearer of a power; it can effect something, it has its own life which reveals itself"; everything may be a
power bearer.[8] Souls, spirits, and ghosts are sacred, and, by association, anything connected with them acquires an indisputable
potency, for example, a fetish, totem pole, a shamanic talisman,
the staff of a king or chief, and so on. Natural objects which display unusual features or irregularities which distinguish them or
set them apart from the ordinary environment also lend themselves to being identified as "power objects".[9] Tools and weapons
also assume sacred importance; they must be powerful to be
effective. Among native North Americans, the shaman's sacred
bundles assured the life and health of the community. Their loss,
theft, or desecration could mean disaster or desolation for the
community. One need only recall the effects of the loss of the
Grail in the Parsifal myths, or the loss of the Ark of the Covenant
in ancient Israel, to get a sense of the ambience of power and
dread surrounding such sacred objects. Additionally, any old
thing handed down by authority or tradition, by ancestors, chief-
tains, or kings, tended to be viewed as sacred, that is, as saturated
with power: old spears, a dagger, an eagle feather, a scripture,
stones, an imperial insignia. In distinction from fetishes, amulets
were reservoirs of power. They needed to be pocket-sized or
wearable around the neck. Effective in warding off evil and sickness (impotence), they could acquire power from a holy person
(shaman, witch, saint, lama, or priest). Natural elements such as
fire, water, stones, and trees could be considered sacred, and are
often employed in healing rituals. Water and fire, for example,
have often been associated with purification rituals. The role of
water in spiritual purification, healing, and exorcism has been

well documented, and Van der Leeuw gives a description of some of the diverse uses of water powers:

> Purifications by water were effective in Ancient Egypt as well as for Roman Catholic piety: the holy water, freed from all damaging influences by exorcism, defends person or object sprinkled with it from all demonic sway, drives off spooks and sickness, protects entrance and egress, house and cattle. And finally in baptism, water expels the devil and pours in sanctifying grace.[10]

TABOO AND POWER

Before we leave the discussion of Van der Leeuw's conceptions of the sacred, we must discuss the relations between the sacred and taboo, since this is a very important relation in shamanic ideology and practice. We mentioned earlier that one of the causes of illness in shamanic ideology is taboo violation, often expressed in the form of offending the spirits; sometimes it is an offense of tribal rules or law. Van der Leeuw tells us that that which is sacred, and thus powerful, is also that which is taboo. In tribal existence, daily life has been heavily circumscribed with taboo, that is to say, with the fear of violating sacred potency. Insofar as certain objects, times, places, persons, or things were charged with power, they were taboo. Van der Leeuw compares power to an electrical charge. It may serve creative purposes, but it is also dangerous. Contact with the sacred, because it is potentially dangerous, is regulated with ritual and imperative (taboo), lest destruction result from casual or unproscribed contact. "Tabu is thus a sort of warning: Danger/High Voltage/ Power has been stored up and we must be on our guard".[11] Approaching the king (or chief), a foreigner, or the opposite sex with proper greeting and due respect are necessary to prevent the dangerous unleashing of destructive energies. Incest was often punished by death, and quickly in the Central Celebs, for example. This was done not in an act of moral outrage, but "merely as a means of limiting the evil results of the outrage to the delinquents".[12] Taboo imposed by shamans is typically for the purposes of limiting the effects of malevolent spirits, or for the purposes of protecting an already weakened individual from contact with other persons or spirits who may further weaken him or her. Shortly, we shall discuss the danger aspect of the sacred under the needs for ritual structure and maintenance of boundaries around sacred space by the shaman. Discussing the sacred in terms of ambivalent attracting and repelling aspects, and in terms of power, provides us with an understanding of the non-rational or feeling side of religious experience presupposed by shamanism. We now turn to Eliade for a discussion of the rational and non-rational aspects of the sacred.

ELIADE: THE SACRED AS ARCHAIC ONTOLOGY

Eliade contrasts the sacred and the profane. Humans become aware of the sacred because it manifests or shows itself as something wholly different from the profane. Eliade proposed the term *hierophany* to designate the act of manifestation of the sacred. He argues that all religions, from the most primitive to the most highly developed, are constituted by various manifestations of sacred realities, that is, by hierophanies. He gives such examples as the most elementary manifestation of the sacred in a stone or tree, to the most supreme Christian hierophany, the manifestation of God in Jesus Christ. No matter what the religious tradition, whether it be archaic or highly developed, in each case there is a confrontation with something of a wholly different order, a reality that does not belong to our ordinary or profane world, but which manifests itself in and through that world and its objects. Any object, person, place, animal, human, or thing in the natural world can become the locus of a manifestation of the sacred. All nature, in fact, is capable of revealing itself as a cosmic sacrality, and the cosmos as a whole may become itself a hierophany. To be sure, it is not the stone, tree, human, or other profane object itself which is venerated, but the sacred which manifests itself through it: "The sacred tree, the sacred stone are not adored as stone or tree; they are worshiped precisely because they are hierophanies, because they show something that is no longer stone or tree but the sacred, the *ganz andere*".[13]

NOSTALGIA FOR THE SACRED

Eliade informs us that the persons of archaic or traditional societies tend to live as much as possible in or close to the sacred. There is a nostalgic longing for the sacred in religious consciousness, which is tantamount to an ontological thirst for Being, for absolute reality, for the "absolutely real, enduring, and effective". Hence "the *sacred* is equivalent to a *power,* and, in the last analysis, to *reality.* The sacred is saturated with *being*".[14]

Eliade, on the basis of a wide sampling historicaly and cross-culturally, abstracted a typology of the sacred, insofar as it manifests itself in certain patterns (archetypes) or universally recurring themes. He articulates them into a three-fold structure: 1) repetition of a celestial archetype; 2) reality as being conferred through participation in the symbolism of the center; 3) rituals and significant profane gestures that acquire meaning through repetition of the acts of the gods, ancestors, or heroes.[15] We shall briefly discuss these themes, since they are of relevance to shamanic cosmology, symbolism, and practice.

CELESTIAL ARCHETYPES

Eliade has drawn comparative data from archaic and ancient societies and civilizations to substantiate his observations that traditional societies tend to become patterned upon a celestial archetype. He refers to the Spanish conquistadors and other Europeans to illustrate the notion that territories, temples, and cities of traditional societies are patterned on a celestial archetype. Drawing upon various civilizations, he cites the Star of the Swallow, which the ancient Mesopotamians believed was the archetypal model of the Euphrates river, and the star Anuit, the celestial model of the Tigris. In India, Eliade points out, ancient and modern royal cities were constructed upon the mythical model of a celestial city where, in the age of old *(in illo tempore),* the universal sovereign dwelt. He illustrates how sacred temples have also been modeled on the celestial archetype. For example he cites Jahweh's giving to Moses on Mount Sinai the form of the temple to be built.[16] Whether it be a city, temple, or territory, all are shown to have an "extraterrestrial archetype, be it conceived as a plan, as a form, or purely and simply as a double existing on a higher cosmic level".[17]

In elucidating the archetypal pattern, Eliade appears to be articulating the deep rational structures of the sacred. But Eliade also believes the sacred has an ordering effect upon traditional societies, not only providing the ground plan for their cities, sacred architecture, and space, but also for their social and ethical relations. This rationality of the sacred runs through Eliade's descriptions. The ordering power of the sacred upon space inhabited by traditional and tribal societies is juxtaposed with the common belief that not everything in the world is ordered. In fact, our world is patterned upon a sacred archetype, but beyond the boundaries of the city or village lies chaos, darkness, and the powers of evil and discord. Desert regions and uninhabited territories constitute the realm of chaos, where dragons and monsters are rampant. These forces of chaos are terrifying, and are also to be found in uncharted regions on land and un-navigated regions of the seas where the marine monster dwells. Insofar as archaic and traditional societies may move about, explore, and conquer new territories, ways of consecrating newly acquired space become necessary. Ways of consecrating space are essential to making them safe and inhabitable, and such has traditionally been the role of shaman and priest. Thus Eliade says, in "Vedic India the erection of an altar dedicated to Agni constituted the taking possession of a territory".[18] Eliade also cites the Spanish and Portuguese erecting of a cross in the name of Jesus whenever they took possession of continents and islands. This is equivalent to a new birth or, in the Christian idiom, to a "baptizing" of the newly acquired territory, remaking it into habitable space. It is important to note here that the consecration rituals serve the purpose of keeping the forces of chaos at bay, which is as much a function of the shaman during a healing ritual as it is in the ritual acts of consecrating and taking possession of a territory. We shall return to this point later. But suffice it to say that the shaman, in his or her healing rituals, typically recites the cosmogonic myth and the myth of the origins of healing, or the myth of the first shaman. These recitations serve the function of returning to the time of the gods and ancestor shamans, when reality and healing rites came fresh from the creator's hands, and thus re-establish order in a situation otherwise experienced as chaotic and threatening. In this way the ancestor shamans, heroes, and tribal deities become the paradigmatic models upon which the healing rites and actions are patterned.

THE PRESTIGE OF THE CENTER AND AXIS MUNDI

Extending his efforts to demonstrate the depth, rationality, and ordering function of the sacred, Eliade argues that *homo religiosus,* the person of traditional societies, seeks to live in an organized and intelligible world ordered by the sacred. The key rational pattern discernible universally in religious experience, especially in traditional societies, is indicated by the "prestige of the center". The importance of the symbolic center overlaps with the ordering and creative function of the celestial archetypes, which also reveal the sacred center from which life and experience must take its orientation. Eliade gives an outline of architectonic symbolism of the center as it appears universally in religious phenomena. The sacred mountain where earth and heaven meet is said to be situated at the center of the world. Eliade cites Mount Meru of India, Mount Sumeru of the Ural-Altaic people, Mount Zinnalo in Laos, and the Christian Golgotha as examples from the great religions and civilizations. We could add the Harney Peak of the Sioux medicine man Black Elk to Eliade's examples to remind us that the mountain as a symbol of the center is extant in shamanic cosmology.

These instances of the symbolism of the center constitute examples of the *axis mundi,* the central axis by which our world is brought into communication with the upper and lower realms. In Christianity, the axis mundi is the intersection between heaven and hell in relation to earth (the analogue of middle world). In shamanism this axis mundi symbolism is often exemplified in the cosmic tree, as well as in the healing ritual shrine, which may also be a symbol of the axis mundi, the origin of the world, and the origin of all healing powers. Thus, center = axis mundi = the meeting point between the three cosmic zones = the creative origin of the world. The center point is an opening, an access to the celestial world of the gods, spirits, and the creative energies of the world. The underworld (understood in Christian culture as the terrifying realm of hell) is the realm of the dead, of ghosts and evil energies. At this point, Eliade's phenomenology of the sacred takes an inward turn, for it is the axis mundi, often symbolized as the cosmic tree or pillar, which connects the lower and upper worlds for the shaman, the ecstatic healer of traditional societies. The shaman, as we have previously mentioned, makes journeys to the lower and upper regions in his or her initiatory and ecstatic ordeals and tasks. The shaman mounts the sacred tree in the celestial ascent to commune with the spirits in his or her mystic flight. It is out of the center that the creative/healing energies of the cosmos issue.

The center, then, is the preeminent ontological zone of absolute reality, the point of contact with that which gives orientation in our world, and of access to that which is absolutely real, enduring, and effective. The center, we should clarify, is not the sole province of the shaman. All transformative religious experience requires contact with the energies of the sacred. The religious person of traditional societies is possessed of an ontological thirst, a profound nostalgia to be near the center. The center as an inward experience, however, is not automatically or easily accessed. Religious geniuses such as shaman, mystic, and guru may have learned how to access it, but only after strenuous effort.

> The road leading to the center is a "difficult road"...and this is verified at every level of reality: difficult convolutions of a temple (as at Borobudor); pilgrimage to sacred places (Mecca, Hardwar, Jerusalem); danger-ridden voyages of the heroic expeditions in search of the Golden Fleece, the Golden Apples, the Herb of Life, wandering in labyrinths; difficulties of the seeker for the road to the self, to the "center" of his being, and so on. The road is arduous, fraught with perils, because it is, in fact, a rite of passage from the profane to the sacred, from the ephemeral and the illusory to reality and eternity, from death to life, from man to divinity.[19]

The symbolism of the center occupies a supremely important position in shamanism: in terms of the shaman's ecstatic experience, in terms of shamanic cosmology, and in terms of shamanic healing rituals.

REPETITION

We are arguing that the symbolism of the center, as Eliade elucidates it, is equivalent to the sacred source of creation, order, and healing/transformative energies. Implied throughout discussion of the celestial archetype and the symbolism of the center is the theme of paradigmatic repetition. This is the theme of repeating the sacred or transcendent pattern or form laid down by the gods, ancestors, or heroes. The city, the royal palace, and the temple repeat the primordial or archetypal forms. In this way, ordinary, profane phenomena become informed by a sacred ordering; hence the importance of consecration as a way of imposing the divine archetypal form, bringing order out of chaos. Additionally, the transformative healing and religious experiences repeat the celestial archetype and the symbolism of the center. Beyond this, every act of creation repeats the paradigmatic cosmogonic act of the gods, heroes, and ancestors. The shaman, too, as we have mentioned, recites the myths of the origins of healing and often the cosmogonic myth, for it is necessary to become contemporary with the gods, in order to reconstitute the creative healing energies. If illness and disease are conceived as the forces of chaos and destruction, then it is the invocation and appropriation of the creative and ordering energies which restores health, and brings healing. The shaman plays a vital role in traditional societies, which are continually threatened by the forces of chaos. It is the shaman as the representative and mediator of the sacred power and order that provides assurance to the community that the forces of chaos will be kept at bay, and that an access to the sacred energies will be available to the community.

Myths, for the religious person of traditional societies, also become the paradigmatic forms upon which life becomes modeled. The repetition of mythic forms provides assurance that things are done properly and in harmony with the ultimate scheme of things. Without the repetition of these transcendent and transhuman models, the person of traditional societies does not consider himself to be truly man except insofar as he imitates the gods, the culture heroes, or the mythical ancestors.[20] To repeat these archetypal patterns is to be truly human, for such repetition assures that one's life is real, enduring, and effective. We shall turn now to a discussion of the relation of the sacred to the transformative ritual process in shamanic and contemporary psychotherapy.

THE SACRED AND RITUAL PROCESS

In traditional shamanic healing there are several basic elements which become integrated in the therapeutic ritual. These elements include the mythology or cosmology of the patient's community, a method of diagnosing the illness in an idiom congruent with the mythological cosmology, and certain methods of treatment. Each of the elements of traditional therapeutics are related in a part-to-whole manner, so that each makes sense only in relation to the others.[21] The category which is central to all of them is the sacred, and nowhere is the centrality of its role more clearly discernible than in the ritual structure and process of traditional shamanic psychotherapeutics. It is in the ritual structure, and in terms of the sacred mediated within that structure, that the ordering myth is recited, diagnosis is made, and the method of treatment determined and applied. In traditional shamanic therapeutics, it is the sacred which is the healing and transformative power. Human efforts are necessary to constitute and maintain a ritual structure within which the sacred transformative energies can be evoked. Eliade is most illuminating on the relation of the sacred to space and transformation.

SACRED SPACE AND RITUAL TRANSFORMATION

We mentioned previously that Eliade documents the universal importance of the "prestige of the center", and that it is the axis mundi which provides an orientation in time and space. Profane time and space, we said, is homogeneous; there is no fixed point from which to gain an orientation. There is no contact with

that which is absolutely real, effective, and enduring. But sacred
time and space are heterogeneous, having qualitative irruptions.
To homo religiosus, certain places and times are qualitatively
other; that is, they are manifestations of the sacred. They put one
in touch with the meaning-giving center from which orientation
is drawn and healing/transformative energies are experienced.[22]

It is this qualitative break in profane space which allows the
world to be constituted, which creates cosmos out of chaos, which
provides an orientation, and which allows the world to be regen-
erated. Drawing upon massive data from ethnology and the history of religions, Eliade notes that the manifestation of the
sacred, a hierophany, permanently changes the quality of that
space, even if the dominant culture or religious tradition constituted by it passes or is relativized. We can see an example in the
Dome of the Rock in Jerusalem, in which three different cultures
and religions have valorized (Judaic, Christian, Muslim) its space
as sacred during periods of historical ascendency in that region.
Thus the manifestation of the sacred (hierophany) is continually
repeated irrespective of historical changes. Eliade says:

> In this way the place becomes an inexhaustible source of
> power and sacredness and enables man, simply by entering
> it, to have a share in the power, to hold communion with the
> sacredness....But however diverse and variously elaborated
> these sacred spaces may be, they all present one trait in com-
> mon: there is always a clearly marked space which makes it
> possible...to communicate with the sacred.[23]

Sacred space cannot be generated by an act of the human
will. It can be provoked, invoked, and prepared for by questing,
fasting, and by various ritual means, but it is beyond the power of
human beings to force its manifestation. Human beings do, however, have important responsibilities in the consecration and
maintaining of the boundaries demarcating sacred space, and
this human function is of paramount importance. The boundaries demarcating sacred space serve as notice that a qualitatively
other space is near, and that proper relations with the sacred
require acknowledgment and respect for these boundaries.

Respect for the boundaries also serves as protection against
the "high voltage," to use Van der Leeuw's expression, of the

sacred. Careless contact with the sacred can be destructive without proper stewardship of its boundaries. Hence the enclosure around the sacred space serves a function of preserving profane persons from the danger of trespassing upon it without due care and respect. The necessity of ritualized relations with the sacred is derived from the fact that the sacred "is always dangerous to anyone who comes into contact with it unprepared, without having gone through the 'gestures of approach' that every religious act demands".[24]

According to Eliade it is one of the primary tasks of the shaman as a technician of the sacred to locate and effectively use the powerful deconstructive/reconstructive transformative energies of the sacred for healing purposes. The primary function of the shaman was that of healing disorders of a spiritual/psychopathological nature, that is, disorders of the soul. Other forms of disorder may be appropriately attended to by other types of healers who need not ritually provoke a strong and safe space for powerful transformative energies. Herbalists, naturopathic physicians, diviners, surgeons, and the like may be employed to diagnose physical illness, treat it medicinally or surgically, or make referral to a shaman. But disorders of the soul, in primitive societies, belong exclusively to the shaman.

The shaman as a technician of the sacred is the psychotherapist of traditional and premodern cultures, who knows how to effectively locate, utilize, and maintain sacred transformative space. Although Eliade indicates that it is always a "clearly marked space" which makes it possible "to communicate with the sacred", he is reluctant to say that such spaces can be found within modern western industrial culture, except in degraded or laicized form.[25]

TRANSFORMATIVE PROCESS AND RITUAL LEADERSHIP

Robert L. Moore has drawn upon the work of Mircea Eliade and Victor Turner in formulating a theory of ritual structure which contrasts with Eliade on this notion of a qualitatively different space which cannot be found in modernity except in laicized form. He finds sympathy with Turner's belief that even under the conditions of modern industrial culture the human

experience of space is anything but homogeneous.[26] Moore
believes Turner's work on space and transformation provides a
significant contribution to our understanding of the relationship
between space and transformational process. Moore notes that,
in a way similar to Eliade, Turner has devoted a considerable
portion of his research to the task of understanding the nature
and meaning of heterogeneous forms of space discernible in
human experience.

Turner's work on ritual process was influenced by Van Gennep's pioneering monograph, *The Rites of Passage,* which distinguished traditional rites of passages into three phases:
separation, transition, and incorporation.[27] Separation was the
ritual phase which drew a distinction between profane space and
time, and sacred space and time. A special cultural realm is created, during this phase, which becomes the locus of the interven-
ing phase of transition. The second or middle phase was termed
margin or *limen* by Van Gennep. In this phase the ritual subjects
pass through a period of cultural and social ambiguity in which
they are relieved of their typical or previous social statuses,
undergo ordeals, painful trials, and dismemberments, and
receive instruction from their ritual elders in mythical lore relevant to their soon to be attained new status. The third, or final
phase, that of incorporation, returns the subjects to the ordinary
space and time, and reincorporates them, with their new status,
into the social structure.

According to Moore, the great contribution of Turner to our
understanding of space and transformation concerns his extensive elaboration of the middle or transitional phase of liminality.
For Turner the distinction between ceremony and ritual is drawn
on the basis of the presence of liminality. Turner views ceremony
as indicative, but ritual as transformative. Transformation, especially those forms respecting life crises, occurs most completely in
liminal seclusion. It is in the liminal phase that the "cognitive
schemata that give sense and order to everyday life no longer
apply, but are, as it were, suspended—in ritual symbolism perhaps
even shown as destroyed or dissolved. Gods and goddesses of
destruction are adored primarily because they personify an essential phase in an irreversible transformative process".[28]

Similar to the danger of the sacred noted by Otto, Eliade, and Van der Leeuw, Moore draws attention to Turner's understanding that liminality can be dangerous. But he adds that more than the destruction of a previous "life world" is going on. Liminality is more of a space/time pod in which the individual is ritually unbound from the binding power of social norms and conventions, and is ritually rebound. In the liminal experience, new meanings and symbols are often introduced, or new ways of embellishing old modes of living, so as to renew interest in them, are portrayed. The danger of the liminal phase is conceded and respected by demarcating it with ritual interdictions and taboos. Moore also draws attention to the distinction Turner makes between *liminal* and *liminoid,* a distinction crucial to Moore's own theoretical developments of ritual prowess and leadership. Liminal phenomena are more characteristic of tribal social crises which naturally occur. Liminal phenomena are typically organized around symbols which are culture-wide, and which have a common meaning for all members of the group. Liminoid phenomena, by contrast, are more typical of modern societies. Rather than being collective products, they are often individual products, with meanings not shared normatively or universally throughout the culture by all members of the society. These meanings are marginal to dominant symbols and cultural institutions. Often associated with leisure time, and with play, liminoid phenomena are more idiosyncratic, and are typically generated by competing individuals or groups. Theater, film, opera, ballet, art, poetry, and pilgrimage are exemplifications of liminoid phenomena.

Moore's own contribution to understanding transformative ritual process in religion and psychotherapy builds upon the insights of Turner, but it begins with a critique. While giving credit to Turner for mapping the distinctions between liminal and liminoid space, Moore argues that Turner did not give enough attention to the relationship between boundary and space in his reflections. Concern with the establishment and maintenance of boundaries, for Moore, is essential to providing effective transformative ritual leadership. Moore claims that the distinctions between liminal and liminoid should not be based on distinctions between whether or not the practices and symbols are culture-wide or not, but "on the basis of how the boundaries that delimit the space are constituted and maintained."[29] Moore holds that it is the permeability of the boundaries of the space involved, and the "relative importance of the leadership of ritual elders or 'technicians of the sacred' in making judgments as to the approximate utilization of the space," upon which the issue should become focused.[30] Ritual leadership becomes the key variable which, according to Moore, Turner failed to isolate.

Moore insists that liminal space requires ritual leadership, whereas liminoid space does not: "A ritual leader may be present in liminoid space, but must be present for liminal space to exist".[31] He says that the reason liminality occurs at or near the center of tribal society is not simply because the social processes are integrated and totalistic, but because of the availability of knowledgeable ritual elders. Moore's concept of the ritual elder echoes Eliade's shaman as technician of the sacred, but Moore extends his concept to and beyond shamanism to contemporary psychotherapists, ministers, film and theater directors, civil rights leaders, and presumably to any figure who can help an individual or a group face powerful conflicts, oppositions, and competing energies in a way which can bring about relatively safe and creative transformation or resolution. The ritual elder is primarily one who knows how transformative space is "located, consecrated, and stewarded."[32] In the culture of modernity, Moore contends, there is a lack of knowledgeable and competent ritual leadership able to locate and effectively utilize such space for transformative purposes. What has been left to fill the vacuum is a plethora of liminoid spaces not so much constituted by boundaries as by being on the boundary. Liminal space, by contrast, requires the constitution and stewarding of strong boundaries capable of holding the intensity of the energies released in the transformative deconstructive/reconstructive process. The availability of such effectively transformative space requires the conscious intentionality of its stewards in maintaining the boundaries. Whereas liminoid space does not require such leadership, liminal transformative space does. A ritual elder is not necessary on a pilgrimage, but is necessary in a transformative life crisis or political crisis.

Moore has been extending his theory into the domain of the ritually transformative processes of psychotherapy and religion. He believes that the time has come for us to recognize that psychotherapy, religious and secular, provides a certain sector of our population with important ritual leadership in times of crisis. Although he does not contend that all psychotherapy is effective transformative ritual leadership, where it is effective, such leadership is implied. Most forms of psychotherapy manifest within their process ritualized submission, containment, and enactment:

> In order to facilitate a needed deconstruction of the old personality structure of the individual, the individual is offered an opportunity temporarily to surrender autonomy, to submit to a total process which has an autonomy of its own and which can enable the individual to maintain the needed orientation and structure during this time of deconstruction. Built into the therapeutic process is the creation of a relatively safe psychosocial space in which this deconstruction and surrender of autonomy can occur. It is in this ritually constructed therapeutic space that the enactment, both playful and painful, of innovative new behaviors and styles of thinking can be tested experimentally before returning to the world of *structure* and its merciless demands for adaptive effectiveness.[33]

Moore emphasizes that, while there are many other ritual dimensions of psychotherapy, the salient issue is that of *containment,* a term underscoring the issue of boundary maintenance.[34] Moore cites psychoanalysts Robert Langs and William Goodheart, who have used the analogous term *therapeutic frame* to suggest the strong boundaries which need to be maintained in an effective therapeutic field. The securing of a stable frame or boundary for therapeutic space has, Moore contends, become more than an expression of professional ethics. Moore contends that a stable frame has become the "sine qua non which must be present for the facilitation of any truly transformative therapeutic space".[35] He argues that maintenance of an effective therapeutic frame is essential for containment. Without a strong enough frame the intensity and depth of the transformative processes become truncated. In such a situation, therapist and patient may collude in resisting truths which need to be faced, and the transformative truth becomes dissipated or extinct.

Moore's thought on ritual leadership has implications far broader than our topic of a dialogue between shamanism and Jungian psychology. Nevertheless, it is of value to us in illuminating how the shaman exerts ritual leadership through the constitution and stewardship of the boundaries of sacred-transformative space. Moore's use of the shaman as a paradigmatic example of ritual mastery is instructive for contemporary psychotherapy and other forms of leadership. His work on ritual leadership will be taken up again when we examine the power of ritual in the transformation of intractable psychological and spiritual disorders in Part Three (Chapter 7).

Part Two
JUNG AND SHAMANISM

Chapter Three

===

Jung the Wounded Healer

SOME SHAMANIC ELEMENTS OF JUNG'S LIFE

It has often been observed that a writer's works reflect, in some way, the writer himself or herself. Perhaps we can extend this to say that an original psychologist's theories will be rooted to some extent in his or her own life experience. On this assumption we will begin exploring a dialogue between Jungian psychology and shamanism by looking first at the life and experience of C.G. Jung to see what might be shamanic in it. We might begin with such questions as: What is there about Jung's life and work that make it a good disciplinary dialogue partner with shamanism? Are there elements in Jung's life and work that are shamanic? If so, what are they? Was Jung a shaman? There are in fact areas of Jung's life that seem to run parallel to the classic phenomena and experience of shamanism. In this chapter we will limit our focus to some key elements in Jung's life and experience that can be said to be shamanic, or are closely parallel to it. We shall save the exploration of similarities and differences in his work and thought, and exploration of some implications for therapeutic practice, for subsequent chapters. To sharpen our discussion, we shall review some basic elements of classic shamanic experience, and then compare them with some important aspects of Jung's life and experience as he described them in his autobiography, *Memories, Dreams, Reflections* (MDR).[1] The period of Jung's life most fruitful to examine is the midlife crisis period beginning shortly after his break with Freud. It is during this period that Jung underwent a profound loss, which he himself considered equivalent to the shamanic conception of soul loss (MDR, p. 191), and had to make an original descent into his own unconscious to recover his soul. Jung's descent, exploration, and soul recovery constituted a self-healing of heroic proportions, since it resulted not only in the personal benefit of self-healing, but contributed an understanding of the self-healing tendencies of the psyche to his tribe of western man.

Up to now, we have claimed that the shaman is to be distinguished from other ritual elders, and medicine men and women, and from herbalists, bone setters, and other traditional healers who employ the sacred in their healing practices. We have followed Eliade in arguing that the shaman's special province is disorders of the soul, the most common disorders being soul loss, loss of a power animal, and sickness caused by spirit or power intrusions (related to a loss of power or vitality). The future shaman, we have said, is typically a wounded and dreamy youth, a loner whose introverted tendencies and unusual interests may make him or her seem strange to peers and community. The future shaman is called by the spirits, often by way of a crackup or life crisis, or by way of a major physical or psychological loss in which he or she is taught by the spirits, often under the guidance of an elder shaman, to heal himself or herself by intentionally and ritually undergoing the deep dismembering and transformative processes of the psyche. In that transformative or death/rebirth experience, the shaman learns what he or she fundamentally *is*, what his or her deepest wounds are, and how to heal them or bind them up. It is as a result of these discoveries, teachings, and healings that the shaman gains the wisdom, vision, and power to see into the souls of other afflicted individuals, to diagnose and treat them by the power of, and under the direction of, the spirits.

We should emphasize that the future shaman not only is singled out by superior psychological and spiritual abilities and then taught shamanic techniques for diagnosing and curing illness. Rather, the future shaman is grounded in a spiritual path and practice that entails discovering a strong center of orientation on which to found a strong sense of self. A hard-won integrity and sense of personal power are rooted in courageous self-examination and trust in, and knowledge of, the spirits. The preparatory and initiatory processes are lengthy and test the mettle the future shaman is made of. The path of the shaman emerges out of a difficult and time-consuming process of acquiring self-knowledge. It is a path that involves being firmly and deeply rooted in the spirit world, and in harmonious relationship to nature. It is out of the shaman's discovery of his or her center, the deepest core of the self where the sacred dwells, and out of the putting of himself or herself in intimate accord with it, that he or she is able to move solidly out towards the world in generosity and compassion as a healer and ritual elder. Without such a solid spiritual foundation, the shaman is likely to be weak and careless at best, or become an ego-motivated sorcerer using his or her talents for his or her own gain. Shamanism without this kind of spiritual foundation is indeed a dangerous thing.

It is from this fundamental understanding of shamanic experience that we shall examine some of the aspects of Jung's life that parallel the classic shamanic experience, and note some of the differences we might expect from a modern Western physician and psychologist.

JUNG'S CHILDHOOD: THE WOUNDING OF A HEALER

Like the childhood of many future shamans, Jung's childhood was marked by some oddities. He was a precocious and dreamy child, a loner who preferred to be out in nature, talking to stones, digging canals in the mud, and exploring his own imagination to being with friends. Jung's introversion was not simply a sign of his precocity or calling to be a great healer, but was also a sign of early childhood woundedness. Some explanation of his marked introversion can be understood in the light of his early childhood circumstances. Jung was born on July 26, 1875, in Keswil on Lake Constance, in the canton of Thurgau, in Switzerland. His father, a classically educated orthodox Protestant, took a pastorate in Lauffen six months later. In his autobiography, Jung describes his childhood as relatively happy, contented, and secure. He remembered the "sense of indescribable well being" of his early years. Yet, what he documents are dreams, experiences, and resulting anxieties that reveal another side to his early experience. Not all was as well as he preferred to remember it in his old age.

Jung remained an only child until nine years of age, when Gertrand, his sister, was born. This lack of siblings allowed Jung plenty of time to play alone, especially to explore his own imagination. There is not much evidence of a bond with playmates during these years, and Jung no doubt experienced more than a deep passion to be alone, but also a deep loneliness that his absorption in imagination and play helped him to abide. Jung describes a strong bond with his mother; he felt she had a hearty animal warmth, was a wonderful cook, and was pleasant and companionable. But he did not experience her as altogether reliable. He experienced different sides of her. One side, which he came to call her "personality No. 1," was well adapted, conventional in thought and attitude, and had a wonderful sense of humor. But she had another aspect, which he came to call her "personality No. 2". This No. 2 personality would now and then suddenly put in an appearance. He experienced this personality as unexpectedly powerful, uncanny, and frightening at times. This No. 2 personality fascinated Jung, but also frightened him. One may wonder what aspects of her No. 2 psychology actually frightened Jung, and if these aspects may have been reflective of deficits in her mothering skills. In Jung's first recalled dream, he goes down underground to a chamber where a large phallus-shaped figure sits on a throne. Jung felt a certain anxiety in its presence, and then he heard his mother's voice shout: "That is the Man Eater", which intensified his anxiety into terror, and he awoke (MDR, pp. 25–26). Jung himself believed the earliest recalled dreams are of great importance for an individual's psychology. If this is true, it is interesting to note that in this dream Jung's mother is not perceived as a figure who exhibits the maternal functions of calming and reassuring the little boy, but one who generates more anxiety. Anthony Stevens has drawn attention to some of the possible maternal difficulties Jung's mother had. He suggests that she was probably not adequately emotionally attuned to Jung in his place of horror; she does not reassure him or comfort him. Her somewhat feeble attempts to do so appear to generate more anxiety.[2] For example, once when Jung expressed anxiety to his mother over the drownings and funeral burials of people around the Rhine Falls, she attempted to comfort him with a song she sang every night: "Spread out Thy wings Lord Jesus mild, and take to Thee thy chick, Thy child". Little boy Jung experienced these words as anything but reassuring. In fact, the implication was that Jesus took you in death down into dark scary places underground. Jung came to fear not only Jesus, but developed a peculiar phobia of Jesuits as well, for they seemed connected to Jesus in some ominous way that Jung could not adequately fathom. There apparently was no further attempt, by Jung's mother, to monitor how Jung was doing with this anxiety, and to further attune her responsiveness to it. That Jung's mother did continually generate anxiety and was unreliably available in his early years becomes more plausible as we learn that she had a nervous breakdown and had to be hospitalized for several months, leaving Jung feeling abandoned, but in the care of an aunt and family maid. Around the time of her breakdown, Jung sensed forebodings in the air, and believed it had something to do with difficulties in his parents' marriage. His mother's maternal difficulties were no doubt rooted in her own psychological pain and perhaps in strained marital relations. Anthony Stevens suggests that her breakdown was a collapse into major depression (*On Jung*, p. 102). This occurred when Jung was age three, around the time he experienced the Man Eater dream. His mother's withdrawal into the asylum forced a prolonged separation from her that Jung no doubt experienced as further damaging to his sense of self. While he became particularly attached to the maid, he also was deeply affected by his mother's absence and developed a case of nervous eczema. Of the negative impact on his future experience of women and of love he said: "From then on, I always felt mistrustful when the word 'love' was spoken. The feeling I associated with 'woman' was for a long time that of innate unreliability" (MDR, p. 23).

Relating Jung's sense of abandonment or detachment by his mother to Bowlby's studies of attachment and detachment phenomena, Stevens suggests that Jung reacted by becoming self-absorbed and self-reliant to an unusual extent. Such defensive reactions to abandonment/detachment can result in an individual who becomes disconnected, remote, aloof from his peers, who has difficulty in integrating socially, and who may seem odd to his peers. By Jung's own account, his childhood solitary activities were fascinating, fun, and filled with exploration of the mysteries of the world of the psyche. To point to their connection with Jung's wound, and to draw attention to their defensive function, however, is not to underestimate their potentially constructive and even creative value. The future shaman typically begins with a wound, and it is through suffering this wound, becoming conscious of it, facing it, and learning to tend and heal it that one becomes truly initiated as a shaman. We may view Jung's childhood wounds and resulting fantasy life as at once a sign of his wounding, and as a sign of his potential as a greater healer. These wounds probably provoked a strong introverted tendency and an attending compensatory preoccupation with the psyche at an early age. Such introversion and fascination with the psyche has been noted as a characteristic of the future shaman.

LATE CHILDHOOD AND YOUTH: THE WOUND DEEPENS

Increasingly the young Jung explored the imaginal world, and found it irresistibly entertaining. By age eleven, when Jung was sent to the *Gymnasium* in Basel, his psychoneurotic constitution became suddenly worse; he felt himself to be in a social world which was disturbingly different from the familiar pastoral life with his country parson father. Basel, the big city with its powerful personages, seemed to shrink Jung's capacity for idealization of his father and his father's world. His classmates were rich and well groomed, their fathers were powerful and "lived in big, splendid houses, drove about in expensive carriages drawn by magnificent horses, and talked a refined French and German" (MDR, p. 24). Jung did not particularly like his polished, bourgeois classmates, and found his own personality quite different from theirs. He no doubt felt insecure and inadequate in this new environment.

Typical of many extremely gifted and creative children in modern Western civilization, Jung found school boring, and withdrew into fantasy: "It [school] took up far too much time which I would rather have spent drawing battles and playing with fire" (MDR, p. 27). Jung found himself wanting to withdraw more and more into the fantastic part of himself, his own "personality No. 2". There was a growing division in himself similar to what he experienced in his mother between inner and outer worlds. In his twelfth year Jung suddenly developed another neurosis. He reported that he was shoved down in the cathedral square and bumped his head, and almost lost consciousness. He took the opportunity to manipulate his father and use this injury as a possible way out of the dull activities of his school life. He did manage to convince his father and the family physician that he was too injured to return to school for awhile. During this time away from school (more than six months) Jung claims that he steeped himself more and more in solitude, withdrawing from ordinary waking pursuits into fantasy and reverie:

> Above all, I was able to plunge into the world of the mysterious. To that realm belonged the trees, a pool, the swamp, stones, and animals, and my father's library. But I was growing more and more away from the world, and had all the while faint pangs of conscience. I frittered away my time with loafing, collecting, reading, and playing. But I did not feel any happier for it; I had the obscure feeling that I was fleeing from myself. (MDR, pp. 30-31)

We could view this "fleeing from myself", from a shamanic perspective, as sign of soul loss, or of an increasing departure of his soul from the necessary responsibilities and obligations to the outer world. Jung, later reflecting on this time of his life from his perspective as a psychologist, saw himself as having become too unbalanced towards introversion (and his No. 2 personality), and claims that he suddenly came to his senses and made a decision to rebalance himself, moving again towards the adaptiveness of his school and social life after he overheard his father telling someone of his despair about Jung's future. It was around this point of his life when Jung began to realize that he himself had what he considered to be two personalities: the No. 1, and the No. 2. Recognition of this duality in himself, and in his mother, would later lend him an interest in dissociative pathology and lay the foundations for his own psychology based on dissociative and integrative processes. Jung applied this conceptuality of personalities No. 1 and No. 2 to this turning point in his youth. Personality No. 1 was considered his outwardly oriented and adapted self, capable of making its way in the world. This personality later became associated with Jung's conception of the ego and the persona. Personality No. 2 was considered by personality No. 1 to be darker, more mysterious, if more intuitive, individualistic, and ancient. Jung reports that he had a eureka experience, a sudden insight into his own duality one day:

> To my intense confusion, it occurred to me that I was actually two different persons. One of them was the school boy who could not grasp algebra and was far from sure of himself; the other was important, a high authority, a man not to be trifled with, as powerful and influential as this manufacturer. This "other" was an old man who lived in the eighteenth century, wore buckled shoes and a white wig and went driving in a fly with high, concave rear wheels between which the box was suspended on springs and leather straps. (MDR, p. 34)

> I always knew that I was two persons. One was the son of my parents, who went to school and was less intelligent, attentive, hardworking, decent, and cleaner than many other boys. The other was grown up—old, in fact—skeptical, mistrustful, remote from the world of men, but close to nature, the earth, the sun, the moon, the weather, all living creatures, and above all close to the night, to dreams, and to whatever "God" worked directly in him. (MDR, p. 44)

While personality No. 1 could be considered the adaptive functioning of the personality consisting of the ego, directed thinking, the persona, and their socially and psychologically adaptive purposes; personality No. 2 was viewed as a deeper self, an unfathomable depth of experience which is associated with processes of symbolic imagination, intuitive perception, and non-directed thinking and which invites solitary reverie and play. Jung found personality No. 1 most demanding and tiring, but the No. 2 personality he found a source of refreshing peace and solitude. No. 2 also seems to have been exalted in a compensatory way, covering over the inadequacies Jung felt from his No. 1.

Jung came to realize that there was a danger in being overly preoccupied or identified with personality No. 2. He considered *Zarathustra* to be Nietzsche's No. 2 personality, and *Faust* to be Goethe's. Nietzsche made the mistake, Jung believed, of identifying with No. 2, and of forsaking No. 1, which led to Nietzche's psychotic disintegration. In terms of his own psychological constitution, Jung appears to have been more fascinated with No. 2, but he found it necessary to readjust himself in the direction of No. 1 when he felt himself too far off balance in the direction of No. 2. Based on this intuition of the dual nature of his own personality, Jung eventually came to the generalized belief that psychological health for all people requires a balance between opposing forces.

Jung believed that the division into No. 1 and No. 2 was not what today is considered a dissociative disorder, but normally occurring aspects of the psychic totality. He also came to believe that it was a mistake to consider oscillations between oppositional forces as pathological, for "on the contrary, [the oppositions] are played out in every individual" (MDR, p. 45). As Jung prepared for his university education it became clearer to him that personality No. 1 needed a good education and grounding in life, that is, in the outer world. This realization probably influenced Jung to choose the sciences, to satisfy the demands of No. 1, but it was, no doubt, personality No. 2 that led him to select psychiatry for his post-doctoral specialty. In this way both personalities got some input in shaping the direction of his life course, although it would be at midlife before Jung's No. 2 personality would begin to more deeply stir and eventually consume his attention. Jung's deep woundings, stemming from his difficulties with his mother, and adolescent difficulties with his father, were by no means healed at this time. Their festering presence would resurface again at midlife and demand that Jung take note and do something with them. But for now, for the period in which he needed to prepare for adult life, he had stumbled on the insight that he must put all of this preoccupation with depths aside for awhile, and focus on the adaptive demands of personality No. 1.

Jung's intuition of the need to compensate for imbalances or one-sidedness in the direction of No. 2 could be considered an insight that provided a temporary self-healing, or at least a containment for wounds that must later be tended. That is to say, Jung's early theory was shaped by his experience of these contrasting opposites within the currents of his own psyche. Although Jung, as we said, found a preference for No. 2, he tells of a dream in which he realizes, just prior to beginning his university studies, that No. 1 is important to his adaptation to the outer world, and to his ability to confront the inner world.

> It was night in some unknown place, and I was making slow and painful headway against a mighty wind. Dense fog was flying along everywhere. I had my hands cupped around a tiny light which threatened to go out at any moment. Everything depended on my keeping this little light alive....This dream was a great illumination for me. Now I knew that No. 1 was the bearer of the light, and that No. 2 followed him like a shadow. My task was to shield the light.... I recognized that my path led irrevocably outward, into the limitation and darkness of three-dimensionality. (MDR, pp. 93-94)

Like the shaman who discovers that he must have one foot firmly placed in "this ordinary world", Jung concluded that the knowledge and experience of the "other world" must be limited for a time, and always supplemented by knowledge and practical competence in "this world". The shaman needs a firm and intentional grip in both worlds. For Jung, the need to rebalance in the direction outward (this world) implied that it was time to put limits on No. 2 and begin the academic development (public initiation of his No. 1) which would give him the firm grounding in the outer world which adult life required. This theme is still articulate when Jung later formulates the task of the first half of life as that of "ego-adaptation" to outer reality, whereby one achieves one's place in the social and economic order. It was the task of the second half of life, Jung came to believe, when No. 2 would again be given its due, for No. 1 (the ego/persona complex) to relinquish some of its dominance to make way for an expanded personality structure created by its encounter with and integration of No. 2.

There are many other inner and outer events in Jung's childhood and youth that could throw further light on his solitariness, his peculiarity, and his woundedness. But we have said enough to clarify the origin and nature of the childhood woundedness of Jung, the future wounded healer. All the precocious fantasy experiences, the mystical experiences, and the paranormal and uncanny experiences that Jung underwent provided rich data for him to experience in his solitude. They increasingly confirmed for him the objective reality of the psyche; and its importance. The fascination with this material was never totally set aside, even when he entered the university and medical school, but he discovered that getting a strong foothold in the outer world was necessary before further exploration of the inner world could safely be undertaken. These beliefs helped to clarify Jung's situation to himself, and helped him to bind himself while his ego acquired the further developments necessary for adaptation in the outer world.

YEARS OF APPRENTICESHIP

We shall fast-forward now up to Jung's University of Basel studies and medical school training in which he was an outstanding student and finished his studies in the shortest amount of time possible. His No. 2 personality interests, however, slowly crept back into his preoccupations, as his chosen medical dissertation topic focused on the spiritistic seances of his cousin Helene Preiswerk. The dissertation title, "On the Psychology of So-Called Occult Phenomena," designates Jung's desire to explore No. 2 interests, but with the now highly educated, scientifically trained intellect of his No. 1. Jung was still interested in the uncanny and the spirits, but now wanted to examine them with a hard-earned scientific, or at least, phenomenological, eye.

The dissertation topic was not a mere regression to the interests of his No. 2 personality, for Jung was clearly moving ahead with the program of personality No. 1, and then, in 1900, on into his psychiatric residency at the asylum at Burgholzli, under Eugen Bleuler (1857–1939), who was one of the most outstanding psychiatrists of his day. Jung's choice of psychiatry as a specialty may have been rationalized as a mere professional or even scientific choice, but it is not likely that Jung's own psychological wounds, and his own psychological giftedness, were not more determinative of this choice. Nevertheless, Jung speaks of his early fascination with psychiatry as if it were an apprenticeship in an area chosen by his own scientifically inquiring mind: "The years at Burgholzli were my years of apprenticeship. Dominating my interests and research was the burning question: 'What actually takes place inside the mentally ill?' That was something which I did not understand then, nor had any of my colleagues concerned themselves with such problems" (MDR, p. 114).

Jung was ambitious in his study, in his questioning and exploring the inner world of his patients. He became Bleuler's chief assistant and withdrew into the asylum's "monastic walls" and devoted every spare minute to reading the entire fifty volumes of *Allgemeine Zeitschrift für Psychiatrie*. Jung worked hard, long days focusing his scientific energies upon the investigation of the inner life of the patients, because he "wanted to understand how the human mind reacted to the sight of its own destruction". During the years at Burgholzli, Jung managed to find time to meet, court, and marry Emma Rauchenbach, the daughter of a wealthy industrialist. He claimed love at first sight. When he proposed the first time, she turned him down, perhaps because of differences in socioeconomic status, but this did not deter Jung. Jung was poor, and working in an unglamorous profession, but he was brilliant and certainly had a promising future. Emma eventually accepted the marriage proposal, and they were married in 1903; she moved into Jung's flat at Burgholzli, and they soon began making a family. Jung continued to pursue his knowledge of psychopathology passionately. His hungry and creative mind was no doubt propelled by the daimon of a wounded healer in the making. In his work with the asylum's insane patients, Jung felt that he was in the realm of lost souls, and this is indeed how a shaman would view the world inhabited by psychotic patients. In a shamanic view, psychotic states are an absorption, a lostness in the non-ordinary reality of the other world, where the person is lost to the social relationships and responsibilities of the ordinary reality of the everyday world. Jung, like many powerful shamans, was highly intuitive and had a knack for accessing the inner world of his patients. A great compassion and sympathy for the tortured soul was no doubt a major factor in his inquiry. He interviewed floridly psychotic patients and felt an urge to piece together their biographies, their stories, so that he might see if their bizarre and florid symptoms (delusions, hallucinations) could be placed in a meaningful context. He found that this psychotic material was not meaningless, but highly intelligible when placed in the context of the person's life story. This was a remarkable realization in his time, because the psychiatry of his time was interested in little else than classification of the various forms of insanity, all thought to be nothing more than symptoms of organicity, of brain pathology:

> Through my work with patients I realized that paranoid ideas and hallucinations contain a germ of meaning. A personality, a life history, a pattern of hopes and desires lie behind a psychosis.... It dawned on me then for the first time that a general psychology of the personality lies concealed within psychosis, and that even here we come upon the old human conflicts. Although patients may appear dull, apathetic, or totally imbecilic, there is more going on in their minds, and more that is meaningful, than there seems to be. (MDR, p. 127)

Jung came to believe that there was no fundamental difference between the sane and insane at the deepest levels of the soul: "At bottom we discover nothing new and unknown in the mentally ill; rather we encounter the substratum of our own natures" (MDR, p. 127). By 1904 Jung had begun laboratory experiments on psychopathology by means of the newly devised word association experiment. In this experiment the subject must respond as quickly to the series of stimulus words as possible. The reaction time was noted, and inordinate delays were made salient for psychological conjecture. Through this experimental procedure, Jung stumbled onto the concept of "feeling toned complexes," the autonomous contents of the unconscious which interfere with the reaction time. He came to believe that complexes were involved in psychopathology, and his method of association experiment using the galvanometer was later adapted to criminal investigation work, and became the basis of the lie detector test. Because of this work, Jung subsequently won some early fame, and traveled with Sigmund Freud to Clark University in the United States to receive an Honorary Doctor of Laws degree in 1909, at age 34. Jung had already met Freud in 1907, and had become interested in Freud's new theories of psychoanalysis after reading his book *The Interpretation of Dreams*.[3] He felt a special kinship with Freud because his theories introduced a psychological approach into psychiatry. Freud's approach was convergent with Jung's own, but Freud was 25 years Jung's senior, had much more experience than Jung, and had developed elegant theories. Jung was naturally attracted to Freud because no one else seemed to speak so knowledgeably and authoritatively to Jung's intuitions in, and discoveries about, the psyche. Another motivation for Jung's taking an active effort to establish contact with Freud, however, involved Jung's own father complex, and a need for a psychological ritual elder.

In order to understand Jung's attraction to Freud we need to understand something about Jung's disappointment with his own father. Jung was not only wounded by his mother's instability and intermittent availability; he was also deeply wounded by his father's lack of guidance of him intellectually and spiritually. Jung's mind was naturally open and inquiring. Jung's father's mind was relatively rigid, orthodoxly Protestant, and closed on the great questions of life. Jung's early experiences of god images were bound up with sexuality and feces, a dream of a phallus associated with Jesus as a man eater, and a vision of God sitting on his throne ejecting a giant turd which falls and crushes a cathedral. The god who had the impudence to show itself in such a manner seemed very different from the orthodox God of Jung's father. Jung had questions, but his father seemed to have stopped questioning. Jung found his father's mind closed, his theology boring and unsatisfactory, and surmised that his father himself suffered from a crisis of doubt, from which he never recovered. When Jung prepared for his first communion, he had hopes of learning something about God, but he was very disappointed to find his father knew little. When Jung asked him about the Trinity, how one could be three simultaneously, all his father could say is, "We'll skip that, for I really understand nothing about it myself" (MDR, p. 62). While this may have been an honest answer, it also must have felt like a discount to Jung's inquiring mind, and it must have been a major disappointment to his passionate No. 2 personality. Jung seemed to be seeking for what self-psychologists call an "idealizing selfobject" in his father, someone who could guide and teach him, confirm his intellectual and spiritual gifts, and acknowledge Jung's future promise. Jung was amazed to find that his father, a pastor and theologian of sorts, had so little of divine knowledge for him. Jung decided that Christian theology was boring and the church characterized more by an absence of God than a fullness of his presence. Jung concluded that his father had nothing of interest to teach him, and he became so disenchanted with Christianity that he decided that "a church is a place I should not go" (MDR, p. 64).

It appears that Jung had not really found an adequate idealizable father figure in his university days, nor in Bleuler, although he was a worthy mentor. By the time Jung had discovered the reality of the soul (psyche) in the insane, he had recovered the passion and interest of his No. 2 personality along with the discipline and power of his No. 1 intellect. Sigmund Freud must have seemed just the right salve for Jung's wounding around his father, for Freud was developing a science of the No. 2 domain. Here, at last, there seemed to be a brilliant older man who had just the kind of interests that Jung had, and who was more experienced and advanced in understanding them. Jung was in need of a spiritual father, and Freud seemed to be in need of a blessed son.

FATHER FREUD

When Freud and Jung met in Vienna in 1907, they were so excited and had so many ideas to exchange that their initial conversation ran thirteen hours non-stop: a sign that the archetypal father and son couplet had been activated. It seemed to be another situation of "love at first sight." Freud valued Jung tremendously, and came to view him as the most brilliant of his students, and the probable future crown prince of psychoanalysis. There was much mutual admiration exchanged, and a great deal of collaboration. From the start, however, this relationship was unstable and problems lay just under the thin surface of their friendship. Freud immediately had an agenda for Jung, and Jung no doubt had his own agenda. It is not likely that Jung wanted to remain a priest of anyone else's dogma, for his own ambitions, in accord with his own unusual gifts and the drive towards individuation, would insure that Jung would not remain Freud's disciple.

Freud's agenda was to have a successor to lead psychoanalysis into the future, a future that apparently involved no possibility of deviating from Freudian doctrine, especially the sexual nature of the libido. Jung's agenda was informed in part by his need for an idealizable intellectual father figure, for someone who could teach him, and for a partner in scientific inquiry, who would work with him in a common cause and common interest. Jung wanted to continue his investigations, add new knowledge to psychoanalysis, even abandon theory when it no longer made sense of the facts. And there was the proverbial rub. Freud's theory of the sexual nature of the libido was set in concrete; for Freud it was fact, not to be modified. A higher or more fundamental level of understanding was not possible. Jung's reflections on his own experience, and upon that of his patients and of cases he'd read about, suggested inadequacies in the Freudian libido theory. Jung thought it ludicrous that the infant's sucking at its mother's breast could be a sexual act. It was also possible, Jung thought, to view the satisfaction displayed by an infant at its mother's breast as a sign of the kind of satisfaction anyone gets from eating. Jung felt Freud's libido theory confused the reproductive instinct with a normal hunger drive. Jung was well aware that sexuality could be present at birth and develop into maturer forms over time. But he felt the libido was more fundamental and psychic in nature, than it was sexual. As psychic energy, it would migrate to whatever zone (oral, anal, phallic, etc.) was seasonally relevant to the child's developmental or maturational schedule. At the phallic or genital stage it would of course be characterized by sexual themes and interests. Jung felt that Freud had overextended the concept of sexuality to describe all developmental stages from birth to maturity. He lacked an adequate understanding of the maturation and transformations of libido in adulthood, at midlife, and in old age.

Jung was convinced that it was good science to modify or abandon theory if it wasn't adequate to the facts, or if they could be better explained by other theoretical constructs. Once he began publishing thoughts to this end, the relationship with Freud began to unravel. But there were other significant differences as well. Jung was increasingly interested in studying reli-

gious and occult material, and by 1911 had begun psychoanalyti-
cally investigating astrology, mythology, and other occult areas
for their psychological contents, with ambivalent blessings from
Freud. Paradoxically, Jung's association with Freud seemed to
consolidate his own scholarly confidence, and was partially healing for him in this way. However, it was the same confidence in
the validity of his own ideas that drove an irreparable wedge
between himself and Freud.

Jung's personal problems with what he later called the
anima, the soul-image, the inner feminine, manifested themselves during his partnership with Freud, and also no doubt
served to caution Freud of Jung's seeming adolescent instabili-
ties. There was no doubt that Jung loved his wife, Emma, but he
felt from early on in the marriage that she could not satisfactorily
contain him or adequately reflect aspects of his anima, especially
those aspects having to do with his feelings of maternal abandonment, and the need for an admiration and soul-to-soul partnership and merger. By the time Emma's energies were invested
in maternal responsibilities, Jung found himself being irresistibly
attracted to a number of other women. Perhaps Emma's maternal investments seemed to him another abandonment, thus activating his old mother complex. Perhaps Jung required more
energies than Emma could give at this point in her life. Perhaps
Jung was naturally polygamous, as he liked to think of it. The fact
is that he was indeed involved in a series of brief amorous entanglements with other women, at least two of which were his
patients. He made no secret of his sexual pursuit of extramarital
relationships, and sought after Freud's advice and help when he
got into a mess. His analysis of Sabina Spielerein went astray and
Freud had to take over. When Jung attempted to become Emma's
analyst and trainer, he quickly made a mess of it, using the analysis as a forum for attempting to manipulate Emma into feeling
comfortable with his promiscuous intentions. It didn't work, and
Emma sought Freud's advice, for Jung seemed blind to the jeal-
ousy, indignation, and anxiety he was arousing in Emma by using
his analysis with her as a rationalization for his own motives.

In 1910 a young woman by the name of Toni Wolff became
Jung's patient. She was an intelligent and mysterious young

woman who suffered a breakdown upon the death of her father, a wealthy Zurich businessman. There is no doubt that Jung was able quickly to help Toni. The death of her father probably left considerable unfinished business with him; Jung, an older man by at least fourteen years, no doubt provided her with a relatively able substitute father figure, enabling her to regain her equilibrium, even if her analysis with him was too brief to work through her father complex and other issues. It may be too much to say that Jung had a corresponding need for an admiring daughter figure; it is probably more accurate to say that he was vulnerable and hungry for a woman to reflect aspects of himself (anima) that were not mediated by Emma. What he seemed to need from Toni was that she be his *femme inspiratrice,* and later a containing vessel for him. The functions of admiration, adoration, comforting, and containing have a maternal ring to them. It is probably the case that Jung's femme inspiratrice (Toni) was more accurately an embodiment of the maternal functions which he languished for and lost to his mother's illness, and which he enjoyed briefly from his nursemaid. Those aspects of Jung's anima more in line with his maternal wounding, and with his additional feelings of letdown and abandonment by his father and by Freud, were apparently picked up or reflected by Toni.

SEPARATION AND SOUL LOSS

Toni Wolff's analysis was evidently brief, and no one is certain how long it lasted or at what point the affair actually began. We do not know when or how the affair became apparent to Emma. By 1911 Emma's letters to Freud revealed that she was very troubled, and later in the year, during the Weimar Conference of the International Psychoanalytic Association, gossip of the affair had begun to circulate.[4] Jung apparently had no intentions of ending his marriage to Emma and would have no talk of a divorce. What resulted was a strange triangle in which both women played a different role and shared differing aspects of the same man: Emma was the nominal wife and true mother of Jung's children. Toni appeared to be the true lover, femme inspiratrice, collaborator, and nursemaid. Like the nursemaid (substitute mother), she was emotionally close to Jung, while he probably experienced Emma as emotionally distant. Toni apparently had an olive complexion and dark hair like the nursemaid that cared for Jung during his mother's long absence. This triangular arrangement entailed significant strain on all concerned, and this strain was probably a factor in Jung's breakdown following upon the break with Freud.

The inevitable and devastating break with Freud came in 1912, and it dramatically initiated Jung's personal explorations into the unconscious. The reader of MDR may be led to think that Jung explored the depths of his own unconscious out of scientific or psychological curiosity or commitment: "From the beginning I had conceived my voluntary confrontation with the unconscious as a scientific experiment which I myself was conducting and in whose outcome I was vitally interested" (MDR, p. 179). But we only need to read the next line to get a hint that it was more than a scientific experiment: "I might equally well say that it was an experiment that was being conducted on me" (MDR, p. 179), and indeed it was conducted on him. While it is true that Jung did confront the unconscious in as objective and scientific a manner as he could, the descent was not altogether voluntary. Immediately following upon the break with Freud, Jung was ushered into a midlife crisis of monumental proportions. Consider that he had lost another significant figure in his life, "Father Freud". His own fragmentation over this was further deepened by the consequences on his social and public life: the necessary resignation from the International Psychoanalytic Association, and from his teaching post at the University of Zurich. All of his psychoanalytic friends and colleagues withdrew from him. In short, Jung's hard-won outer world collapsed. All that he had built in the first half of his life, on the basis of his No. 1 personality, crumbled, and he was set adrift in a seething sea of doubt, lost and directionless as to his own ideas and his life's course: "After the break with Freud, all my friends and acquaintances dropped away. My book was declared rubbish; I was a mystic, and that settled the matter" (MDR, pp. 162–163). Jung's own mature psychology and theory had not yet emerged in a clear and distinct form. He had used Freud's edifice for his own intellect to react against, to begin defining his own position, in a parasitic, if creative, manner.

Suddenly, he no longer had a Freudian framework, nor did he yet have a "Jungian" framework. Jung was no doubt deeply, narcissistically wounded by the public loss, embarrassment, and lack of appreciation for his solid work. The resulting feelings of rejection, loss of appreciation, and lack of sense of his own mature framework ushered in a period of profound disorientation; he was betwixt and between firm structures.

According to Stevens, in the weeks and months following the break with Freud, Jung became seriously depressed and close to psychosis. The insult to Jung's self-esteem, his lostness with respect to his own psychology and his future, released a powerful upsurge from the unconscious. From a shamanic perspective, Jung was now suffering a form of soul loss, and his life (his future, his work, and the well-being of his marriage and family) was at stake. Shamanically speaking, soul loss has traditionally been associated not only with a loss of will, such as we find in depression, or with a loss of vital powers, such as we find in pathological dissociation, but also with a loss of connection to community, to the social sphere. In soul loss, one may be so lost in the "realm of imagination", in altered states of consciousness, that there is little relatedness to the outer world. In this respect, Jung must have felt very "lost" indeed.

During this liminal period Jung was so frequently absorbed in non-ordinary reality (Castaneda) as to substantiate Stevens' belief that he was nearly psychotic. Jung temporarily and intermittently lost his foothold in the realm of No. 1. He heard voices, had visions, dreamt of rivers of blood, talked with spirits as he walked in his garden. He was so absorbed in the altered states of consciousness associated with psychotic, mystic, and shamanic realms that he had to remind himself that he was a doctor, a really existing person with a family, patients, and responsibilities. In talking to himself in this manner, he was seeking to regain and maintain the foothold in both worlds, of No. 1 as well as the No. 2 he was so nearly irresistibly immersed in.

JUNG'S RITUAL ELDERS AND TRIBE

During a shamanic initiatory crisis, the initiant has available ritual elders, master shamans to whom he or she can go to guide and safely contain the transformative process. The wounded healer learns to heal himself or herself partly through the encounter with the spirits, and partly under the necessary structuration and guidance of the ritual elders. Jung had no ritual elder, no analyst to help him sort through and understand the emerging material, and no professional therapeutic containing vessel was available. Going to an asylum was not an option. There weren't even any helpful books on what he was experiencing to help guide him though the process. The ritual responsibilities, perhaps by default, fell to Emma and Toni. With their valuable help, he was able to respond to this "upsurge from the unconscious" with the intentionality and courage of a shaman, and the desire for objectivity and understanding of a scientist. Perhaps it is too simplistic to say that Emma provided much love and faith in Jung, and domestic and financial security (material container), and Toni provided love and possibly some esoteric knowledge that helped to psychologically structure the process (psychological container) for Jung, but it is probably not far off the mark.[5] Recalling James Hillman's conception of "relationships as containers", the idea that "the deeper the relationships go, the more they can contain", the matrix of relationships between Jung, Emma, and Toni must have run very deep. This brings to mind the powerful containing roles of the community when illness occurs in tribal life. The shaman will often call together the patient's extended family or clan, and involve them in the preparations and procedures of the healing ritual. Sometimes, the entire tribe is invited to participate. The weight of the community, their love and concern, not only provides safety and security for the healing ritual, it sends an important loving and supportive message to the afflicted. In his midlife initiation Toni and Emma, and perhaps Jung's family, were his personal tribe, albeit a small but loving tribe or clan. Their very real love for him and relatedness to him, in combination with his own determination, somehow constellated a good enough ritual space/time pod. It was only by such a vessel provided by these relationships that he could safely make the nekyia into the water of the collective unconscious, and undergo the necessary and heroic transformation that midlife was requiring of him. It was in this makeshift ritual context that Jung underwent the most profound experiences with non-ordinary reality, the collective unconscious; and this ritual context made it possible for his encounter with numinous spirits, visions, dreams, and voices to become a transformation of shamanic proportions. Like the shaman and the archetypal hero, Jung, as we shall see, was able to return from his journey not only with benefits for his own life but with a boon for his collective tribe (western society) as well.

THE DESCENT: JOURNEY AND SPIRIT GUIDES

For a while, Jung was uncertain how to approach his own emerging unconscious material with a method that would be useful and reliable in yielding insight into it. Recalling his doctoral thesis on his mediumistic cousin, Helene Preiswerk, where he suggests that the doubling of consciousness (as in dissociative states, mediumship, multiple personality) is fundamentally "new character formations or attempts of a future personality to break through", Jung hit upon an insight into how to approach his own unconscious material. If he approached it with an attitude that the events emerging in his dreams, fantasies, and visionary material were suggestive of his future personality, a greater personality, then the results of his encounter might be fruitful. This idea in itself became a type of container, and inspired him to search further within himself. With trust in the emerging material as purposeful, Jung began to experiment with ways to intentionally enter various altered states of consciousness, and to even evoke the experiences with the numinous figures himself. On December 12, 1913, Jung was sitting at his desk pondering his fears. On that day he took a decisive step: "Then I let myself drop. Suddenly it was as though the ground literally gave way beneath my feet, and I plunged down into the darkest depths" (MDR, p. 179).

The language of "dropping down into dark depths" is reminiscent of shamanic trance-journey language for a descent into the underworld. Jung, seeking to avoid notions of hypnosis, or mystical trance, preferred to use his own term, which he coined for the process, "active imagination". In the process of learning to do active imagination, Jung began by visualizing a descent, a passage downward. He kept at it until he began to see that he was arriving somewhere in an other world.

> In order to seize hold of the fantasies, I frequently imagined a steep descent. I even made several attempts to get to the very bottom. The first time I reached a depth, as it were, of about a thousand feet; the next time I found myself at the edge of a cosmic abyss. It was like a voyage to the moon, or a descent into empty space. First came the image of an empty crater, and I had the feeling that I was in the land of the dead. The atmosphere was that of the other world. (MDR, p. 181)

Traditionally speaking, shamans have used some form of percussion to facilitate trance states and enhance or vivify the imagination. Jung's method of active imagination apparently involved no percussion to facilitate trance or intensify visualization; he apparently did not need it. He seemed to have found through persistence and concentration that he could enter the underworld through this method and make his own nekyia (journey) much as Odysseus journeyed through the land of the dead. As such, Jung's journeys eventually yielded impressive results. On one occasion he encountered a couple of spirit figures, an old man who called himself Elijah, and young girl, called Salome. Jung was able to converse with them, and listened to what they had to say. They claimed to have been together from all eternity. Jung, kicking in his left brain, his psychological understanding, interpreted Salome as an anima figure, and thought of Elijah as a personification of the archetype of the old wise man, embodiments of the eros and logos principles. In interpreting the spirit figures that appear in psychological terms, Jung differentiates himself from the traditional shaman who takes the phenomena just as they appear, as spirits. But Jung does not seem to deny their objectivity or value by interpreting them psychologically, although this respect for their objectivity only becomes clear to him after his encounter with another spirit figure, Philemon.

Jung tells us that Philemon emerged out of Elijah, as if Philemon is a higher or more complete manifestation of the psychical entity. This phenomenon is not new to shamans. In classical shamanic understandings, spirits and spirit guides are thought to be very old spirit entities. A spirit guide or power animal eventually may leave a shaman and be replaced by another, or it may reappear when it shape-shifts or changes form. When a shaman's spirit guide or power animal changes form, this is often because the shaman is ready for a fuller revelation of its reality. It first relates to the shaman in a form he or she can understand. As the shaman matures, a higher form is manifested. This in turn may even be superseded by higher forms. In this way the shaman's consciousness is gradually expanded. Something similar may have been going on with the transformation from Elijah to Philemon. While Philemon was later superseded by another figure, Ka, Jung chose not to tell us much about it except for offering a few Egyptian amplifications. Instead of telling us more about Ka, he decided to focus on the importance of Philemon. This may be because Philemon opened the initial door to a deeper understanding of the psyche for Jung.

Philemon first appeared to Jung in a dream, in the image of an old man with a long white beard, the horns of a bull, and the wings of a kingfisher. He flew to Jung holding four keys in his hand. Jung considered him an ancient Gnostic figure who revealed the objectivity of the psyche to him. At first Jung did not understand this dream figure, so he carefully and lovingly painted his image, which he placed in his secluded, pastoral solitary retreat at Bollingen. During the days when Jung was painting this picture he was thunderstruck to find a dead kingfisher, while walking in his garden. Kingfishers are rare in the vicinity of Bollingen, and Jung never saw one in the area again. This event he felt to be highly synchronistic, an outer confirmation of the objective reality of the inner world. Jung was very struck by the sense of importance to him that Philemon evoked, and he became drawn to engage him in dialogue through active imagination. Jung had a series of important conversations with Philemon, and would take walks in his garden holding philosophical discussions with him. In his discussion about Philemon, Jung reveals just how struck he was by his objective inner reality, and by his message about the objectivity of the psyche:

> Philemon and the other figures of my fantasies brought home to me the crucial insight that there are things in the psyche which I do not produce, but which produce themselves and

have their own life. Philemon represented a force which was not myself. In my fantasies I had conversations with him, and he said things which I had not consciously thought. For I observed clearly that it was he who spoke, not I. He said I treated thoughts as if I generated them myself, but in his view thoughts were like animals in the forest, or people in a room, or birds in the air, and added, "If you see people in a room, you would not think that you made those people, or that you were responsible for them". It was he who taught me psychic objectivity, the reality of the psyche. Through him the distinction was clarified between myself and the object of my thought. He confronted me in an objective manner, and I understood that there is something in me which can say things that I do not know and do not intend, things which can even be directed against me....Psychologically, Philemon represented superior insight. He was a mysterious figure to me. At times he seemed quite real, as if he were a living personality. I went walking up and down the garden with him, and to me he was what the Indians call a guru. (MDR, p. 183)

Jung's need for a ritual elder to help him during this chaotic time of his life seems to have been met by Philemon: "I could have wished for nothing better than a real live guru, someone possessing superior knowledge and ability, who would have disentangled for me the involuntary creations of my imagination" (MDR, p. 184). Jung had not heard of the idea of an inner guru until fifteen years later when talking with a friend of Ghandi's who said his own guru was Shankaracharya, the commentator on the Vedas who died centuries before. In learning that it was possible for a Hindu devotee to have a ghost guru, Jung felt even more confirmed in the belief in Philemon's objectivity as an inner guru (spirit guide). Philemon came to be understood as an aspect of his higher Self, and after his encounters with it and his confrontations with the anima, Jung realized that all the visionary activity had to do with his own condition, his own actual life, whatever else it might be about: "No matter how deeply absorbed or how blown about I was, I always knew that everything I was experiencing was ultimately directed at this life of mine" (MDR, p. 189). Over a period of several years Jung gradually experienced the outlines of the inner change.

VISIONS OF THE DEAD

If Philemon was a kind of spirit guide or inner guru who opened Jung up to the objectivity of the psyche, it was the visionary activity subsequent upon his encounters with Philemon that yielded insights into additional pieces of the framework of Jung's mature psychology. Jung had been thinking about, and struggling with, his own theory of the psyche. It had not yet emerged in its clear and mature form, but through these encounters with Elijah and Philemon, and the anima figures, it began to gradually emerge into conscious formulation. By this time Jung already had a theory of the collective unconscious, an awareness of the archetypes, and a view of the psyche's personifications as representations of a greater personality. He also intuited the self-healing tendencies of the psyche and knew that trusting it was important. But the hub of his psychology, the goal, and its basic structures were still not crystal clear to him. Jung felt compelled to express and formulate what might have been said by Philemon on this subject. Out of his struggle with these questions, and the pressure of trying to solve them, a period of strange and synchronistic phenomena, followed by dramatic visionary activity, developed.

"It began with a restlessness", Jung claims, and he and his family felt as if there were spirits in his house that wanted something of him, only he did not know what they wanted. "Then it was as if my house began to be haunted. My eldest daughter saw a white figure passing through the room" (MDR, p. 190). Jung reports that a second daughter related that twice her blanket had been snatched away. The same night his nine-year-old son had an anxiety dream. Jung's entire environment seemed to be highly charged; he and his family experienced a type of mystical merger, a *participation mystique* (Lévy-Bruhl). We won't repeat the entire description of the pressure building up in Jung's household, but it was uncanny. Jung describes the situation and what follows, reporting that the door bell began to ring frantically, but no one was found to be there:

> The atmosphere was thick, believe me! Then I knew that something had to happen. The whole house was filled as if

there were a crowd present, crammed full of spirits. They
were packed deep right up to the door, and the air was so
thick it was scarcely possible to breathe....I was all a-quiver
with the question: "For God's sake, what in the world is
this?" Then they cried out in chorus, "We have come back
from Jerusalem where we found not what we sought". That
is the beginning of the *Septem Sermones.*

Then it began to flow out of me, and in the course of
three evenings the thing was written. As soon as I took up
the pen, the whole ghostly assemblage evaporated. The
room quieted and the atmosphere cleared. The haunting
was over. (MDR, pp. 190–191)

No doubt Jung's family was glad Jung had a creative breakthrough, and what a breakthrough it was. The *Septem Sermones ad
Mortuos,* while given as the Gnostic "Seven Sermons of the
Dead," which Jung wrote down in a Latin script, set out a number of the basic ideas of Jung's mature psychological theory,
most notably the theory of polar oppositions and of masculinity
and femininity (intimations of the anima and animus theory),
and the relation of sexuality and spirit. It was as if out of Jung's
confusion and tremendous desire for some clarity about his psychology, a eureka experience had occurred, which finally
reduced the tension in him, and in his household, by giving him
more details of his own psychology. A kind of gestalt closure/sat-
isfaction relieved the situation for everyone. The psychological
ideas which came forth were not worked out consciously, however, but were given as a gift from beyond, it seems, through a
process that Jung is unclear about, but which appears to have
been automatic writing, perhaps a form of active imagination for
him. Jung repeatedly had revelatory dreams or visions of this
sort, where he gained tremendous psychological and spiritual
insight. He tended to interpret such experiences in psychological
terms as information coming from the collective unconscious or
from the greater personality. In these psychological interpretations, Jung takes care to remain respectful of their objectivity,
emphasizing at the very least that they do not come from his own
ego-consciousness.

THE ANIMA: RECOVERING SOUL AT MIDLIFE

Experiences such as the hauntings and visions around the *Septem Sermones* give us an inkling of just how stressful it must have been to be around Jung at this time in his life, and more than an inkling of how precarious his own psychological condition was. Jung worked hard at trying to understand the meaning of this material for his own life. Like the shaman who must directly experience, know, and learn from the spirit revelations, Jung adopted a creative attitude towards these unconscious contents. This creative attitude of trying to understand every image and act with its implications probably prevented the experiences from becoming destructive. The shaman, too, must adopt such a constructive attitude in becoming a self-healer. It is not likely, however, that Jung could have "healed himself" without the help of the women in his life, his family context, his very human ritual elders. Stevens suggests that Toni Wolff was especially helpful to Jung during periods when he felt he was losing his sanity, and that this may be why Emma Jung was able to tolerate her presence, even accept her into the family circle for a time. The relationship of Toni to Jung's experience of soul loss is worth considering. Around the time of the *Septem Sermones,* Jung described having a fantasy that "my soul had flown away from me" (MDR, p. 191), and Jung likened his own situation and experience to the primitive experience of soul loss (MDR, p. 191).

Midlife, that time when a person has climbed the ladder and realized it is against the wrong wall, is a time of profound change, for women as well as men. Since we are attempting to understand Jung's experience, we will make a few comments on the male midlife crisis, and relate it to anima activity. For a man, midlife is a time of reevaluating and, often, of feeling dissatisfied with one's achievements, with the values and orientation by which one has led one's own life. Discontent and depression often attend this condition as a man loses his bearings. He wants something more, needs something more, but does not yet know what. At midlife the anima typically becomes powerfully aroused. Those aspects of a man's life that have been unacknowledged or not made conscious and integrated often become activated by a lover. Powerful romantic longings, sexual lusts, desires for carefree playing, or a desire to throw off old stultifying commitments arise. Additionally, old wounds resurface and clamor for attention. This can be a most critical challenge to a man's sense of identity and continuity. It can be an opportunity for self-transformation or self-destruction.

Jung recalls a story. He was writing down a fantasy one day and suddenly heard a voice from within call what he was doing art, rather than psychology. Jung felt this as a seductive and tempting voice, and a dangerous one, for he already had a life, a wife, and a career, and he recognized that acting on such a voice could cost him his hard-won life structure (e.g., his marriage, his livelihood, his career). It was too late, in any event, to start over from scratch, and he felt his psychology was more important to him than just doing art. He feared that if he listened to her he would end up high and dry in some Bohemian garret. He was struck by the feminine feel of this part of himself, and was "intrigued by the fact that a woman should interfere with me from within" (MDR, p. 186). After some conjecture that this voice might be from a bit of undeveloped feminine personality that was developing within himself, he came upon the idea this was his soul, in a primitive sense, and had a feminine quality. He quickly became aware of a duality to the anima, that it had a positive aspect as well as a negative aspect. It could be a femme inspiratrice or a femme fatale, for example. It all depends on the man's psychology and what he does with it.

At midlife, if a man has been neglecting his anima, she may become so charged that she arouses powerful compensatory urges. For example, if a man has been one-sidedly goal-focused and overrational in building his career, neglecting the more feeling, intuitive, playful, and sensual aspects of his life and relationships, he may become seized by anima-generated fantasies. These may become projected onto a special type of woman who fascinates the man and becomes an object of obsession. Such a man may be attracted to passionate embraces in a lustful relationship, or he may seek femme fatales who ultimately will destroy him if he does not become conscious and change his course of action. Through the passion, sensuality, and carefree and non-rational spirit such a passionate relationship evokes, the

psyche is attempting to compensate for its neurotic onesidedness. If the man is fortunate enough to become conscious of his
onesidedness, and if he realizes that the problems stem from
within himself (neglect of his anima), he may become able to
consciously integrate these anima aspects (the non-rational, playful, sensuous, intuitive, and wounded aspects) into his personality organization. If all goes well, the anima then becomes a
positive force, a guide or pathway into his own depths.

The concept of the anima is of major importance to Jung's
soul theory, and it is important to note that Jung's understanding of it emerged out of his own midlife crisis. Jung did not
learn of the anima by conjecture or studying books; he learned
about it through direct experience, the way shamans best learn
about the soul. There is a sense in which only in a midlife crisis
does a man come fully to encounter the anima and begin to
understand it. It can not be understood from book learning
alone, for it must be experienced. At midlife its power is tremendous indeed. Jung used the term *anima* in a number of different
but related aspects. It is the Latin word for soul, and Jung
described it variously as the "soul image" of a man, as the
"archetype of the inner feminine" in a man's psychology, just as
the animus is the "inner masculine" in a woman's psychology.
As an archetype, the anima is a "bridge" to the deeper depths of
the psyche, to the archetypes of the collective unconscious. As a
bridge, it is a kind of psychopomp, or guide into the collective
unconscious.

A man's experience of the anima is colored by his early
experience of significant females, his mother, sisters, aunts, girl-
friends, first love, and later, other women. In the process of
falling in love a man projects his anima, his soul image, onto the
woman. This projection makes her highly attractive, numinous.
Such attractions may insure the survival of the species, but they
also insure drama further on down the line. The woman is compelling precisely because the anima projected onto her mediates
the man's unconscious. Of course, if the man has been wounded
by women (e.g., his mother), this will be reflected in his anima.
Midlife crises have a way of rubbing a man's nose in his wounds
and vulnerabilities by way of the anima.

In the case of Emma Jung and Toni Wolff, Emma was encumbered with focusing her maternal energies on the children and providing the home and economic stability, and attendant feeling of safety that a nice setup provides. Toni seemed to represent an inspiring muse, a woman who was intelligent, wise, admiring, and comforting. But Toni was also young, wounded, and probably in need of a father figure. For a middle-aged man who felt wounded by his mother, to be admired by a young woman must have seemed most attractive. Toni possessed another important quality as already mentioned. Her dark hair and olive skin reminded Jung, apparently, of the nursemaid that he had become attached to during the period when his mother had been institutionalized. As a target for Jung's anima projections, the dual role of muse and nursemaid to Jung's wounded psyche fell upon Toni. It is possible that one aspect of the Elijah and Salome figures had been to mirror the anima/animus relationship of Jung and Toni. The motivations to cooperate with Jung's demands upon her may have been complemented by her own need for a wise father figure. In this view, those aspects of her animus colored by her experience of her father were caught by Jung. Without going into the thorny question of the professional ethics of Jung making her his lover and confidante, we may suggest perhaps that both individuals were wounded, and were able to help each other out in some way, however incomplete Toni's analysis with Jung must have been. Certainly Jung could not have come upon the conception of the anima without real relationship entanglements, and his entanglement with Toni (and Emma). For Jung, this help seemed vital to the recovery from his soul loss. Having lost his mother to depression, at a young and critical age, he recently lost Freud's admiration and love. These losses would be profound since they were highly important figures in Jung's life. While Freud was a father figure, he was also a parent figure providing certain emotional supplies that Jung needed, such as confirmation of his value, of his gifts, and of his future. To lose Freud must have felt analogous to the magnitude of the loss of his mother, thus evoking Jung's mother complex and the vulnerabilities associated with it. Toni Wolff, who greatly appreciated and believed in Jung and his destiny, must have served a compensatory healing function. She admired, confirmed, and contained him, and through his relationship with Toni, Jung's self-understanding increased as he became aware of his anima, and gradually learned to withdraw it from her, thus recovering his soul or his soul image. She provided a valuable reparative function for him. Stevens speaks of the personally difficult but important role she played in Jung's own soul recovery:

> She carried the full burden of his anima projection, as well as his terrors and despair, until the personification of the anima in his fantasy life became sufficiently differentiated for him to be less in need of an outer woman to mediate his work with the unconscious....Toni evidently advanced Jung's individuation by enabling him to integrate the unlived feminine in himself and bring it to maturity. There is little doubt that the relationship was of equal importance to her.[6]

Through understanding Jung's concept of the anima in the context of his midlife illness, we come to see how he arrived at an understanding of soul recovery as a psychological process of reclaiming aspects of the greater Self that have been dissociated or projected. From Jung's relation to Toni Wolff we can see how important it can be to have a human relationship to mediate the process of reclamation and recovery. This has two fundamental implications. First, like most shamans undergoing crisis and initiation, Jung did not self-heal completely on his own. Although he did tremendous work, mustering great courage and self-discipline to heal himself, he still required his little tribe or clan to help him. The importance of the weight of the family or community in healing is well established. Second, like a shaman undergoing initiation, Jung also required a ritual elder to provide structure, to provide the container. There were no knowledgeable ritual elders available in his society to help him. He thus allowed Toni and Emma to provide a human ritual container for his initiation. Like the shaman relying on the spirits for guidance and healing, Jung had to rely on Philemon and other figures as they revealed themselves to him. It was through his confrontations, conversations, and reliance on the insights gleaned from these numinous figures that Jung can be said to have self-healed by virtue of their inner help.

The necessity of human relationships, especially with ritual elders, in a safe and secluded ritual space/time pod is fundamental to shamanic initiation. The traditional shaman has played the role of such a human mediator for the shaman-to-be in the past, as the modern urban shaman still does. However, without psychological work and effort on the part of the patient in welcoming home (Ingerman) and integrating the recovered soul or aspects of the soul, the recovery will be in vain as the soul will become lost again. Without the process of psychologically recognizing how the recovered soul or soul parts fits within a person's life context and relationships, and within their own habits of living, it is also unlikely that soul recovery in any lasting sense is possible.

DISCOVERING THE GOAL AND RETURNING WITH THE BOON

Jung's midlife crisis came to resolution around 1918–1919 when he was drafted into the military. He acted as commandant in a prisoner of war camp at Chateau d'Oex, and found time to continue his inner work. In the mornings he would sketch a circle in his notebooks, a mandala (Sanskrit for sacred circle), and within it he would draw what he felt to be his inner situation at the time. This method appeared to be a type of active imagination, and Jung discovered that through such drawings he could observe his own psychic transformations from day to day. Gradually it began to dawn on Jung that the mandala is really a mirror of the psyche in its totality: "Only gradually did I discover what the mandala really is: 'Formation, Transformation, Eternal Mind's eternal recreation'. And that is the self, the wholeness of the personality, which if all goes well is harmonious, but which can not tolerate deceptions" (MDR, pp. 195–196).

Jung had a strong awareness of the Self crystallizing at this time, but he still was missing its fundamental importance for his life and his mature psychological theory. This became resolved with a marvelous revelatory dream. In the dream, Jung found himself in Liverpool. There was a central square in the city around which were organized four quadrants. In the center of this mandala-like dream image resided a round pool with a small island in the middle of it. A magnificent magnolia tree stood in the center of it. While the rest of the city was enshrouded in a fog, the tree blazed with a numinous light. "Everything was extremely unpleasant, black and opaque—just as I felt then. But I had a vision of unearthly beauty, and that was why I was able to live at all. Liverpool is the 'pool of life'" (MDR, p. 198). Jung said that the dream brought with it a sense of finality and that finally the goal had been revealed. What was this goal? It was the center, the axis mundi, represented by this magic tree. The magic tree is what the shamans mount in their journeys to the upper world, or descend via roots to the underworld. It is the axis mundi, at once a symbol for the center of the world, a symbol for the center of the psyche, the center point of orientation. From this dream Jung realized the *telos* (goal and purpose) of his life and of his mature psychology: "One could not go beyond the center. The center is the goal, and everything is directed toward that center. Through this dream I understood that the self is the...archetype of orientation and meaning. Therein lies its healing function" (MDR, pp. 198–199).

Jung had found the key to his own healing, to his own psychology theory, and to others in his tribe of western society. The Self is the goal of his of his personal quest and simultaneously the goal of his mature psychological theory. In this insight we have Jung the shaman becoming healed, and returning with the boon for his tribe: the individuation process is a path towards self-realization. The understanding of the Self and its realization as the goal of the life process, the individuation process, became the program and mission for the second half of his life. From this point on, Jung had a clear sense of his mission (purpose), and a valuable psychology to offer the modern western world. He devoted the rest of his life to elaborating it for his people. Looking back on this period of midlife crisis, Jung realized that his mature psychology, his true life work, began then: "The years when I was pursuing my inner images were the most important in my life—in them everything essential was decided. It all began then; the later details are only supplements and clarifications of the material that burst forth from the unconscious, and at first swamped me. It was the *prima materia* for a lifetime's work" (MDR, p. 199).

WAS JUNG A SHAMAN?

It is difficult to say that Jung was a shaman in the classical sense of the term as suggested by Eliade, Harner, and others. There do appear to have been strong shamanic elements in Jung's life. If we can suspend, for a while, the cultural differences between shamanic terminology and conceptuality, and Jung's psychological terminology, we perhaps may see that Jung can in some sense be called a shaman.

We have described the development of Jung's life from early childhood through his midlife period as the story of the making of a wounded healer. The wounded healer is a fundamental aspect of the shaman. It is through the tended wound that the shaman is able to see, to empathize, and heal. Jung possessed empathic abilities in a high degree, and his abilities increased immeasurably after the resolution of his midlife crisis. Like the traditional shaman, Jung was a loner, an individual who preferred solitude and absorption in the non-ordinary or imaginal dimensions of what he later came to call the *collective unconscious.* Jung does not specify that he had a power animal, but he is clear that he had a spirit guide—more than one.

Like the traditional shaman, Jung also had a fascination with the soul—especially with its numinous contents—that remained with him all his life. Our focus has been on early childhood and midlife, but if we focused on the second half of his life, we would see that Jung continued his interest in the uncanny, in synchronicity, in the parapsychological, and underwent a near-death experience, where he left his body, had a life review, and learned that he must return to earth because he still had work to do. We would see that he continued to have visions, that he became very interested in alchemy and astrology, and even had one of his assistants cast horoscopes on his new clients, so he could get an astrological and synchronistic perspective on his patient's life. This practice is reminiscent of the Tibetan Buddhist shamans and the Tibetan

Bon Po shamans who make astrological and oracle consultations
for the same reason.

Just as the classic shaman's province is the soul and its disorders, based on a very ancient theory and therapeutics of the soul,
so Jung's psychology is a theory and therapeutics of soul, and one
that developed, like shamanism, out of his own confrontation
with it, out of his own initiation into it. Just as the shaman moves
about intentionally in non-ordinary reality, in the lowerworld,
middleworld, and upperworld, Jung navigated similar realms,
perhaps the same realms, in what he called the collective unconscious. Just as the traditional shaman has mapped this non-ordinary and sacred geography for his or her people, so did Jung. Just
like the vision quester discovering his or her life's purpose and
then offering it to the benefit of his or her tribe and piece of
earth, so did Jung offer the results of his nekyia to western culture. Such a journey is heroic, involving a descent, an important
discovery, and a return with it to benefit the people and the earth.

Unlike most traditional shamans, Jung did not use percussion to enter trance, to enhance imaginal processes, but he
employed a similar method of descending downward, a "letting
himself drop" and intentionally encounter the spirit presences he
met in the unconscious (active imagination). Surely the personal
and collective unconscious are modern designations of the old
non-ordinary reality, the three-storied imaginal cosmology of the
shamans. Jung had his spirit guides (Elijah, Salome, Philemon,
Ka) who lead him to discover himself, and discover the objective
transpersonal psychical dimensions that are beyond himself. He
sometimes referred to the entities he had conversations with as
spirits, although he remained cautious about using a spirit idiom
before a modern scientific readership. Like the traditional
shaman, it was through his concourse with such spirit presences
that he learned much about the human soul, and thus fashioned
his own psychological theory and method of therapy. This is not
unlike the traditional shaman who is led by the spirit, or by the
spirits, in how he should live, work, or heal others.

Jung was not a psychopomp in the traditional sense of
escorting the souls of the dead to their abode in the other world,
the land of the dead, or a realm of light. He had a profound

insight into the psychological meaning of death and its relation to the death and rebirth process, and believed he underwent a psycho-spiritual death/rebirth process at midlife. This death/rebirth was his initiation into the underworld at midlife. Jung also felt his mental patients at the asylum of Burgholzli were lost souls, hanging out in the land of the dead, an intuition that persons undergoing psychosis are lost to the everyday world of ordinary reality and are lost in the imaginal realm of non-ordinary reality (the collective unconscious). On occasion, Jung was able to pull such persons out of this lost realm and back into ordinary life. Certainly through his analytic and psychotherapy practice, he was able to facilitate the recovery of souls, not through trance journeys, but through analysis of dreams, of transference and counter-transference, and through the power of a deep relationship with him.

Shamanism has always had a close relationship to nature, to the earth mother and the nature spirits. For Jung, nature was alive and sacred (numinous). Jung had a profound love and respect for nature and solitude, and knew that he needed to take periodic "vision quests" at his Bollingen retreat. There, he felt at one with nature, and describes a mystical merger, as if he were the splashing waves, the wind in the trees, the substance of the stones and earth. Like the traditional shaman who heals himself or herself through solitary retreat, by taking mini vision quests, at Bollingen Jung felt he could touch his core, the Self, recharge and renew himself and his vision, and heal from the strains of living. He felt that at Bollingen he was in the midst of his true life. At Bollingen, Jung lived very simply. He chopped his own wood, drew his own water, lighted kerosene lamps, cooked his own meals. He meditated and engaged the spirits through active imagination and analysis of his dreams. He only accepted visitors there when he flew a special flag from the tower. Bollingen constituted Jung's personal sacred space, the locus for his highly disciplined psycho-spiritual practice, the place of his renewal and vision questing.

We have examined Jung's early and middle life and found many shamanic elements. Jung seemed to have stumbled on a shamanic way of being, knowing, and healing, without the standard supports of traditional shamanic culture, which shamans have traditionally enjoyed. In the absence of the traditional shamanic ritual elders and thought systems to serve as a framework, Jung had to undergo his own original experience with the help of Emma Jung and Toni Wolff. He underwent his own courageous initiation, and had to arrive at his own methodology and his own language of soul. Because of this original quality of his discovery, he developed some new approaches and novel conceptions which are at once compatible with shamanism and which may extend it beyond its traditional domain into the world of post-modern Western culture. In the chapters that follow, we shall bring Jung's resultant ideas into dialogue with shamanism, and explore some implications of the interface of a Jung-shamanism dialogue.

Chapter Four

Jung's Theory of the Soul

COMPARISONS AND CONTRASTS WITH SHAMANISM

The most salient common ground of the shamanic and Jungian perspectives is the valuation of the soul. Jung often translated *psyche* by the German word *Seele,* meaning soul, especially when he wanted to emphasize the depth and plural nature of the psyche, emphasizing its multiplicity. The shaman views the soul as a plurality of psychical energies which must exist in some loose harmonious balance within the individual; Jung similarly viewed the soul as a multiplicity-in-unity. When stressing its mystery, variety, and impenetrability, he tends to use the word *soul (Seele).* When stressing its integrity, ordering, archetypal patterning, and striving towards wholeness, he tends to use the term *psyche.* Whatever the terminological usage, psyche and soul are largely synonymous for Jung. There are many parallels which can be drawn between the primitive view of the soul and Jung's view. As James Hillman has recurrently pointed out, there is a certain animistic feel to the psychic contents and structures named by Jung.[1] It is important to note that this animism tends to be self-consciously metaphoric in Jung. For example, his main psychological terms are not affects, cognitions, volitions, and other such behavioral terms, although he does use them at times, but highly suggestive, poetic, and animistic terms which are often personifications of psychic energies and structures, such as the shadow, the old wise man/woman, the anima/animus, the trickster, and the like. The use of such evocative language is intended to bring the imaginal realities of the psyche to life, to give them a numinal status and importance of their own. Jung and the shaman both approach the psyche in this imagistic way.

Jung also conceived of the psyche in structural language,

and at times used the language of secular psychiatry, psychology, neurology, and biology. However, in his later work, he came to prefer the more imagistic or symbolic way of approaching and relating to the psyche. Regardless of the language style, Jung's writings always reflect an underlying view of the psyche as mysterious, numinal, and of infinite value. Like the shamanic view of the soul, Jung's attitude towards the psyche gives his psychology a spiritual or numinal aura, a religious feeling tone, if you will.

The soul was so important to Jung that he wanted it to be understood as something in itself, and not simply the epiphenomenon of biological processes. In its broadest sense, Jung understood the psyche as a totality or unity composed largely of conscious and unconscious aspects. The field of conscious experience was understood as a relatively limited area of psychical experience involving discrimination, awareness of contrasts, of opposites, emerging from the more developmentally and phylogenetically primitive and ancient layers of the unconscious. Following Freud, Jung termed the center of the field of consciousness the ego *(das Ich)*. His understanding of the ego moves beyond the cognitive and perceptual and discriminative identity and continuity of self. For Jung, however, the ego was not the whole personality. While it was essential for daily living and functioning, it was really only the tip of the psychic iceberg. Although the ego has a tendency to want to direct the life of the individual, Jung believed that it must relativize itself, subordinating itself to a deeper center of order and meaning within the psyche. This deeper center Jung referred to as the Self archetype, of which we shall say more later. The unfathomably deep reservoir supporting consciousness, Jung sometimes referred to as the unconscious. In this he followed Carus, Freud, and others who conceptualized this underlying substrate to conscious experience as the unconscious *(das Unbewusst)*. Freud, as is well known, viewed the unconscious as largely consisting of repressed, forgotten, or preconscious memories, cognitions, affects, and instinctual energies. His view gave a negative tone to the concept of the unconscious. Jung also acknowledged this Freudian dimension of the unconscious, and termed it the "personal unconscious". Jung diverged from Freud's view, however, by positing the unconscious as creative and purposive in its strivings, and as having deeper, more ancient, and more universal layers than the personal unconscious. He called these deeper layers the collective unconscious, because they were shared by human beings universally, historically, and cross-culturally.

THE ANCESTRAL AND ARCHAIC LAYERS OF THE SOUL

Jung's understanding of a deeper collective dimension to the psyche brought him close to the ancestral soul theory of primitive psychology and shamanism. The belief that ancestral spirits play a significant part in the daily life of the tribe, as well as in causing and curing illness, has been well documented. In many cultures where shamanism is practiced, the shaman enters his or her ecstatic trance state and apparently accesses these ancestral dimensions, often having concourse with the helping or malevolent ancestral spirits. Such a view presupposes that the psychic interior of the so-called primitive is somehow open to, and in touch with, significant influences from the past. Assuming the shaman is able to access such ancestral layers, Jung's mapping of the psyche can help illuminate the experience of, and belief in, such layers. Jung's first intuition of the multi-layered structure of the psyche came to him in a dream around the time he was trying to differentiate his views clearly from those of Freud. Such extraordinary dreams and visions revealing the nature of psychical reality, and serving as a map for the shaman, abound in the literature on shamanism. The central dream image which awakened Jung and served as a lifelong map and guide to psychical reality was that of a multi-layered house:

> I was in a house I did not know, which had two stories. It was "my house." I found myself in the upper story, where there was a kind of salon furnished with fine old pieces in rococo style. On the walls hung a number of precious old paintings. I wondered that this should be my house, and thought, "Not bad." But then it occurred to me that I did not know what the lower floor looked like. Descending the stairs, I reached the ground floor. There everything was much older, and I realized that this part of the house must date from about the fifteenth or sixteenth century. The furnishings were

medieval; the floors were of red brick. Everywhere it was rather dark. I went from one room to another, thinking, "Now I really must explore the whole house". I came upon a heavy door, and opened it. Beyond it, I discovered a stone stairway that led down into the cellar. Descending again, I found myself in a beautifully vaulted room which looked exceedingly ancient. Examining the walls, I discovered layers of brick among the ordinary stone blocks, and chips of brick in the mortar. As soon as I saw this I knew that the walls dated from Roman times. My interest by now was intense. I looked more closely at the floor. It was of stone slabs, and in one of these I discovered a ring. When I pulled it, the stone slab lifted, and again I saw a stairway of narrow stone steps leading down into the depths. These, too, I descended, and entered a low cave cut into the rock. Thick dust lay on the floor, and in the dust were scattered bones and broken pottery, like remains of a primitive culture. I discovered two human skulls, obviously very old and half disintegrated. Then I awoke.[2]

As Jung pondered the dream imagery it struck him that the psyche was much more complex and deep than Freud suspected. Interpreting the dream, Jung said it suggested to him that there were further reaches beyond the personal unconscious. The long uninhabited ground floor in medieval style, the Roman cellar, and finally the prehistoric cave signified not only the past in human biological and cultural evolution, but past stages of consciousness. The dream pointed to the cultural and historical foundations of human consciousness, a kind of Hegelian history of the successive layers of consciousness. The dream postulated an impersonal foundation underlying the human psyche. It seemed to constitute a structural diagram of the psyche in imagistic/metaphoric terms. Jung says that it became a guiding image which was confirmed over and again throughout his life as he studied the psyche and its cultural and historical manifestations. It was his first inkling of a collective a priori beneath the personal psyche. He notes that he first understood the contents of the lower layers to be traces of earlier modes of functioning, but later he recognized them as forms of instinct which he came to call archetypes.[3]

As Jung's thoughts about the various layers of the psyche grew more subtle and clarified, he proposed an alternative structural diagram of the psyche as being layered from the most personal levels to the deeper pre-human and transpersonal levels. According to Barbara Hannah,[4] Jung once used a large colored diagram during a lecture to illustrate the layers in the unconscious. She reports that Jung colored the lowest level in crimson and called it the "central fire", apparently representing a cosmic source of energy which gives off sparks which ascend upward through all the layers, touching them with its luminous energy. The next to the lowest layer he called the layer of animal ancestry, which he believed was present in every human psyche, and above that was the layer of primeval ancestors. Above this was a layer representing the psychical deposits and structures of a large cultural group such as Europe or Asia, each with deep unconscious connections to the other. These deep layers supply most of the archetypal images which form the human patterns of behavior. Above these, the layers are less collective, and more culture and individual specific. These layers include the nation, above this the clan, above that the family, culminating in the individual person. In any individual all these various layers have some efficacy in structuring experience; most of them normally operate unconsciously. In special altered states of consciousness induced by psychosis and other forms of psychopathology, and in the creative and mystical altered states of consciousness, the most archaic levels of the psyche become activated in such a way that they give rise to archetypally patterned imagery experienced in dreams, hallucinations, visions, artistic products, and in the imagery of mystical or transcendental states. Such imagery often has a very numinous feel, compels attention, entices the imagination, and involves archaic or mythological forms. Jung in fact believed that the collective unconscious was the source of the imagery which rises to the surface in cultural myth and ritual, which informs and structures religious and moral ideation, and which provides the ideological ground of socio-cultural ordering.

ARCHETYPES

Jung believed the collective unconscious was structured by archetypes, the forms which pattern and direct instinctual energies into purposive channels, leading to distinct psychological processes and behaviors:

> We can also find in the unconscious qualities that are not individually acquired but are inherited, e.g., instincts as impulses to carry out actions from necessity, without conscious motivation. In this deeper stratum we also find... archetypes....The instincts and archetypes together form the "collective unconscious". I call it collective because unlike the personal unconscious, it is not made up of individual and more or less unique contents but of those which are universal and of regular occurrence.[5]

Jung considered the archetype to be an inherited part of the psyche, initially developing through repeated experiences of pre-human and human evolution. This conception of characteristics acquired through individual experience and passed on to subsequent generations was originally conceptualized by Jean-Baptiste de Lamarck (1744–1829). This view apparently influenced Jung's early formulation of the heritability of the archetype. While de Lamarck's view has been discredited, and has been supplanted by Darwinian natural selection and Mendel's laws of inheritance, Jung's conception of the heritability of the archetype can be explained in terms of natural selection.[6] The fear and fascination with snakes, for example, appears to be a universal human reaction, which Jung believed may be due to an archetypal pattern which formed through countless aeons of human experience of fear and fascination with snakes, so that the emotional reaction arises in each person's initial encounter with a snake. Alternatively, it could be that a mutation involving a fear of snakes proved useful to the species. In the view of natural selection, genetic mutations which enhanced survival meant that the mutants would reproduce and supplant previous generations. Thus archetypes emerged, in this view, in a seemingly random way, but proved useful for the survival of the species. A genetic structure that insured the survival of an infant (e.g., attachment/bonding,

the genetic programming for motherhood, i.e., the mother archetype) would be passed on to succeeding generations and thus
become universally accessible to a mammalian species, helping to
insure its survival. There are also philosophical-theological views
that explain archetypes as Platonic forms, or as Whiteheadian
"eternal objects", which exist as potentials in the mind of God,
and which inform the world.[7] In Whitehead's view, the eternal
objects are the potential patterns and forms that inform the
world. God contemplates every creature in the cosmos in its context, and offers it forms of possibility for becoming the most harmonious and intense occasion of experience it can be. For
Whitehead this is true whether the creature be a simple sub-
atomic particle, a complex animal body, or the human psyche. In
this view an archetype is a complex eternal object, which has
entered into the conceptual feelings of God, and into the usually
non-conscious conceptual feelings of the creatures of the actual
world. In the process of biological and psychological evolution
certain complex eternal objects have become selected because
they enhance not only survival, but harmonious and intense experience. However these recurrent forms of experience are
explained, Jung believed there to be a seemingly endless variety
of archetypes universally appearing across cultures. Only certain
archetypes are salient in Jung's writings because they are typically
recognizable in familiar human behaviors, especially those which
configure around fundamental human experiences: crises and
challenges, such as birth, death, loss, motherhood and father-
hood, creativity, healing, and psychological transformation.
There are, for example, certain recognizable mental states and
behaviors which are clearly characterizable as fatherly as opposed
to motherly, or characterized as creative rather than destructive.
Among the common archetypal patterns which dominate the psychic life and behavior of humans are those which Jung termed the
anima in men and the animus in women, the shadow, and the persona. Other prominent archetypes in Jung's understanding were
those of the hero, the trickster, the old wise man/woman, and the
archetypal Self. Each of these archetypal structures plays important roles in giving meaningful shape and direction to the psychical energies of the libido. Jung came increasingly to believe that

the archetypes are not the instinctual energies themselves, but the aim and form of the psychological states and behaviors. An instinct may be conceived as the energetic force behind the archetypal pattern, but the archetype is what gives the instinct its purposeful direction, its telos.

It is possible to note a certain affinity between an archetype and a Platonic idea. Both the archetype and the Platonic idea can be experienced as a form, an image; as something "seen" or intuited. However, Jung placed the archetypes on an empirical and evolutionary basis as well. Platonic forms or ideas were conceived as immutable, transcendent, a priori forms of experience. By contrast, Jung conceived the archetypes as forms arising out of evolutionary process, subject to change with time and evolution.[8] Even new archetypes could form, he believed, with sufficient evolutionary time. Nevertheless, in his later years Jung's theory of the archetype became increasingly Platonic, that is, concerned with their formal and transpersonal (transcendent) quality, but he never gave up the biological grounding of the archetype.

Jung's theory of the archetype developed in several stages. In 1912 he coined the term *primordial image* as a result of noticing certain regularly occurring psychological themes and images in the unconscious productions of his patients. As he studied comparative religion, myth, and ritual, Jung found regularly occurring motifs there as well. The similarities in motifs between cultural myths and psychological productions (dreams, visions, and hallucinations) were first documented at length in his book *Symbols of Transformation,*[9] a book that heralded his break with Freud. Shortly after that publication, Jung began speaking of "nodal points" and "non-personal dominants" which influence a person's functioning by attracting psychical energy. Eventually he began using the term *archetype,* and made a distinction between the archetypal *image* which empirically manifested itself, and the archetype *per se,* as an abstract form transcendent to empirical manifestation, that is, as an "in-itself" *(an sich).*

The archetype must be understood as neither a purely biological phenomenon, nor as a purely mentalistic phenomenon. Jung sought to avoid a dualism which placed one dimension in a dominant role. Rather he saw the physical and psychical as polar aspects of the same underlying reality (world), as aspects which find their manifestation in psychical life. Jung, it seems, had a philosophical view of the psyche approximating panpsychism in which psyche, at its deepest and most fundamental level, emerges out of the material world. The more deeply one penetrates into the psyche and its origins, the more physical and mental distinctions become blurred:

> The deeper "layers" of the psyche lose their individual uniqueness as they retreat farther and farther into darkness. "Lower down", that is to say as they approach the autonomous functional systems, they become increasingly collective until they are universalized and extinguished in the body's materiality, i.e., in chemical substances. The body's carbon is simply carbon. Hence "at bottom" the psyche is simply "world".[10]

For Jung the archetype is a psychosomatic concept which involved linkages between image and instinct, between psyche and soma. The psychosomatic nature of archetypes was important for Jung in preventing a mere reduction of imaginal and psychical contents to mere representations of biological drives. Archetypes sometimes come into play seemingly automatically, as in the maternal response to a newborn infant. However, such activation of the maternal archetype is in part a response to external demands and a deep and intelligent response to outer demands from the numinous archetypal patterns lying dormant in the collective unconscious. Certain other archetypes are best activated through ritual. For example, various rites of passage are often employed in tribal societies to evoke/activate, in masculine initiations, such archetypal patterns as the archetypal hunter, the archetypal warrior. In female puberty rites the culture-specific feminine archetypes have also been activated through an analogous ritual process.[11] The ritual transformation of a child into a mature and responsible adult is the objective of puberty rites. Often considerable ritual action is required to activate the adult archetypal patterns, and switch off the childhood patterns, in a young man or woman. That ritual action is required to turn off some powerful archetypal patterns can be observed in the fate of many Vietnam veterans, who returned from brutal battle circumstances without a national public ritual to help transform their psychological organization from the warrior to the civilian pattern. The lack of such a turnoff ritual made it difficult for many to re-enter their normal daily roles as worker, spouse, and parent. Many suffered chaotically from warrior-aggressive impulses which were inappropriate for civilian life, and expressed them destructively after returning home. Thus, archetypal patterns typically lay dormant, only potentially activated, awaiting inner or outer signals for their activation or actualization. Some archetypal patterns are activated and developed through ritual and educative processes, some through responses to significant life events, some as the result of psychotherapy, and some as the result of mental imbalance and breakdown.

ARCHETYPE AND NUMINOSITY

Archetypes are considered numinal by Jung. They have the power to arouse affect, to take possession of the will, to bedazzle consciousness, and to blind one to other realities. Jung described the *numinosum* as

> a dynamic agency or effect not caused by an arbitrary act of will. On the contrary, it seizes and controls the human subject, who is always rather its victim than its creator. The *numinosum*—whatever its cause may be—is an experience of the subject independent of his will....The *numinosum* is either a quality belonging to a visible object or the influence of an invisible presence that causes a peculiar alteration of consciousness.[12]

Like the Platonic forms, the archetype exerts a numinal attraction upon and within the psyche, providing structure and direction for psychical energies (libido). The patterns of behavior exemplified, for example, in mothering, fathering, in becoming a hunter, a food gatherer and preparer, a warrior, a witch, a priestess, or a shaman, are felt as irresistibly alluring; or as a compelling force. They may gradually emerge into consciousness and behavior as the personality develops and matures, or they may burst suddenly into consciousness with a power and violence in which the subject is over-powered, seized, or possessed. Typically, in a healthy individual, the attracting power of an archetype will be subtle, gentle, if also effective. The so-called maternal instinct, for example, often dawns on a young woman as an urge, perhaps a deep but quiet desire to bear children, and to mother them. However, in cases of psychological crisis, or in cases of severe pathology or mystical experience, the archetypes may burst upon the stage in raw or near-pure form. In such cases their power, for good or ill, is overwhelming. Their efficacy in seizing consciousness, or in possessing the will, is compulsory. In cases of religious or mystical consciousness, the effect may be desirous or threatening. This is true also in the province of pathology.

The numinosity of the archetype also has a religious quality to it, compelling the attention and loyalty of ego-consciousness, and giving a sense of meaning and purpose, even if it manifests itself in pathologically truncated and fantastic form. Jung seemed to view the mythological gods as archetypal images, that is, numinal representations of the presence and power of certain archetypes, or archetypal configurations. Archetypes thus become the driving structures behind religious images, behind god-images. Zeus and Hera, for example, could be considered as archetypal images (representations) of the king and queen archetypes, or of the central archetype of the personality which Jung called the "Self" (capital "S" is used to distinguish it from the ego-identity, which is referred to as self, small "s"). Drawing conclusions from comparative study of religions, Jung inferred that each culture has an array of religious images, all structured by archetypes. It is as if the gods and goddesses of traditional societies have particular cultural clothing and expression, exemplified in myth and ritual, but are patterned upon underlying universal or archetypal forms. The cultural masks and clothing account for the differences in emphasis. Historian of dynamic psychiatry, Henri F. Ellenberger, argued that Jung was indebted to the anthropologist and explorer Adolf Bastian for his understanding of the distinction between the archetypal representation and the underlying universal form (archetype *per se*). Bastian had noticed numerous recurring patterns of myth and belief in various cultures, as he traveled about the world in the late 19th century. He made a distinction between the basic form and its culture-specific manifestation. The former he called elementary ideas *(elementare Gedanke),* which correspond to Jung's term *archetypes.* The latter, cultural masks, he referred to as cultural ideas *(Volkesgedanke).*

THE NUMINA: SHAMANIC AND JUNGIAN PERSPECTIVES

It may be useful to pause and contrast, for a moment, Jung's view of the numina, from the traditional shamanic view. Shamanism and Jung converge in the area of numina and animism. Like the shamanic belief in a numinal world of invading spirits, ghosts, and demons, Jung also affirmed the reality of certain powers, which could be characterized as spirits, ghosts, demons, and the like; but he interpreted them in a psychological framework. When Jung sometimes spoke of psychological phenomena in an animistic way, he was apparently addressing the phenomenology of the numinous mythico-symbolic clothing of various archetypal forms. As a psychological theorist, Jung did not address the question of whether or not some spirits might exist transcendent to the human psyche. He did address the phenomena of spirits as a psychologist, viewing them as psychological facts, as always appearing within the psyche. The key to understanding Jung's affirmation of spirit powers lies in his employment of the concept of the numen. Jung occasionally characterized the numinal powers of the psyche, in animistic terms, as

> certain dynamic factors that we conceive as "powers": spirits, daemons, gods, laws, ideals, or whatever name man has given to such factors in his world as he has found powerful, dangerous, or helpful enough to be taken into careful consideration, or grand, beautiful, and meaningful enough to be devoutly worshiped and loved.[13]

Jung borrowed the term *numen* from Rudolf Otto, whose book *The Idea of the Holy* appeared in 1917.[14] It is not known when Jung read the book, but in 1934 Otto's term *numinous* began appearing in Jung's writings. Otto had a catalyzing effect upon Jung's understandings and theorizing. The ground for Otto's influence was prepared by Jung's interest in the non-rational aspects of symbol, myth, and dream imagery, and by the fact that Jung found archetypal imagery to have the dual aspect of being fascinating and attracting, and of being repelling and terrifying. Jung conjectured that what the shaman believed to be benevolent or threatening spirits were actually archetypes exercising their numinal effect through various animistic forms of images, which symbolically represented them. From Otto, Jung found a conception which could illuminate these ambiguous, non-rational, and dual effects of images upon the psyche. Otto's term also suggests that there is a religious quality to the numinous, associated with value and meaning. But Jung made a selective use of Otto's concept. Whereas Otto intended the term ultimately to refer to the transcendent God of theology, Jung attempted to employ it in a non-metaphysical way, withholding theological speculation. Jung ambiguously reshaped the transcendent meaning of Otto's term into an immanent (psychological) framework. That is to say, Jung attempted to understand numinosity from within the psyche, and believed numinosity, as any form of religious experience, must always be a psychological experience, because it must take place within a psyche. Unfortunately Jung did not address the possibility of independently existing spirits, nor did he speculate on the relationship between such spirits and the archetypal structures of the shaman's mind.

If the archetypes have a numinous quality, for Jung, and if they give rise to numinous imagery, the phenomenology of the numina (of their empirical manifestation as ghosts, spirits, demons, etc.) is affirmed, but is given a psychological interpretation. The traditional shaman could not, and probably would not, offer a psychological (secular scientific) interpretation. In the shamanic view, spirits are a *sui generis* reality; they simply are what they are, and should not be reduced to other terms. According to anthropologist Michael Harner, they (spirits, numina, etc.) are experienced in a shamanic state of consciousness (SSC), and not in the ordinary state of consciousness (OSC). In the shamanic state of consciousness the spirit beings are real. To the ordinary state of consciousness spirits and other numinous entities may look like illusions, or like mere psychological apparitions. However, in the shamanic state of consciousness, they *are* spiritual realities, having an objective ontological status outside any presumed personal mental structures. According to Harner, the mental structures of the imagination open a door into the alternative, non-ordinary reality.[15] By passing through this imaginal door of the mind, one may enter into the realm of spirits, who also manifest themselves in terms of images. The shaman's mind is used, then, as a door to pass through into another reality which exists independently of that personal mind. The soul perceives the numina of the other reality by means of images. Thus, the traditional shaman would claim that such spirit entities exist external to the individual psyche, and occasionally invade or possess it. By contrast, Jung would claim that the spirits (numina) are immanent within the psyche, and that they only appear to be outside the psyche, but we can only say that they are transcendent to ego-consciousness, and may be imagistic representations of complexes and archetypal patterns.

A Jungian perspective on the shamanic states of consciousness, might claim that it is a right-brained mode of accessing the collective unconscious, which Harner and Castaneda have referred to as the nonordinary reality of the shaman. It is because archetypal contents may seize, invade, or possess the ego, that they are experienced as ego-alien powers. The ego is bedazzled by them because they are other than it, appearing strange, mysterious, and sometimes threatening. But being other does not mean exterior to the psyche, but outside the field of ego-consciousness. Additionally, the Jungian understanding also views the numina as manifest in images, and accessible by images. The psyche may be said to perceive the realities of the other dimension (that is, the collective unconscious) as images, and by means of images. For Jung, image is psyche,[16] regardless of the dimension from which it arises, or to which it refers.

INDIVIDUATION AND THE RELIGIOUS OUTLOOK

Jung had a teleological view of the psyche, in which everything in it had purposive intentionality aiming at wholeness and an unfolding realization of potentiality which he called individuation. The unconscious contents inherently strive toward outward expression and realization in the actual world: "Everything in the unconscious seeks outward manifestation".[17] The psyche as a whole strives toward an unfolding of the personality into a distinct and individual unity in a developmental process. This unfolding development is much like the transformation from the proverbial acorn into the proverbial oak. That is, the originally enfolded psychic implicate potential becomes unfolded into explicate psychological fact. Jung called this unfolding development of the personality the individuation process, because it is the "process by which a person becomes an in-dividual, that is, a separate, indivisible unity or whole".[18] Jung uses the term in a way synonymous with coming to selfhood and self-realization.[19] By self-realization, however, Jung does not mean ego development. Ego development is a precondition to self-realization. Jung refers to a self deeper than the ego, but including the ego, which he sometimes simply termed the psyche, sometimes termed the Self, and at other times termed soul. Individuation requires the aid of the ego in making deep unconscious contents conscious, and is a precondition for the uniqueness and differentiation of the personality which may begin with the second half of life. But the promptings to individuate, to be true to the self, come not from the ego, but from deep within the psyche itself, and appear to be intrinsic to it.

The individuation process, proper, is at once the unfolding development of becoming differentiated and unique, and a process of becoming an integrated whole. In becoming an individual, one differentiates one's psyche from the collective (i.e., the crowd) and affirms the individual differences. Jung's archetypal concept of the persona as a social mask which a person wears for various roles he or she must play is considered necessary for socially adaptive purposes. To fail to develop a persona would leave the individual vulnerable if not disabled. It is necessary to have a persona in order to have a recognizable place within the social order. However, the persona is not the true self in its most authentic sense: "One could say, with a little exaggeration, that the persona is that which one in reality is not, but which oneself as well as others think one is".[20] Individuation involves a process of methodically differentiating from one's persona so

that one recognizes that it is not the deeper self, and that this
deeper self is distinct from social roles and expectations. It is also
important to become differentiated from the inner collective,
that is, from the contents of the collective unconscious. Archetypes, for example, can possess and consume one. They care little
for the individual. They are like the Greek and Roman gods and
goddesses who are jealous, and who may compete for the person's
total allegiance. It is possible, for example, for a woman to be so
consumed by a need to mother that she has no identity separate
from that archetypal pattern. The archetype consumes the
woman in a compulsive way. Part of Jung's understanding of individuation is its characteristic freedom, the freedom to set limits
upon the outer and inner collective structures. It presupposes the
freedom to give each relevant archetypal energy its due, without
destructive imbalance, and it presupposes the freedom to differentiate oneself from the outer collective, or social demands and
influences. Such freedom presupposes a conscious relation to the
inner and outer worlds. Such consciousness strives for a balance
between competing and opposing forces. Wholeness is the aspect
of individuation which presupposes this delicate balancing act of
holding the oppositions in tension. It is strenuous conscious work.
But it is work which is deeply fulfilling and personally meaningful. The teleology of the individuation process is directed towards
differentiation and wholeness, leading to a sense of meaning or
fulfillment which has a spiritual character. Echoing the Socrates
of Plato, we might say that, when intentionally undertaken, individuation is "care for the soul and what becomes of her".

For Jung, the individuation process is an archetypally structured or patterned process of unfolding development. It is not irra-
tional, although it involves the integration of so-called non-
rational (symbolic and affective) contents. Jung did not spend as
much energy writing about the developmental processes of children as he did of adults, perhaps because Freud and his followers
had given much study to those processes already. Jung's concept of
individuation did place greater emphasis upon adult development,
an area which Freud neglected. He divided the major developmental steps into two complex sets of tasks. The task of the first half of
life is to develop the ego as an effective adaptive structure. The first

half of life, until about thirty-five or forty, Jung believed, was oriented towards primarily the ego and persona which develop in this phase of life. The psychological achievements of this first half of life involve separation from the mother and father, relinquishing childhood and adolescent status, and acquiring adult identity and capabilities. The task is to grow up and takes one's place in the social order, to acquire a financial means of survival, to achieve a necessary measure of social status and skill, and typically, to purchase one's house and raise children. The tasks of the first half of life typically burden the individual with the consumption of most of his or her energies, and leave little time or energy for solitary pursuits, or for greater differentiation from collective demands. The deeper self is typically stifled. However, the first half of life has a positive and purposive function: to set the stage for the tasks of the second half of life, providing the necessary ego strength for greater exploration and development of the deeper self.

The tasks of the second half of life shift from preoccupation with the external, collective dimension, to a conscious relationship with the inner life, with intrapsychic processes. It also involves a shift from the personal ego-centric guiding principles of life, to those principles which are more objective, and other-centered. We might characterize the task as a shift from an ego-centered attitude to an ego-transcending attitude. This is a way of saying that the ego, being fully developed and actual, now has to be relativised, giving allegiance to values which may be considered higher, or deeper than those which have dominated it up to this point. Dependence upon the ego must give way to a subordination to the deeper self, to a relationship with the Self and its concern with meaning and spiritual values. Subordination of the ego to the central archetype, this deeper self, may result in commitment to higher social values (exemplified in such figures as Ghandi, Mother Theresa, Martin Luther King), as well as to objective values flowing in upon the psyche from that center itself.

With the emergence of the second half of life, the individual may find himself or herself dissatisfied with the collective values by which he or she has been living. The values which previously guided the person's development may suddenly seem dry, inauthentic, and the person may feel estranged from the authentic self, from life, or from spiritual concerns. Life seems to lack something, and a hunger for zest and meaning arises. Such persons, after enjoying the rewards of having arrived into adulthood, may find themselves asking the question, "Is this all there is?" In the second half of life the reality of death enters on the horizon and brings the question of life's meaning to the fore. The task is to find a way to affirm and accept approaching death, so that one may more deeply affirm the life that remains before one. Jung believed the refusal to honestly face death was a refusal to accept life, especially life at its most meaningful level. What seems to be involved is to ultimately gain a measure of self-acceptance, and a willingness to live in accord with the promptings of the archetypal Self. From the perspective of psychological structure, this means living in conscious relation to the center of the personality, the archetypal Self. Failure to face death, to accept life, and to live in accord with one's deeper self results, Jung believed, in a pathological condition. This pathological condition could be considered a form of soul loss since lack of conscious relation to the archetypal Self, and to the anima/animus, has the effect of leaving the individual with a loss of something vital which parallels the primitive phenomenon of soul loss. It is connection to the numinous meaning-giving power of the archetypal Self which gives the process a spiritual feel. The problem at midlife is to discover a religious or spiritual outlook on life, by consciously submitting to the values and direction of the archetypal Self. Jung considered the midlife problem a religious one, which if not resolved would lead to a spiritual neurosis characterized by bitterness, emptiness, and despair:

> Among all of my patients in the second half of life—that is to say, over thirty-five—there has not been one whose problem was not that of finding a religious outlook on life. None of them has been really healed who did not regain his religious outlook.[21]

By "religious outlook", Jung did not mean living by a particular creed, nor by church membership. He meant a connection to the numinal energies manifesting themselves in the soul, living in accord with the promptings of the archetypal Self, which gives rise to authentic spiritual experience and valuation, and which gives a sense of meaning, of fullness, to an individuating life.

INDIVIDUATION AND TRIBAL SOCIETIES

In tribal societies in which shamanism has been traditionally practiced, Jung believed that individuation has not been as highly valued as participation in the collective life of the tribe. The emphasis upon the collective, however, does not mean that personal or unique experiences are not acquired in the process of individual development in these cultures. Psychological development, although not called by that name, is a process of maturation assisted by rites of passage which help transform pubescent children into responsible and capable adults. Typically these rituals facilitate psychological transformation through allowing the initiates contact with numinal powers, objectified and encountered in the myths, costume, and ordeals which the initiates experience or undergo. The major rites of passage in tribal societies include those surrounding birth, puberty, marriage, and death, and include initiations into special statuses (warrior, kingship/queenship, or into a medicine society). The purpose of these rites is to facilitate, through ritual procedures and community support, the development or transformation of individuals within the society. Tribal myth provides the ordering necessary for natural unfolding development through the stages of the human life-cycle. Jung believed that modern people, by contrast, had lost meaningful connection to the orienting myth of their culture, and live in a culture where communal-participative ties are weaker, and where independence from the collective is valued.

Paradoxically, although tribal societies stress participation in the collective, there is considerable value placed upon inner experience. Historically, for example, in native North American tribes there has been an emphasis upon personal interior experience through vision quests. Meaningful contact with numinal entities, such as ancestral spirits, power animals, and the like, are encouraged, and this personal religious experience is highly valued because it is believed to serve the individual and social good. Jung believed the shaman had more independence from the collective norms of his or her community, and actually practiced an archaic form of individuation. More will be said when we discuss Jung's view on shamanism. Suffice it to say here that shamanism involves ecstatic and revelatory experiences which differentiate the shaman sharply from the communities in which he or she serves. Some shamanic and medicine societies consider the personal experiences to be secret. These unique experiences are not totally for the individual benefit of the shaman. The results of such secret ecstatic or mystical encounters are also contributed back into the collective good, usually in the form of healing, myth making, divination, or other ritual practice. This is a perspective close to the Jungian understanding of individuation. Both views presuppose the heroic archetypal pattern of detachment from the collective, discovery of the boon (insight, healing power, knowledge, etc.), and return with the discovery to the collective, where it contributes to the collective good.[22] It would appear that the main difference between the personal developmental process of traditional (tribal) societies, and that required by the individuation process, is a matter of accent. In tribal societies, the accent appears to be on the collective participation. In the Jungian view of individuation, the accent is on the differentiation from the collective.

THE ARCHETYPAL SELF (THE INNER AXIS MUNDI)

The individuation process, when analytically assisted or intentionally entered upon, has the feel of a spiritual path. This is in part due to the fact that it is not a linear progression, but a circumambulation around a numinous nuclear center point, the central archetype, the archetypal Self. The archetypal Self, as we have noted, is not the center of the field of consciousness (i.e., it is not the ego), but is a deeper organizing principle to which ego-consciousness must become related. Originally Jung regarded the archetypal Self as comprising the totality of the conscious and unconscious.[23] Later he described it as the ordering, regulating, harmonizing, and meaning-giving agency of the psyche.[24] Jung also uses the term in such a way as to include both the contents of the total personality, and the ordering and structuring factor which contains the contents, when he says that the "self is not only the center but also the whole circumference".[25] The archetypal Self is at once the psyche's centering point, and its circumference; it is the origin of psychic development and the goal of integration and wholeness. It is the psychic totality of which all psychic contents are partial manifestations or reflections. As the totality it is far greater than the ego can conceive or integrate.

As the goal of the individuation process, the archetypal Self evokes images of the fullest potential and unity for the personality as a whole. As the unifying principle, it has a position of authority in relation to psychic life and individuation. In life, the archetypal Self makes a demand upon the ego to be consciously recognized, integrated, and actualized. In its role of prompting the personality to develop, differentiate, and integrate, it has something of a spirit or god-like quality. Jung called this prompting function of the archetypal Self the *spiritus rector*. It is this aspect of the Self which brings the concept close to the primitive conception of the spirit guides and power animals of shamans. Amplifying Jung's conception, Marie Louise von Franz has likened the spiritus rector aspects of the archetypal Self to the ancient notions of great spirit, genius, or power animal:

> Throughout the ages men have been intuitively aware of the existence of such an inner center. The Greeks called it man's inner *daimon*, in Egypt it was expressed by the concept of the *Ba soul*, and the Romans worshiped it as the "genius" native to each individual. In more primitive societies it was often thought of as a protective spirit embodied within an animal or fetish.[26]

Von Franz goes on to mention the Naskapi Indians of Labrador. Being simple hunters who live in isolated groups which make collective custom, ritual, and belief impossible, they have relied on their spirit helpers as inner voices to guide them daily in their economic, moral, and psychic life. The Naskapi believes this inner voice to be his or her best friend, an inner companion *(mista'peo)* to be consulted and lived in accord with. From a Jungian perspective, the helping spirits and power animals could also be understood as the spiritus rector of the shaman. That such helping spirits possess greater wisdom and knowledge, and that they serve as inner guide and companion, distinguishes them from the contents of ego consciousness, and gives them qualities in common with the archetypal Self in its prompting and directing capacities.

The archetypal Self is never experienced directly, *per se,* but always by means of representations, that is, by images. Symbols of the Self often possess extraordinary numinosity, giving them a sense of transcendent priority, as if before a god-image. Jung believed the various images of God around the world were projections of the archetypal Self. The symbols of the Self which appear in dreams and active imagination also have a god-like quality. Jung was unwilling to say, as a psychologist, that such god-images might actually be referent to a divine or ultimate reality which prompts the psyche towards wholeness, but the richness of his thought does not foreclose such possibility. Jung did believe his discovery of the archetypal Self, as it manifests itself in god-images, mandalas, and other central numinous images found the world over, should be of special interest to empirical theology. "Its relatively frequent occurrence seems to be a noteworthy fact for any theologia naturalis".[27] When Jung spoke personally and confessionally, he sometimes suggested that God had a direct effect upon his own vocation, and destiny: "Nobody could rob me of the conviction that it was enjoined upon me to do what God wanted."[28] An examination of Jung's personal letters and his autobiography (MDR) supports the idea that Jung personally believed in a divine reality present and manifest within the deep center of the person, the archetypal Self.

MANDALAS: IMAGES OF SELF AS AXIS MUNDI

The archetypal Self has the characteristics of an axis mundi, a center of the psychological world of the individual. If the axis mundi be understood as a center point of order and orientation for the collective life of a tribe or community, then the archetypal Self may be considered an axis mundi for the individual world. Just as every tribe, every village, every church, has an image of the axis mundi, symbolizing a sacred center point of orientation, so the psyche has the archetypal Self as the center from which it takes its orientation.

Jung believed he found in the mandala the special symbol of the archetypal Self. The word comes from the Sanskrit word meaning "magic circle". It is usually a circular image which may be squared, or contain a square within it. It may be divided into a quaternary structure, and be further divided into regular subdivisions, all of which seem to radiate from or move toward a center point. A major theme of mandalas is the integration, balancing, or harmonizing of opposites. Mandalas have been used as aids in meditation and healing in cultural contexts as diverse as Tibetan Lamaism and Navaho medicine societies, where mandala-like sand paintings are employed. The Islamic geomatrix and the Gothic rose window and Christian crucifix are examples of mandalas used for religious devotional purposes. Jung believed the mandala was a projection of the archetypal Self, and may emerge not only in religious traditions, but in the dreams and active imagination of individuals in analysis. Mandalas represent potential for wholeness on both cosmic and personal levels. They have been used by shamans and medicine societies for healing purposes, and Jung noted that they tended to spontaneously emerge in his patients who were undergoing crisis. Jung noted that spontaneous mandala images appeared in some individuals who were fragmenting, and that these images seem to have had a calming and integrative (cohesive) effect upon them.

Shamans, and medicine men and women, have often had recourse to mandalas, as aids in the healing process. The building of sacred shrines for the healing seance, the drawing of magic circles within which the patient is to lay and the shaman to perform, the construction of sand paintings upon which the afflicted sit, and the employment of tribal myth as a means to re-establish the order and keep chaos at bay, all suggest an attempt to evoke a sense of a central orienting point, a zone of the "absolutely real, enduring, and effective", as Eliade would say. Mandalas apparently function as a way of evoking or reconstituting an axis mundi (sacred center) and so provide a sense of order and safety. Whether they be employed in shamanic ritual, or emerge spontaneously from the unconscious of troubled modern individuals, mandalas seem to impose order on psychic chaos, perhaps by establishing a central focus (sacred presence) while providing a protective enclosing circle (ritual boundaries).

Individuals living in tribal or traditional societies, had recourse to the axis mundi mediated through their myths, rituals, and sacred architecture. Today, many modern individuals are unable to affirm the myth of their Judeo-Christian culture. Few public center points of orientation are trusted, and few satisfying religious institutional containers are available in which to live a symbolic life. However, Jung believed that it was possible to find meaning and inner security in living one's own myth, in taking one's orientation from the inner center, the psychic axis mundi which he called the Self. This, as we shall see, is also what he thought the shaman has always been able to do. The shaman individuates by living from the heart.

JUNG'S THEORY OF PSYCHOLOGICAL DISORDER

Every theory of disorder presupposes some theory of order. In the shamanic view, balance is the key word. To be healthy requires that one live harmoniously, keep in balance. Disorder, in the shamanic view, is the result of some imbalance, caused by the intrusion of some spirit or object which upsets the balance, or of the loss of some vital part of the individual (e.g., soul loss). In the Jungian view, wholeness and integration are key terms suggesting an order and balance which, when disrupted, results in pathology. This brings the shamanic and Jungian views very close together. Let us give a schematic diagram of the shamanic and Jungian views on health and pathology:

Shamanic View: Health = living in accord with the will of the sacred.

Pathology = imbalance caused by violating the will of the sacred.

Jungian View: Health = result of wholeness, living in accord with the promptings of the archetypal Self.

Pathology = imbalance (one-sidedness), caused by violating the wholeness and integration demanded by the archetypal Self.

In Jung's view, factors which contribute to mental disorders are psychological imbalances between the archetypally patterned psychical energies. He considered the personality to be composed of numerous polar energies, archetypal patterns which come into conflict and tend to pull the individual towards one pole or the other. The psychological task is to consciously hold the opposing forces in some type of dynamic tension promoting wholeness. Jung expresses this as a process of holding the opposites in tension, and it is considered to be strenuous psychological work, requiring conscious effort and courage. Inevitable imbalances occur in the course of living, giving rise to disorder and various forms of psychopathology. Psychopathology has a purposive or teleological function since the psyche is attempting to call attention to the imbalances and correct them through compensation: "But since everything strives for wholeness, the inevitable one-sidedness of our conscious life is continually being corrected and compensated by the universal human being within us, whose goal is the ultimate integration of conscious and unconscious, or better, the assimilation of the Ego to a wider personality."[29]

COMPLEXES: THE "LITTLE DEVILS"

As we have mentioned elsewhere in this study, one of the most common shamanic theories of psychological disorder is based upon the belief that invading and possessing spirits can seize and possess the person, or steal away the soul, giving rise to pathological imbalances requiring shamanic restoration. Jung sometimes speaks in a similar manner, although with psychological intent, of those "little devils," which account for various psychopathological manifestations, but which he psychologically reinterprets as feeling toned complexes. The traditional shaman confronted the problem of diagnosing and treating what we, from our Western medical or psychological idiom, call mental disorders. The shaman has to draw terms from his/her own cultural worldview in which the sacred is presupposed, and those terms would of necessity be animistic or demonological in idiom. The modern scientific worldview of the west, which dominates the process of diagnosing and treating mental disorders in

industrialized or westernized societies today, constructs its conceptions and terms out of a secular worldview. Jung's worldview
was heavily shaped by the secular scientific tools of modernity.
However, Jung had great respect for the worldview of traditional
peoples, and a great affinity for the numinal which showed up in
his rhetorical style. This blend of modern scientific and numinal
terminology in Jung's writings may sometimes be confusing, for
Jung often tried to interpret religious or animistic perspectives in
modern psychiatric terms, and often interpreted psychological
data and processes in spiritual terms. This mixing of spiritistic
and psychological idioms seems especially apparent in his discussion of the complexes.

For Jung, the ideal of health is psychological integration,
and it is complexes which account for the dissociative divisions
manifest in psychopathology. Complexes are Jung's secular psychological interpretation of the (shamanic) numinal spirits that
cause psycho-spiritual disorders, by invading and taking over the
conscious organizing center (will) of the personality:

> Complexes are autonomous groups of feeling toned associa-
> tions that have a tendency to move by themselves, to live
> their own life apart from our intentions. We like to believe
> in our will power, in our energy in what we can do, but when
> it comes to the real showdown we find we can do it only to a
> certain extent because we are hampered by the "little dev-
> ils", the complexes.[30]

Jung's conception of the complex contributes to the traditional theory of spirit and demonic possession, as well as its
modern successor, multiple personality (MPD, now dissociative
identity disorder, or DID). However, Jung, at least early in his
career, wrote that belief in actual spirits should be ruled out as
superstitious, and replaced by the modern concept of the psychological complex. Jung explains in what ways he considers
demonic possession to be a reality, if understood as possession
by a complex in personified form:

> I may say here that the superstition held by all races that hys-
> terical insane persons are "possessed" by demons is right in
> conception. These patients have, in fact, autonomous com-

plexes, which at times destroy self control. The superstition is therefore justified, inasmuch as it denotes "possession", because the complexes behave quite independently of the Ego, and force upon it a quasi-foreign will.[31]

Jung's first piece of psychological scholarship, his medical dissertation, was itself a study of complex-related dissociation phenomena, which has traditionally been understood as possession, and in modern psychiatric terms, as dissociative disorder. Jung's dissertation, entitled "On the Psychology and Pathology of So-called Occult Phenomena,"[32] was based upon a psychological case study of a young woman who performed mediumistic feats in spiritistic seances. The young woman was Jung's cousin, Helene Preiswerk. With his supervisor's (Eugen Bleuler) encouragement, Jung attended the mediumistic seances regularly for some time, and studied the phenomena of Helene's possession states from a psychological perspective. That is, Jung bracketed out any consideration of the possessing spirits as actual occult spirits existing independently in time and space from Helene's psyche. Although Jung had not yet formulated the term *complex*, his observations were actually prefigurations of the concept. The seances gave Jung insight into a number of phenomena which would later support Jung's theory of the complex.

Observing the many enactments of spirit possession by his cousin, Jung categorized them into several classes. There were various masculine figures, which Jung later interpreted as animus personifications, a female personality who appeared more mature than Helene (a representation of Helene's archetypal Self), personifications of past lives, complete with historical references, which Jung would later see as suggestive of historical archetypes, the revelation of a psychological cosmology, and the spontaneous appearance of a mandala imagery (image of archetypal Self, or of wholeness). Jung came to understand these manifestations as dissociated and/or projected aspects of Helene's personality, and prefigurations of a future and more mature self. Although Jung did not classify Helene as suffering from multiple personality, one recent study of the case, reflecting on the child abuse Helene experienced, has suggested that Helene probably suffered a dissociative disorder, and possibly from multiple personality.[33] Jung believed Helene's spirit possession states could be explained in psychological terms. He later articulated such possession states as the result of the activity of feeling toned complexes which had become dissociated or split-off from ego-consciousness, and became personified in the various figures which spoke through her. Since they were experienced as dystonic (separate from) the ego, she felt compelled to believe they were independently existing spirits, rather than manifestations of her greater Self.

Jung gained his first world-wide notoriety for his studies of word-association experiments at the Burgholzli Hospital, under Eugen Bleuler, in Zurich. These studies led Jung to establish his theory of the complex. The research involved the construction of 100 neutral but emotionally charged words, which were carefully mixed and presented to patients and to normal control persons. Reactions to the stimulus words were carefully recorded in terms of response times, response content, and perseverations, and any other uncommon reactions were noted. The empirical data suggested that unusually long response times (hesitations, confusions), failures to respond, unexpected responses, seemingly unrelated responses, or other atypical responses, indicated the presence of complexes outside the field of conscious awareness, such as he had encountered with his cousin Helene. Complexes became the foundation of Jung's understandings of psychopathology:

> Complexes are psychic fragments which have split off owing to traumatic influences or certain incompatible tendencies. As the association experiments prove, complexes interfere with the intentions of the will and disturb the conscious performance; they produce disturbances of memory and blockages in the flow of associations [q.v.]; they appear and disappear according to their own laws; they can temporarily obsess consciousness, or influence speech and action in an unconscious way. In a word, complexes behave like independent beings, a fact especially evident in abnormal states of mind. In the voices of the insane they even take on a personal Ego-character like that of spirits who manifest themselves through automatic writing and similar techniques.[34]

At the Australasian Medical Congress in 1911, Jung presented the results of his association researches, concluding that he had actually studied the behavior of complexes accounting for a wide variety of psychopathological symptoms, including demonic possession, dual personality, psychotic hallucinations, fantasies of dementia praecox (schizophrenia) patients, hysteria and related conversion symptoms, and obsessions arising from catatonic impulses.[35] In the same paper Jung draws attention to Freud's researches along the same lines, in studying slips of the tongue (Freudian slips) as suggesting the presence of alternative and unintegrated psychological viewpoints within the person which slip out when ego-consciousness is weak, fatigued, or caught off guard. Jung argued that hysterical symptoms are caused by "autonomously acting complexes", but that the hysteric's complexes are continually subject to changes in response to environmental fluctuations. He found the fantasy life of schizophrenics also to be dominated by complexes, but the libidinal charge of these complexes was so strong as to rigidly fix the attention of the schizophrenic on them. Jung believed schizophrenic complexes to be more rigid, or fixed, than those of the hysteric. He also noted that while the schizophrenic personality may outwardly appear to be in a state of deterioration, the inner fantasy life is exceptionally lively, dominated by imagery and hallucinatory voices organized into symbolic patterns revolving in theme around an archetypal core (pattern). The direction of thought and libido, on the other hand, is turned away from external reality and over-invested in inner reality. Such overinvestment was understood to be a kind of possession by the complexes dominating the schizophrenic's psyche. Because the ego-personality is so fixed on the imagery dominated by complexes, the progress of general personality development becomes radically one-sided (radical introversion) and arrested.[36] Adaptation to outer reality (via normal extroversion) becomes maladaptively impoverished.

Jung did not believe complexes were confined to pathological individuals, however. Complexes develop in every personality, healthy and unhealthy. It is a matter of how strong or autonomous such complexes may be, and whether or not they seize and take over the ego. Jung believed that complexes showed up in the dream material of ordinary as well as pathological individuals. The complexes emerge as themes in ordinary dream activity, and in ordinary behavior, giving substance and dramatic character to the dream contents and fantasy life of the person.

Every person has a number of complexes. A complex itself is not harmful or resultant in significant self-defeating behavior. It is the autonomous complexes, usually the result of childhood trauma, that create profound difficulties in living. Complexes consist of a collection of ideas and images organized around one or more archetypes at the complex core, and having a certain feeling tone and energy charge. All of us, for example, have a mother and father complex. They may not be harmful, but simply a collection of ideas, memories, fantasies, and emotions which are constellated around our own experiences of our parents, and which are finally organized by the mother and father archetypes. What distinguishes a pathological complex from a more or less ordinary one is the emotional charge of the nuclear core of an autonomous complex. If inner and outer events become sufficient to provoke the constellation of a complex in a strong and discordant way, it may be said to be pathological, because it remains unconscious, and tends to be autonomous in working against the part-to-whole integrity of the psyche. An autonomous complex can usurp the role of the ego, can even use the ego for its own purposes.

Psychological disturbance may be potential or actual with a complex, depending on whether or not the inner and outer events are sufficient to activate it, or are insufficient, leaving it latent. Once activated, the complex resists the executive functions and intentions of the ego. Jung also considered the ego to be a complex, the ego-complex, since it also consists in a collection of ideas and images with a feeling tone. It is the center of the field of consciousness, and plays the role of being the conscious executive of the personality. It is only one complex among at least several, but it is of central importance in everyday living tasks. It can be invaded, thwarted, used, and seized by other complexes. "Every one knows that people have complexes," Jung wrote, but "what is not so well known...is that complexes can have us".[37] A sufficiently strong complex can thwart the adaptive purposes of the ego and lead to serious psychopathology in which the ego is seized and controlled by the complex's dictates.

Jung's therapeutic response to the pathological complex is the process of making it conscious. This response is not as simple or as simplistic as it sounds. Countless persons have found that intellectual knowledge of their problems may be illuminating at first, but insufficient to bring about resolution. Jung's understanding of "making conscious" implies more than intellectual knowledge. It requires a courageous effort, a strong ego, and the capacity to accept suffering, which facing of complexes entails. Only when the complex has been discharged, its emotional element assimilated, or its energy transferred to another tension gradient can the affective charge of the complex dissolve. Only then can the contents be integrated in a relatively harmonious way which contributes positively to the whole personality.

As long as complexes remain unconscious they can grow and become harmful to the integrity of the psyche. Remaining unconscious, the archetypal core of the complex acts like a magnet, continuing to attract images, ideas, affects, and other associations until it can become very swollen and powerful. The complexes of psychotic individuals, such as schizophrenics, tend to take on an archaic mythological character. Their unconscious productions (hallucinations, dream images, fantasies, beliefs, etc.) become less personally symbolic, and more universal or mythic. In proportion as they distance themselves from ego-consciousness, their numinosity increases, and this numinosity puts the subject in a state of will-less submission to the complex. This is a kind of possession, since the splinter psyche, or complex, has totally taken over the individual's psyche and life. In cases of psychosis and pathological dissociation, the complex may take on the quality of a possessing spirit, demon, god, or ghost. It may appear as one or more alternate personalities, or even as a soul stealing parent, lover, or sorcerer.

MAKING COMPLEXES CONSCIOUS VS. SHAMANIC EXORCISM

Jung's approach to such possession is not exorcism or extraction, as it might be for the traditional shaman dealing with possession or intrusion. Jung's underlying therapeutic purpose is not one of removal/extraction of a pathogenic force, which is what exorcism implies, but of integration. The structure and energy of the complex is a valuable part of the psychic whole. It must not be removed, but restored to harmonious relations within the totality. This requires the kind of consciousness which we just described. If there is a congruent way to think of Jungian therapeutics as exorcistic, it would be that of considering the process of becoming conscious as a therapeutic method of casting out (casting off) the compulsive-autonomous character of the complex. In the Jungian view, what needs to be removed is not the complex itself, but its inordinate cathexis of energy, and its destructive intrusiveness whereby it interferes with the personality's integrated functioning. In the Jungian view, the removal of inordinate energy and intrusiveness could be said to be the goal. This requires conscious work and effort on the part of the patient. In traditional shamanic therapy, this type of conscious work is at a minimum, and the shaman may rely upon the power of suggestion to abreact pent-up energy (affect) and then reinstate repression and therefore relativise the functioning of the complex in the overall psychological economy of the patient. Psychoanalytic studies of shamanism have sometimes interpreted the shaman, when exorcising destructive spirits, as actually sending them back down into the unconscious via ritual means, and reinstating the repression barrier. In a Jungian view, shamanic extraction could be understood as the analogue of removing a pathologic complex from control or influence over the ego. We might say the complex is extracted from the egoic field of influence, so that the ego's repressive powers are reconstituted. This seems to be a fair psychological interpretation of shamanic exorcistic practice. I have recently viewed videos brought back by an anthropologist from Southeast Asia which show shamans performing exorcisms only after exhausting their patient's consciousness through the ordeals of the ritual. At the moment of neurophysiological exhaustion, when the patient's consciousness is likely to be attenuated, the shaman commands the spirit to leave, and it typically does leave.

Voluminous reports of field studies by anthropologists indicate that there will often be recurrences of possession, or new molesting spirits will enter as the old one leaves. Some shamans give amulets and sacred charms to help preserve the healing effects, and to prevent re-possession (relapse), or prescribe periodic returns to the shamanic shrine for what amounts to check-ups. Such sacred objects are no doubt helpful, and the western practitioner could benefit from the wisdom of shamanic experience with regard to giving our patients such significant objects. In psychoanalytic terms, the sacred objects, and check-up visits with the shaman, could be understood in terms of providing the patient with transitional objects, and in terms of providing the patient with object constancy. Both of these concepts relate to the need for the patient to keep something of the healer's presence with them, as an aid in keeping the repression barrier instated. A Jungian slant on this phenomena might suggest that the sacred amulets, charms, and check-up visits actually serve to give the patient an image by which to relate to the central integrative force of the psyche, the "doctor within," which Jung calls the archetypal Self. Being related to a greater center of power and order provides the security that the forces of chaos will be kept at bay, and help to inspire the confidence and courage that further disintegration will not occur. At least in those cases of possession where the subjects are, in Western psychological terms, hysterical or suffering from multiple personality (constructed in the familiar demonological idiom of their culture as demon or spirit possession), the interpretation of reinstating the repression barrier, after allowing the patient to discharge (abreact) pent-up affects attributed to the possessing entity, seems plausible.

FORMS OF COMPLEXES

Complexes may manifest psychic or somatic aspects, or both. In conversion hysteria, the complex is behind the physical symptom. In perverted masturbatory fantasies, a complex is behind the perverted fantasy and the masturbatory compulsion. One ordinary form of complex has such a low energy charge that it seldom intrudes into consciousness, and does not operate independently of consciousness. Another form is the unconscious complex which is so swollen that it acts like a second ego-consciousness, and comes into conflict with the executive ego. Persons with this type of complex often feel caught between two competing value systems, truths, or streams of will. When a complex splits off dramatically from the larger organization of the psyche it becomes what Jung called autonomous, accounting for the phenomena of possession, dual and multiple personality (Janet), or dissociation into several partial personalities. Another form of harmful complex consists of identification with the complex, as in a mother or father complex. The values, opinions, dogmas, or wishes of the parent are carried around unconsciously. It is as if the individual were the mere instrument or mouthpiece of the parent. These individuals may not have the slightest idea of what is going on. The projected form of complex attributes the complex to an outward object or person, or to a spirit. Often these projected complexes are colored by the shadow qualities which the individual has not the courage to face. This form is observed in paranoia and in homophobia, and it is also believed to be present in primitive psychology, for example, in fetishism, totemism, and animism. A complex may also be intellectually conscious, but remain harmful because the individual is not wholeheartedly facing it, assimilating it emotionally, and bringing it into alignment with the adaptive purposes of the ego.

In the Jungian view, the inability or unwillingness to distinguish conscious from unconscious contents is psychologically risky, for it may prevent outward adaptation, thwart one's larger purposes, and interfere with human relationships and intimacy. The phenomenon which anthropologist Lucien Lévy-Bruhl (1857–1939)[38] called participation mystique, which, he observed, was characteristic of primitive psychology, is also characteristic of the effects of autonomous complexes. Participation mystique is basically the same as what object-relations psychoanalysts call projective identification, in which inner and outer events are merged or confused. It is basically an inability to distinguish inner from outer reality. It is found not only in primitive psychology, but also in the thought processes of children, and in modern neurotics. The stronger the tendency towards participation mystique, the less the ego is able to discriminate and delimit the inner and the outer. The result is increased vulnerability to inner or outer domination and loss of freedom.

Psychological health and maturity, for Jung, implies that the different parts of the psyche are consciously acknowledged, recognized, and brought into adequate (harmonious) relation to one another. Distinguishing and delimiting the different parts of the self is essential to such harmonious integration. It requires a strong ego, courage to become conscious and face the disagreeable contents of a complex. The ego must have the courage and strength to take negative elements into its own self-affirmation, if it is to become richer, more flexible, and thus stronger.

WHAT IS THE STATUS OF SPIRIT GUIDES IN SEEING SHAMANICALLY?

Jung's view that feeling toned complexes are normal is a refutation of the modern monolithic conceptions of the personality. In a way very convergent with traditional shamanic views of the soul, the psyche, for Jung, is a plurality, albeit within a greater unity, which he calls the Self. Freud also viewed the psyche as a plurality; it contains a trinity of intrapsychic systems: id, ego, and superego. But Jung's view greatly complexifies the psyche's plurality, since the number of archetypes and complexes may be beyond anyone's ability to number. In a traditional shamanic view, there may be vital souls, dream souls, free souls, and other entities within a person, including the souls of ancestors and the spirits of the clan, tribe, and sometimes of a sorcerer. Only in biological death have all souls fled. In soul loss, typically only one soul, or perhaps several soul parts have wandered off, been stolen, or become lost. When most of a person's vital souls or soul parts have departed he or she may become comatose, psychotic, or die. It is as if more of the person is in non-ordinary reality than in ordinary reality.

A problem with Jung's interpretations of shamanic phenomena is that he tends to interpret spirits as manifestations of the unconscious, and possessing spirits as complexes or archetypes, which we will examine further in Chapters 5 and 6. Unpublished anecdotes from some of Jung's analysands are rumored to reveal that Jung did give personal acknowledgment to the reality of such independent spirit entities, but our discussion of Jung has had to rely on what he actually said (or published) publicly. This might lead one to conclude that spirits are finally nothing but psychological contents. For Jung the unconscious is very large, growing beyond the personal unconscious of Freudian psychology, and including the collective unconscious or objective psyche, which makes it largely an unknown: an unfathomable mystery filled with numinous presences. When Jung speaks of these numinous presences or spirits as a psychologist, he tends to schematize them as complexes, apparently adjusting his discussion to a relatively skeptical scientific audience. However, if we recall that Jung's midlife crisis was an initiation in which he encountered spirits, held lengthy dialogues with them, received guidance and revelations concerning his life's work and his psychology, and spent a great deal of the rest of his life fascinated with Gnosticism, alchemy, astrology, and synchronistic phenomena, it is perhaps not too difficult to conceive that Jung's private interests in the spirit world may have exceeded what he felt that he could express publicly. That Jung had great respect for the spirits that manifested themselves in his own inner life, or in those of his patients, is beyond question. Jung is remarkable for his great respect for the psyche and psychic phenomena in modern western psychology.

It is tempting to think about what real spirits might be like if we modified the publicly published Jungian theory to account for them. Jung claimed that there were limits to what psychology could know. All we can ever know appears first to our psyche, and within psyche. We should keep in mind that Jung's conception of the objective psyche is equivalent to Castaneda's nonordinary reality, even if Jung endows it with archetypal patterns. It is filled with numinal mystery, it is unfathomable, and it is the locus of near-death experiences, out-of-body journeys, and shamanic journeying. It is the locus of ancestral memory, of transpersonal guidance, and of numinous healing power. By virtue of Jung's belief in synchronistic phenomena, including ESP, clairvoyance, clairaudience, precognition, synchronization of inner and outer phenomena, and so on, Jung's model of the psyche may have little trouble making room for telepathy, out-of-body journeys, objectivity of spirit guides, and telepathic healing at a distance. We are all "in" the collective unconscious, the objective psyche, and we are all related. The "we" of this relatedness includes the spirit world, material world, the plant, mineral, and animal kingdoms, the galaxies and star systems, as well as other humans. For Jung, the psyche has subjective (personal) as well as objective (transpersonal) dimensions. The collective unconscious is the ultimate context in which all experience occurs. If spirits manifest themselves, it is always in and to the psyche. If there be independently existing spirit entities, their dealings with humans must pass through archetypal structures. There is no getting around it: whatever appears as a spirit must manifest itself to a human through structures of the psyche and the central nervous system.

When traditional or contemporary urban shamans speak of their spirit guides (or power animals) it is often with great reverence and respect for them. Their trust in these spirits, whatever their psychological or ontological status, is essential to the efficacy of their healing work. It is the spirit guide which diagnoses the patient's illness and which instructs the shaman on how best to engage in the healing work. The shaman, by virtue of these spirit guides, is able to see shamanically into the patient's body (etheric aura or subtle body) and locate intrusions and extract (remove) them. The shaman enters non-ordinary reality to find, by the help of the spirit guide, the lost vital souls or soul parts. Reports of the efficacy of these methods by shamans and their patients are voluminous. Increasingly there are reports of shamans who can traverse thousands of miles in their journeys to heal a patient in another locality geographically. While Jung may have been reticent to speak in non-psychological terms about what such guiding spirits really are, or how they can do such seemingly magical things as heal at a distance, he had no trouble taking such reports seriously. To go a step further than the official and public views of Jung, a slightly extended Jungian view needn't have many problems with the independent reality of spirit guides or of their efficacy in healing, even at a great distance. If the objective psyche is the locus of the world, or of all that occurs, then its embracing unity is like a vessel that contains and inter-relates all entities. Jung's views on synchronistic activity regulated by the archetypes, and especially by the archetypal Self, can easily account for such synchronistic phenomena as telepathic diagnosis and healing at a distance. Jung can say with psychological certainty that the shaman's spirit guides are experienced as ego-dystonic, as outside the agency of the shaman's ego-identity. According to Jungian analyst John R. Haule, the experiencing of the spirit guide as independently existing, as beyond the shaman's ego, as ego-dystonic, enables the shaman to be freed from the limited knowledge and experience of the ego-identity and its self-generating monologues.[39] The shaman thus becomes open to a knowledge, wisdom, and healing power that far surpass that of the ego. Regardless of whether one interprets the spirits as archetypes and complexes or as independently existing spirits, Jung has wisely seen that they exist independent of the human ego and its familiar ego-identity.

Another problem arises from Jung's tendency to interpret the psyche's spirit manifestations as he does the complexes and the archetypes, as partial manifestations of the totality of the psyche, the Self. We shall see the ways Jung does this in Chapter 5, where we examine Jung's sparse writings and views on shamanism in his *Collected Works*. For now we wish to call attention to Jung's interpretation of the shaman's spirit guide (or power animal) as a manifestation and representation of the archetypal Self, the greater wholeness of the person. At first this may sound like another psychological reduction, and it is as if Jung wished to say that all spirits who manifest themselves in the psyche are manifestations of a person's archetypal Self. He does not say this, even if it seems implied. He does suggest, as we shall see, that the shaman's spirit helpers are manifestations of the Self. Even if Jung did insist that the spirit guides are nothing but manifestations of the archetypal Self, there is plenty of room in his psychological theory to account for the factuality and importance of the spirit guides as sui generis. We must remember the great respect and seriousness with which he took his own spirit guides, especially Philemon. We must again remember that Jung's view of the psyche is very expansive, much larger than the ego-personality and its personal unconscious. If the cosmos of the shaman is vast enough to include journeys to various planes, and concourse with spirits, Jung's psyche is also vast and unfathomable, consisting not only of the archetypes and spirit presences, but of ancestral memories, of prehuman memory and, at bottom, the structure and memory of the world and greater cosmos. Jung was not Cartesian in his view of psyche and world; they are at bottom the same thing, viewed and experienced in differing aspects. Jung also does not assume that we are independent of one another, or that the outer and inner worlds are fundamentally separate. We are all interrelated by virtue of being of and in the collective unconscious. If we are all intrapsychically related, then telepathy becomes an outmoded concept, and long-distance journeying to heal a patient is not really long distance at all; it is a matter of tuning in to the collective unconscious, and to the being which the shaman seeks to heal. The collective unconscious, like non-ordinary reality, includes everything, and, from a metaphysical perspective, has its locus in the ultimate reality, call it God, Allah, Brahma, Wakan Tanka, Kitchimanitou, or by whatever name you prefer. Jung, of course, tried to avoid public metaphysical speculation, so this kind of metaphysical conclusion must be inferred.

Perhaps an illustration can help us understand how to conceptualize Jung's understanding of shamanic phenomena. Imagine that our psyches overlap and interpenetrate one another like the circles of a Venn diagram, and perhaps all our circles are encompassed by a greater circle, the divine reality. Then it is possible for my spirit guide to enter your psyche, or more accurately, it would tune in to your psyche through a shamanic altered state of consciousness. The journey of the shaman would in effect be a tuning in to your frequency, rather than a literal traversing of external space and time. You might even access my spirit guide, and see it in an altered state of consciousness. Even if my spirit guide is a manifestation of the archetypal Self, it is none the less real. My trance journey with it is just as much a shamanic journey, and its ability to see into your psyche and diagnose and instruct me on how to help heal it is just as effective as it would be if it were an independent spirit. According to John R. Haule, the value of the shaman believing it is an independent spirit is that it makes its otherness to his ego more apparent, and allows the greater knowledge, wisdom, and power of the archetypal Self to be accessed for healing purposes. This keeps the shaman's ego from trying to run the show. In this view, the shaman's power is from his connection to the archetypal Self, mediated through the spirit guide or power animal. The sorcerer, by contrast, is not individuated, and lacks the direct access to the Self of the shaman. The sorcerer steals power from others, from the outer collective. The shaman, by contrast, has great authority because his or her power is accessed from within. Furthermore, if God is accessed by coming into relation with the archetypal Self, then it is ultimately divine wisdom that directs the shamanic journey and healing process.[40] This view, while not explicitly Jung's, is consistent with his understanding of spirit phenomena.

THE SELF-SELF CONNECTION IN SHAMANIC SEEING

In his book, *Pilgrimage of the Heart,* John R. Haule provides a Jungian discussion of how shamans may access another psyche to see into it and diagnose illness and perform healing functions. Haule explores the similarities between shamans and lovers in their ability to see into one another's souls. The reader may wonder what a book on romantic love has to do with shamanism. At first thought, they may seem to be as far apart as roses and sage, but Haule reveals that they are in fact both paths of the soul that correlate and correspond in interesting ways, while also diverging substantially. Both shamanism and romantic love are passions of the soul, both involve being caught up, inspired by daimones, being dismembered, being initiated into various transformations of soul, to name just a few similarities. Both also have treacherous ground to be traversed, and both can plummet one into unfathomable abysses. Haule argues that romantic love can be something more than a passing experience of youth; it can be an opportunity for initiation into a path of soulful realization and living. Because this work is also illuminating of the psychology of shamanism, we want to draw attention to that aspect of this work here. Haule makes comparisons between the psychological effect of the passion-producing love potion (Tristan and Isolde) in bringing the lovers into a mystical participation (participation mystique) and enabling them to see deeply into each other's soul.

In the alchemy of romance a deep connection signaled by love's passionate energies activates deep archetypal structures of the Self/soul, and it is this activation that makes it possible for lovers to see into each other's soul, in a way that others cannot. Such abilities to see into the soul are due to the accessing of the archetypal Self of the other, in romantic experience. Haule maintains a classic Jungian affirmation of the importance of the archetypal Self. He thus describes an underlying model of the psyche with two major levels, and three sub-levels:

PERSONAL PSYCHE: EGO CONSCIOUSNESS
                     PERSONAL UNCONSCIOUS

COLLECTIVE PSYCHE: Level 1) Mythic Images (mytho-
                     poetic imagination)
                     Level 2) Self (archetypal Self, deep
                     center)
                     Level 3) Instincts (inborn releasing
                     mechanisms)

When the lover drinks the love potion, or when the shaman enters ecstatic trance, both become able to see into the soul of the other. Haule claims that there are two ways of accessing the world: 1) Through ego-consciousness, which includes directed thinking and feeling, and use of the sense organs, and 2) through the Self level of the psyche. Our mental level can be lowered by erotic involvement, bringing about a state of merger not unlike the participation mystique described by anthropologist Lucien Lévy-Bruhl. An experience that involves the activation of an archetype brings about a drop in the level of consciousness, giving access to other individuals through the Self, which is the second sublevel of the collective psyche (Level 2).

Shamanism, the author argues, is found world wide and consists of individuals who have a special talent for deliberately passing into ecstatic trance in order to gain access to a very similar state of unity or mystical participation with nature, nature spirits, and with their patients. By virtue of calling, talent, and training, the shaman learns to gain access to the soul of any individual, whereas lovers only gain access to each other's souls.

Haule makes some interesting observations about shamanism. He notes that Eliade's classic work on shamanism is restricted in focus primarily to cases where the shamanic calling is limited to an elite who have a special calling and talent. But Haule argues that shamanic powers are more universally accessible, and cites the instance of the !Kung tribe who believe that all individuals have shamanic power and abilities. This would of course follow from Haule's thesis that lovers and shamans are able to see by virtue of their access to the Self level of the collective psyche. He mentions the fact that in Castaneda's eight books there is a gradual reduction in the connotation of seeing as Castaneda matures and learns what Don Juan Matus has been trying to teach him all along, that seeing should be practiced as a daily event, and not given such a grandiose, fanciful, and radiant content as Castaneda does for so long in his apprenticeship.

Haule describes the !Kung shaman's journey in terms of this Jungian model. The !Kung shaman actually enters a kind of dreamscape and goes in search of his patient's lost soul. We might add that if the shaman's spirit guide be a manifestation of the archetypal Self, or of God, it still is a reality, a mode of access that allows the shaman to see into the other's psyche through a Self-Self relation. The journey is not a private dream of personal significance for the shaman, for it has an objective quality about it. It is a dream about the Self level of connectedness between psyches of shaman and patient. The shaman obtains a true (effective) insight into the psychological condition of the woman.[42] The shaman's method is interpreted as 1) diagnostic seeing by way of a direct, imageless intuition (Collective Level, Level 2), the level of Self. The shaman's grasp of the problem at this level is non-specific, because there is no image of it. Hence the shaman must 2) rise to the mythopoetic imagination (not Haule's term) where a mythic image is given to the experience. In other words, the shaman must access a level of psyche (Collective Level, Level 1) where mythic images are given to deep but inarticulate psychical experiences, to "where those deep, unarticulated interpersonal facts (the patient's deceased father is seen as having possession of the patient's soul) can be represented in a useful manner".[43] Haule has brought into bold contrast, through his Jungian based analysis, a two-step process to shamanic seeing that is very similar to the creative process. It calls to mind Silvano Arieti's distinction between the preliminary stage of the endocept wherein the artist feels an intuition, an inspirational urge that is experienced or felt as quasi-physical and, which may be uncomfortable until expressed, and the conceptual stage, when an image or concept is given to the inarticulate endocept. Once given such form, there is a release, a sense of eureka, and a satisfaction for the artist. In addition to formulating a Jungian understanding of how shamanic seeing is possible, Haule's work helps us to see the creative dynamic in shamanic seeing. The mind of the shaman creates a reality that is at once subjective and objective, allowing the shaman to tune in to the psyche of another person by passing through his or her own dreamscape into that of another. The locus of both the shaman's dreamscape and that of his or her patient is the collective unconscious, the objective psyche, or, if you will, non-ordinary reality.

Chapter Five

Jung's Interpretation of Shamanism

SHAMANISM AS A PRECURSOR
TO JUNG'S ANALYTICAL PSYCHOLOGY

In the previous chapter we reviewed the basic principles of
Jung's psychology, of the soul and its disorders, and compared
and contrasted it with shamanic views. One purpose was to provide a theoretical context for examining more closely Jung's own
views of shamanism which we shall offer here. Jung had some
very definite views of shamanism, but these views are anything
but coherent and systematic. It is easier to explore the shamanic
implications of Jung's theory than it is to develop a coherent picture of Jung's understanding of shamanism based on his writings
on the subject. This is largely because more of his statements
about shamanism were offered as secondary amplifications or
illustrations of other archetypes and psychological processes,
especially on mystical alchemy. Aside from Jung's own direct and
personal shamanic type of experience, Jung apparently read little
about shamanism. Among the main documented sources in his
investigations of shamanism was Eliade's classic study, *Shamanism: Archaic Techniques of Ecstasy*. Many of Jung's interpretations of
shamanism are based upon Eliade's descriptions of the structure
and symbolism of shamanism. Other sources include the writings
and theories of Lucien Lévy-Bruhl, and various sources in the history of dynamic psychiatry. Additionally, Jung had encountered
medicine men in his expeditions to Africa and to the Taos
Pueblo, but neither of the medicine men is identified strictly as a
shaman in Eliade's restrictive definition. Jung's writings about
shamanism are thus based on a narrow range of the literature on
shamanism, and probably on no direct experience with a traditional shaman. His comments on shamanism are all too few, given

the magnitude of the *Collected Works* and the range of topics he gave exhaustive discussion to. The reader will find no systematic and thorough discussion of Jung's view on the subject here. What we offer are a sampling of a broad range of descriptions, interpretations, and correlations Jung made between his own thought, alchemy, and shamanism. Some of the statements appear to be contradictory, but we offer them here to show what Jung actually thought about the subject as revealed in his public writings.

In 1918 Jung's first references to shamanism appeared in his writings. He wrote an essay entitled "The Role of the Unconscious,"[1] where he described the historical forerunners of his analytical psychology. He drew attention to the Romantic and Victorian revival of interest in the ancient synchronistic phenomena, the non-rational, the occult, the spiritistic seances, and in Mesmerism (hypnotism). Jung viewed these as immediate precursors to the development of analytical psychology. Jung, however, claimed that shamanism was the earliest forerunner of analytical psychology. He argued that early hypnotism, Mesmer's "animal magnetism," was not so much a rational scientific concept, as a revival of the primitive-animistic concept of soul force and soul-stuff: "This is nothing but a rediscovery of the primitive concept of soul force or soul-stuff, awakened out of the unconscious by a reactivation of archaic forms of thought."[2] Historian of dynamic psychiatry Henri F. Ellenberger corroborates Jung's view of Mesmer in considering him more like a shaman drawing upon numinous healing power (animal magnetism), rather than upon scientific methods, to treat his patients.

Jung, while discussing the historical forerunners of analytical psychology, implies that the archaic concepts employed in animism and shamanism live on in the concerns of analytical psychology, and that Mesmerism represents a kind of historic transition phase between the archaic and modern conceptualizations of the same phenomena: soul force, and the numinosity of unconscious contents. Jung argues that even as animal magnetism became legitimated and renamed by modern psychiatry as medical hypnosis and spread through the modern (Western) world of the 19th century, spiritualism, with its form of possession, mediumship (today's channeling), and table turning, spread throughout the popular culture of Europe and America. Jung considered the fascination with spiritualism as a revival of shamanistic forms of religion, and as attempts at a type of individuation process. Much could be said of the New Age revival of ancient forms of gnosis and cosmic consciousness in the 1990s wherein a wide variety of synchronistic phenomena, channeling, near-death experiences, and spiritual healing are becoming popular. New Agers often feel they are discovering a new age of spiritual consciousness when, in fact, they are re-discovering the non-ordinary reality that the archaic shamans discovered in the Paleolithic era. Jung considered such modern fascination with spirits and synchronism: "a rebirth of the shamanistic form of religion practiced by our remote grandfathers".[3] Jung also considered Christian Science to be a precursor of analytical psychology, and a "higher form of shamanism".[4]

As we already mentioned, when Jung wrote of shamanism, it was illustrative of some other point. That is, he drew upon shamanic parallels to amplify other symbolic, mythic, or archetypal phenomena. So often did he do this that there are enough various interpretations of shamanic phenomena for us to present a loosely organized synopsis of Jung's reflections on it. Although these writings are scattered throughout a dozen or so volumes of the *Collected Works,* the largest percentage of them are to be found in the volume entitled *Alchemical Studies* (CW 13), of the *Collected Works.* In fact, Jung draws more parallels between shamanism and the symbolism and methods of alchemy, than with any other religious or mythological form. The largest percentage of Jung's interpretations of shamanic methods and symbolisms is thus to be found as amplifications of the methods and symbolism of alchemy. We shall begin by discussing these views on shamanic and alchemical phenomena, and then move to other categories by which Jung interpreted shamanic phenomena throughout his *Collected Works.*

JUNG ON ALCHEMY AND SHAMANISM

In addition to shamanism, Jung also believed that alchemy, if viewed through a symbolic-psychological lens, rather than through the lens of scientific chemistry, could be understood as a precursor to the modern psychology of the unconscious. Jung believed that alchemy was actually the projection of symbolic processes arising from the unconscious, and the imagery it produced, like that of shamanism, abounded in themes of ritual transformation. However, the ritual transformation processes of alchemy were believed by Jung to be disguised in terms of imagery of a chemical basis, a schema organized into oppositions. With the various magico-chemical operations performed upon these elements (*divisio, solutio, coagulatio,* etc.) the alchemist attempted to turn base metals into gold. This aim of turning base metals into gold, however, was more a mystical art than a scientific art, and hence led to projection of unconscious contents onto the elements, the *opus,* and the goal. Jung interpreted the gold, along with sacred stones like the crystal and the lapis lazuli, to be a symbol of the Self, and the chemico-transformation processes of alchemy to be a type of ritual transformation akin to the transformation involved in the individuation process.

The alchemist, like the shaman, practiced a secret, sacred, and esoteric art. Much ritual preparation and care went into the work *(opus),* and ritual boundaries (alchemical *vas*) were carefully stewarded so that nothing essential could escape or be contaminated. The alchemist often had a female to assist him in his magical labor, much like the shaman's celestial wife; and the alchemist, like the shaman, practiced his secret art at the margins of his society. Jung believed that medieval and renaissance alchemy, like modern depth psychology, arose as an attempt to compensate for the one-sidedness of Christianity. By drawing upon pagan themes, and rich archetypal imagery, it contrasted with the overly dogmatic and sexless expressions of Christianity, and its devaluation of the earthy and the feminine. Jung also believed that alchemy dealt better with the problem of the opposites (seeking a *conjunctio* rather than repression or dissociation), and incorporated rather than repressed the dark, shadow side of reality. Like shamanism, alchemy also placed a priority upon original experience, and did not fear heretical opinion. The convergence of alchemical themes and the similarities of alchemical symbolism is due more to the alchemists' individual discoveries of archetypal symbolism and transformative processes, and perhaps a comparing of findings amongst alchemists, than to dissemination by dogma. In this way, alchemy is akin to shamanism, which also has developed through individual experience of underlying archetypal and transformative processes, and through a sharing of findings (dissemination) amongst and between fellow shamans. A number of Jung's important statements about shamanism are made in amplification of various alchemical symbols. We shall review the more salient alchemical-shamanic comparisons made by Jung.

THE STONE AS SACRED OBJECT

In the context of discussing the alchemical significance of the philosopher's stone, the lapis lazuli, the crystal, and gold as psychological symbols of the archetypal Self, Jung reviews the significance of the numinosity of crystals in North American shamanism and mythology. The crystal, mounted in the head of the Cherokee dragon serpent Uktena, is desired by shamans, and pieces of it are used in shamanic healing rituals. Jung argues that crystals have a numinous status giving them paramount importance as ministering spirits in shamanism:

> In shamanism, much importance is attached to Crystals, which play the part of ministering spirits. They come from the crystal throne of the Supreme Being, or from the vault of the sky. They show what is going on in the world and what is happening to the souls of the sick, and they also give man the power to fly.[5]

The power of crystals to know what is going on, and what is wrong with the sick, is characteristic of the powers of the archetypal Self, in its capacity as regulator of all psychic processes, and as goad towards integrations and healing. Additionally, Jung suggests that the attributes of the stone are also those used symbolically to represent the archetypal Self. These are the attributes of "incorruptibility, permanence, and divinity".[6] The symbolism of alchemy, like the symbolism of shamanism and that of the unconscious of modern man, is polyvalent, consists of numerous and overlapping meanings. Hence, Jung sometimes interprets the same symbols differently, and sometimes interprets one symbol as meaning the same thing as another symbol. Jung thus interprets the magical tree in a way similar to the way he treated the alchemical tree, as having a variety of meanings, depending upon the context and particular facet of functioning of the tree under consideration.

THE ALCHEMICAL TREE AND THE MAGICAL TREE OF THE SHAMAN AS SYMBOL OF ARCHETYPAL SELF

The cosmic tree (world tree) is a symbolic motif common to alchemy and shamanism. Jung's understandings of the significance of the alchemical tree were based, in part, upon Eliade's understanding of the shaman's cosmic tree as an axis mundi, a center of the world which connects the three cosmic zones of shamanic cosmology. The cosmic tree is a kind of ritual passage way by which the shaman may mount up or ascend into the upper world, or descend into the lower world. Jung claimed the symbolism of ascent by means of a ladder, a stairway, or mountain, was found in the dreams of many of his modern patients, and was patterned upon the same archetype as the cosmic tree. Although Jung claimed that he never saw a cosmic tree appear in one of his patient's dreams, John Weir Perry, a Jungian analyst and psychiatrist, has documented the appearance of the cosmic tree motif in the hallucinatory images of various schizophrenic patients. Perry argues that the emergence of this tree symbol heralds a connection with the archetypal Self by the schizophrenic undergoing a transformative psychotic process. Jung also likened the cosmic tree symbolism with the central archetype. Since this type of axis mundi symbolism is so central to shamanic cosmology, it became rather natural for Jung to interpret it as a symbol of the Self, as a union of opposites, and as a means of access to the collective unconscious (symbolized as upper world and lower world).

In a passage in which Jung borrows from Eliade, with reference to a shaman's inverted cosmic tree which has the image of a face carved on it, Jung suggests that the tree is a symbol of the Self:

> "The inverted tree plays a great role among the East Siberian shamans....The roots signify hairs, and on the trunk,

near the root a face has been carved, showing [that] the tree represents a man." ...Presumably this is the shaman himself, or his higher personality. The shaman climbs the magic tree in order to find his true self in the Upperworld.[7]

Jung goes on to elaborate the shaman's need to climb the tree and ascend or descend into the upper and lower worlds as an urge towards mystical experience of the archetypal Self as a greater, more spiritual and true self. This urge of the shaman towards mystical experience is interpreted as the urge to individuate, to become a whole self, to live in connection with the deeper and more authentic Self. Such experience seems to be mandatory for the shaman, who cannot refuse its call without peril to himself or herself, and perhaps without madness. It is essential to the constitution of his or her personality: "Eliade says in his excellent study of shamanism that the Eskimo feels the need for these ecstatic journeys because it is above all during trance that he becomes truly himself; the mystical experience is necessary to him as a constituent of his personality."[8]

SHAMAN'S SELF AND THE SYMBOLISM OF THE INDIVIDUATION PROCESS

Jung links the ecstatic state in which the archetypal Self is encountered by the shaman with the notion of possession by helping guardian spirits, as aids or guides to an individuation process for the shaman. The symbolism of shamanism, like that of alchemy, is interpreted as projections of the individuation process. Again Jung relies upon Eliade for the basis of his interpretation:

The ecstasy is often accompanied by a state in which the shaman is possessed by his familiars or guardian spirits. By means of their possession he acquires his "'mystical organs,' which in some sort constitute his true and complete spiritual personality". This confirms the psychological inference that may be drawn from shamanic symbolism, namely that it is a projection of the individuation process. This inference we have also seen is true of alchemy.[9]

CELESTIAL BRIDE SYMBOLISM AND
THE SHAMANIC ANIMA

Another aspect of the symbolism of the world tree is the feminine aspect, its connection to the shaman's celestial wife, its connection to earth mother symbolism, which Jung interprets as due to the projection of the anima. Eliade documents the motif of the shaman's bond with the sacred, that is, with the numen of the other world. Eliade argues that the celestial wife serves as a spirit guide and instructor to the shaman, helping him navigate the mysteries and dangers of the other world. The role of the shaman's celestial bride (wife) is echoed as an archetypal theme found the world over in myth and literature, for example, as Dante's Beatrice, lure and guide to the other world, spirit guide on the path through the under world (Inferno) and into the upper world (Paradise). It is echoed in the alchemist's female assistant helper, in Orpheus mythology, and in Tantra.

Jung interprets the functioning of the celestial bride of the shaman as an anima figure.[10] He considered the anima to be an inner figure of contrasexual feminine within the psyche of a man. It corresponded to the animus in the woman, as the counterpart of the contrasexual masculine within her psyche. Unfortunately, Jung did not reflect on the role of the animus in the psychology of female shamans. Presumably it would operate much as the anima does for the male shaman. But here we will stay with what Jung did discuss. The anima, for Jung, is like a bridge to the deeper Self, to the unconscious psyche. She is usually perceived in the form of feminine images, and sometimes comes to represent the entirety of the soul (anima = soul). We should recall that the anima, as Jung understood it, may be beneficial, if related to and integrated in a positive manner, but it may also be dangerous, have a negative aspect, if inappropriately related to, neglected, or ignored. The anima is typically projected by men onto real women in the outer world. In projection, the numinosity may attract attention in the form of lovers, mysterious and alluring women, or as ordinary wives and female friends. In myth and folklore, the anima has been projected into concrete mythic personages such as Helen of Troy, Athena, the Virgin Mary, Sophia, Dante's Beatrice, Aphrodite, and Psychopompoi (guides of the

soul). The appropriate way of dealing with the anima, for Jung, is
to relate to her as an inner figure, as a guide to the depths of the
psyche. This is what Jung believes the shaman is able to accomplish, even if it is understood in ecstatic projected form. The
ascent of the cosmic tree is an inward journey to the other world
of the collective unconscious, where the shaman meets his anima
figure: "The climbing of the magical Tree is the heavenly journey
of the shaman, during which he encounters his heavenly spouse.
In Medieval Christianity the shamanic anima was transformed
into Lilith, who ... was Adam's first wife."[11]

For Jung, the anima also represents the "not-I", that is, the
"non-ego". In the analytically assisted individuation process, the
anima is typically one of the first important figures from the collective unconscious which must be brought into conscious relationship. Her importance is due to the fact that she represents
something of the totality of the psyche (soul). Along with the psyche's feminine aspect, the male personality's experience of the
archetypal and personal mother, as well as his experience of
females in general, colors his experience of the anima. Hence
the anima lies close to personal experience, on the one hand,
and collective or transpersonal experience on the other, thus
making her a bridge figure between ego and collective unconscious. It is as a bridge figure that the anima is seen to be a guide
to the other world, that is, of the collective unconscious. Not only
the celestial wife but the cosmic tree itself are also understood by
Jung as feminine, and carry a projection of the maternal and psychopompous aspects of the anima:

> Our material is fully in accord with the wide spread, primi-
> tive shamanistic conceptions of the tree and the heavenly
> bride, who is a typical anima projection. She is the ayami
> (familiar, protective spirit) of the shaman ancestors....The
> tree represents the life of the shaman's heavenly bride, and
> has maternal significance.[12]

THE SHAMAN AND ARCHAIC INDIVIDUATION

For most individuals within the collective life of archaic and
traditional tribal societies, individuation was not as definite a

possibility as it is with modern individuals, since the collective aspect of life in a participation mystique type of consciousness prevented the kind of conscious differentiation possible to today's individuals, living in modern western societies. However, Jung believed the shaman was able to undergo the individuation process on an archaic level, that was later possible in an increasingly sophisticated way as human culture and religion evolved:

> The numinous experience of the individuation process is, on the archaic level, the prerogative of the shamans and medicine men; later of physician, prophet, priest, and finally, at the individualized states of philosophy and religion [of individuals].[13]

SHAMANIC TRANSFORMATION AND THE HERO ARCHETYPE

Jung links the death/rebirth experience of shamans to the archetype of the hero. His understanding of the ritual transformation process of archaic shamanic individuation could not be understood without understanding the role of the hero archetype and its relations to ritual transformation. The hero journey, for Jung, is a process of moving from a lesser to a greater consciousness, by means of a descent into the unconscious. Jung considers the hero figure to be the finest of the symbols of psychical energy (libido) because it is a transformation symbol:

> The finest of all symbols of the libido is the human figure of the hero...a figure who passes from joy to sorrow and from sorrow to joy, and like the sun, now stands high at the zenith and now is plunged into the darkest night, only to rise again a new splendor.[14]

This passage of the hero from joy to sorrow to joy again is, for Jung, the equivalent of a passage from the naive or pre-morbid ego structure, into the suffering and dismemberment in the unconscious (ritual death), and a return (ritual rebirth), but with a greater consciousness. Joseph Campbell, the mythologist who was influenced by Jung, has characterized the hero journey as consisting of three stages: 1) Separation, 2) Initiation, and 3)

Return (with the boon). Campbell claims that the hero mythic pattern underlies the process of ritual transformation which the shaman must undergo. The first stage represents a separation from normal ego-consciousness, from the collective (society with its norms, conventions, and everyday perspectives), whereby the shaman goes off alone into the woods or the wilderness to enter the other world. There the second stage, involving the dismemberment, the contemplation of the skeleton, and the reconstruction of the shaman's mystical body, is a period of learning and discovery of the mysteries, sacred power, or insights. Stage three, the return with the boon (the insight, increased consciousness, or healing power), is the stage whereby the hero or shaman benefits his or her tribe or social group with what he or she obtained on the journey. Campbell emphasizes that this is the feature of the hero journey which differentiates it from mere psychopathological regression. The hero pattern objectified in shamanic experience is beneficial socially, and thus is creative.

Jung links the death/rebirth archetype and the dismemberment the shaman must undergo with the hero pattern:

> The dismemberment motif belongs in the wider context of rebirth symbolism. Consequently it plays an important part in the initiation experiences of shamans and medicine men [or medicine women] who are dismembered and put together again.[15]

SHAMANIC INITIATION: TRANSFORMATION

The shamanic initiatory ordeal of being dismembered and reconstructed is interpreted as a psychological and spiritual transformation (individuation). It is symbolic of the transformation of consciousness from a primitive to a differentiated state characteristic of the path of individuation.[16] Jung also observes the similarity of dismemberment symbolism to the alchemical symbolism of divisio-separatio-solutio. Commenting on the shaman's initiatory dismemberment Jung wrote:

> He is essentially unconscious and therefore in need of transformation and enlightenment. For this purpose his body

must be taken apart and dissolved into its constituents, a process known in alchemy as divisio, separatio, and solutio, and in later treatises as discrimination and self-knowledge.[17]

The transformative processes observed in the shaman's dismemberment and reconstitution are thus interpreted by Jung in terms of an archetypal configuration involving death/rebirth, ritual transformation, and the hero pattern. This archetypal configuration underlying shamanism is discernible in mythology and religion the world over. Jung believed the transformation symbolism of the Catholic Mass to be a kind of heir to a progressive deepening of consciousness which began many millennia before Christianity, but which probably had its origins in the initiatory experiences of shamans:

> The shaman's experience of sickness, of torture, death, and regeneration implies, at a higher level, the idea of being made whole through sacrifice; of being changed by transubstantiation and exalted to the pneumatic man—in a word, of apotheosis.[18]

SHAMAN: TRICKSTER

If the shaman can be considered a kind of hero, there is a negative side to the heroic pattern exemplified in the archetypal figure of the shaman as a trickster figure. The typical antics of the trickster include the tendency to accomplish things through trickiness, slyness, buffoonery, and pranks, what others can only accomplish, if at all, with a concentrated and methodical effort. Jung observed that the trickster holds a compensatory relationship to ego-consciousness, and to rational order, often upsetting the rational order.

Jung catalogued the attributes of the trickster as a shapeshifting figure, akin to the alchemical Mercurius, to parapsychological phenomena, and to the tradition of the medieval carnival with periodic reversal of the social-hierarchical, ecclesiastical, and political orderings. As a shadow figure the trickster plays a compensatory role in relation to the dominant attitude of consciousness or of society. In this form of the jester, for example,

King Lear's fool can humble the king with his wisdom in the way no other member of the society can, and he shows himself to be a wiser fool than Lear. The trickster is often portrayed as a comical and ignorant figure, who can sometimes get himself or herself into trouble by his or her foolishness. In its highest expression the trickster serves the creative and life-enhancing tendencies of self and society. In its lowest expression, the trickster has a self-serving sociopathic aspect that entails tricking and hustling for the sheer heck of it. Individuals in whom the trickster is strongly activated can be socially useful if they are guided by social and spiritual values. They may be sociopathic and socially destructive if guided by narcissistic goals, or by no goals at all. For the great shamans, the value commitment to society overrides selfish or narcissistic aims. Jung believed the traditional shaman and medicine man to have some of both the constructive and destructive characteristics of the trickster archetype. He commented upon the danger of the negative characteristics:

> His [the trickster's] universality is co-extensive with shamanism, to which, as we know, the whole phenomenology of spiritualism belongs. There is something of the trickster character in the character of the shaman and medicine man, for he too often plays malicious jokes on people, only to fall victim in his turn to the vengeance of those whom he has injured. For this reason his profession sometimes puts him in peril of his life.[19]

SHAMAN AS SHAPE-SHIFTER/EPISTEMOLOGICAL MEDIATOR

Another duality in the trickster archetype is the simultaneous appearance of wisdom and folly: the paradoxical image of the wise fool. On the surface level, the trickster appears to be ignorant, immature, and full of mischievous folly. On a deeper level, it can be a folly guided by the deeper wisdom of the unconscious, of the archetypal Self. It is the trickster which upsets the stale routine, the too certain rationality, the too familiar and rigid boundaries of ordinary everyday consciousness, and mocks them. The shaman, in his or her trickster function, plays a similar role with respect to the personal and collective cultural boundaries and orderings of his or her society. In the trickster aspect, the shaman serves as a mediator between the non-ordinary reality of the sacred, and the ordinary reality of everyday life. As a mediator the shaman is able to shift epistemological boundaries through his or her illusive shape-shifting capacities, and place them elsewhere, thus expanding the consciousness of his or her people. The shaman is able to bring findings from the non-ordinary realm back to the people and thus help by communicating it, as much as he or she can, in the mythic and cultural idiom familiar to his or her people.[20]

In this shape-shifting capacity the shaman is also able to share his or her ecstatic-revelatory experiences, and show that ordinary reality is somewhat constructed by arbitrary boundaries. On the other hand, the shaman knows well that the arbitrary boundaries of everyday life are important, and that no one can dwell only in the non-ordinary reality without becoming lost. This is the lesson which Yaqui shaman Don Juan teaches Carlos Castaneda, that the shaman must have one foot firmly planted in both realities. Understood in psychological terms, the shaman must have a firmly developed ego if he or she is to be able to tolerate and survive the numinous and sometimes chaotic power of the collective unconscious, and not get swallowed by it. Finally, if the shaman is to render his or her ecstatic visions and powers into a socially useful form, he or she must do so in terms which his or her people can understand, that is, in terms of the mythology or cosmology of tribe. The shaman requires the shape-shifting subtlety of the trickster in order to expand the consciousness of his or her people within the terms of their ordinary linguistic and mythic conceptual equipment.

SHAMAN AS WOUNDED HEALER AND SAVIOR (SOTER)

The shaman, as we have seen, insofar as he or she begins the vocation with an illness from which he or she must cure himself or herself, and insofar as he or she is dismembered in the other world, is a wounded healer. The shaman's giftedness at healing arises, in part, from the fact of his or her own wound, and from his or her mastery in tending to the wound. It is as if he or she heals out of the wound. The wounded healer motif, according to Jung, is also a trickster characteristic. Of the trickster as *soter*, Jung wrote: "His approximation to the 'savior' is an obvious consequence...in confirmation of the mythological truth that the wounded healer is the agent of healing, and the sufferer who takes away suffering".[21]

It is the qualities of the shaman as trickster, as shape-shifter, and as wounded healer, which enable him or her to mediate the healing power of the sacred to his or her people, to turn the meaningless into the meaningful, and to turn the wound into the gift. Although every person may encounter the trickster, the shaman has it constellated in a high degree, as essential to his or her character and to his or her professional activities.

JUNG ON SOUL LOSS, POSSESSION, AND EXORCISTIC RITES

Jung considered soul loss as a pathological deformation of the personality. The primitive phenomenon of soul loss, diagnosed and treated by shamans, is interpreted by Jung primarily in terms of a diminution of personality, and in terms of possession by a complex. With respect to the diminution of personality, Jung argued that it had the features of Pierre Janet's "abaissement du niveau mental", in which ego-consciousness is attenuated, and the psychical energy (libido) withdraws from the ego. Jung described the condition phenomenologically:

> The peculiar condition covered by this term ["loss of soul"] is accounted for in the mind of the primitive by the supposition that the soul has gone off, just like a dog runs away from his master overnight. It is then the task of the medicine-man to fetch this fugitive back. Often the loss occurs suddenly and manifests itself in a general malaise.[22]

Jung argues that this phenomenon is closely tied to the condition of primitive consciousness, which he believed lacks the coherence and firmness of the ego-consciousness of modern men and women. Jung argues that the primitive does not have the control of his or her willpower that modern individuals do, and so is vulnerable to emotional, instinctive, and archetypal forces from the unconscious. Modern people, by contrast, are viewed by Jung as having a much more rational and reality (external) oriented ego-structure, making it safer and more dependable in being able to resist the whims of the unconscious. Jung believed that the primitive had to perform complicated exercises if he or she was to pull himself or herself together for any activity that is conscious and intentional, not just emotional and instructive.[23]

Because of the unfirmness of the primitive's ego-structure, Jung believed the primitive was especially sensitive to upsurges, invasions, and fantasies arising from the unconscious. Emotions and instincts were amongst the powerful forces which could cause the primitive's nascent ego-structure to break down leading to psychological pandemonium, and a loss of order:

> Primitives are notoriously subject to such phenomena as running amok, going berserk, possession, and the like. The recognition of the daemonic character of passion is an effective safeguard, for it once deprives the object of its strongest spell, relegating its source to the world of demons, i.e., the unconscious, whence the force of passion springs.[24]

If psychopathology and chaos are sometimes the result of passion, emotion, and instinctual upsurges of the primitive, the concerted efforts of exorcism rituals are necessary for sending the erupted psychic energies back down into the unconscious. Jung says of exorcistic rites that they are "effective in causing the libido to flow back into the unconscious".[25] This amounts, as we have already suggested, to a ritual re-instating of the repression barrier, reconstituting a stronger ego for the primitive. Jung also characterized loss of soul as a form of possession by a complex:

> Loss of soul amounts to a tearing loose of part of one's nature, it is the disappearance and emancipation of a complex, which there upon becomes a tyrannical usurper of consciousness, oppressing the whole man. It throws him off course and drives him to actions whose blind one-sidedness inevitably leads to self destruction.[26]

Again, it is the purpose of exorcistic rites, Jung believes, to restore order by wresting the soul from its enchantment with the complex. This is what the shamanic ritual of soul recovery, by means of trance and use of the imagination, does for the victim. The shaman is able to navigate in the waters of the collective unconscious, and by means of imagery derived from it, and by his or her ritual structure and process, free the patient's ego from seizure by the complex. The bringing back of the soul amounts to a recovery of psychical energy (libido), which was entrapped in the unconscious complex, and which the primitive's ego is normally invested with. The restoring of this psychical libido from its enchantment (possession) in the complex, and the similarity between soul loss, major depression, and the hysterical anesthesias and dissociative disorders of modern individuals did not escape Jung's attention. He wrote as if depression and hysteria were the primary modern psychiatric analogues to primitive soul loss.

> Occasionally something similar can happen to civilized man, only he does not describe it as "soul loss" but as an "abaissement du niveau mental", Janet's apt term for this phenomenon. It is a slackening of the tensity of consciousness, which might be compared to a low barometric reading, presaging bad weather. The tonus has given way, and this is felt subjectively as listlessness, moroseness, and depression. One no longer has any wish or courage to face the tasks of the day. One feels like lead, because no part of one's body seems willing to move, and this is due to the fact that one no longer has any disposable energy. This well known phenomenon corresponds to the primitive's loss of soul. The listlessness and paralysis of will can go so far that the whole personality falls apart, so to speak, and consciousness loses its unity; the individual parts of the personality make themselves independent and thus escape the control of the conscious mind, as in the case of anesthetic areas or systematic amnesias. The latter are well known as hysterical "loss of function."[27]

In Jung's discussions of soul loss and possession, and exorcistic rites, he fails to articulate the relation between trauma or psychic shock and soul loss. When he speaks of the primitive as having a less firm ego-structure and as susceptible to invasion by unconscious contents or seizure by a complex, he also confuses things by not connecting these phenomena to their origins in trauma and shock. Whether so-called primitives have a less firm ego-structure and are more susceptible to soul loss is a debatable point. Many neoshamans and modern urban shamans report that soul loss is widespread amongst modern men and women, living in industrialized society, and much of it is reportedly attributable to trauma (e.g., sexual abuse, rape, auto accident, surgery, war, etc.). We will discuss contemporary forms of soul loss and its causes in Chapter Six, but we wish to draw attention here to the inadequacy of Jung's psychological understanding of soul loss and of primitive mentality by today's standards. Nevertheless, Jung was the first major psychologist to take shamanism and soul loss theory seriously, and find ways to correlate it with modern psychological experience. He did call attention to the fact that modern men and women in western society are desperately in search of soul, implying widespread soul loss, but he did not articulate this well in the context of his discussions on shamanism.

RITUAL AND PSYCHOLOGICAL TRANSFORMATION

If primitive psychopathology may be considered a disorder of the psyche (soul), shamanic psychotherapeutics may be considered a ritual re-ordering of the soul, or a re-establishing of order within the psyche. For Jung, ritual functions as a psychic container for transformative processes when psychic integrity and balance is threatened by the unexpected power of the numinosum of the unconscious. Jung believed that ritual served psychological purposes by imposing a restrictive form upon instinctual or archetypal energies.[28] By imposing form upon instinctual and archetypal energies, some restriction and control of these energies became possible. The shaman has been the master, par excellence, of imposing ritual form and order upon unruly and powerful psychic energies.

Jung believed that ritual is so bound up with primitive societies that it means their cultural and spiritual destruction when those societies lose their ritual forms. This is one of the effects of Christian missionaries upon primitive cultures, which, Jung claimed, leads to a "loss of soul for the tribe".[29] Traditional ritual functioned to facilitate the important transitions which members of primitive societies had to undergo, for example, the transformation of a child into an adult, or the change of status obtained in birth, death, marriage, and profession or secret society. Ritual also served to reconcile oppositions.[30] The exemplary type of ritual for Jung was the initiation rite, especially those called puberty rites. At puberty, when a young male displays increased size, strength, intellect, and sexual capability (and thus poses a threat to social/cooperative purposes), he is typically "stolen" by the male ritual elders of the tribe and taken off into the bush, where he must undergo challenging and painful ordeals designed to transform him into a responsible and contributing adult member of the tribe. Under the ritual mastery of shamans, the youth must learn to suffer, to endure difficult things, and learn the mythology and adult moral codes of the tribe. He is taught how to be a contributing adult member through training in hunting and warrior skills, and learns that he must serve the good of the tribe. Jung believed these puberty rites serve to activate archetypes, or archetypal configurations, within the psyche of the initiant. For males, in order to be a good hunter and warrior, the archetypal hunter and warrior must be ritually activated in the psychology of the adolescent initiant. The archetypes are usually disguised as culture-heroes, gods, or ancestors, whose paradigmatic acts serve as a model for the young men. This activation of such powerful and numinous energies are organized in the initiant's psyche by the restrictive ritual forms, placed upon those energies by archetypal patterns. The effect of the imposition of these forms upon the psychical energies of the youth, is to effect a transformation of libido into a higher form of consciousness, in this case, adult consciousness.[31] All shamanic ritual can likewise be understood as having a very similar structure and function of providing a safe container in which to undergo transformation through imposition of restrictive form, into more organized and mature levels of consciousness. Ritual, as Jung understands it, effects a transformation, a death of an old self and the birth of a new self, a transformation from a lower to a higher level of consciousness.

THE UNDERLYING ARCHETYPAL STRUCTURE OF SHAMANISM

For Jung, shamanic imagery is fundamentally a set of concrete symbolic expressions of an underlying archetypal pattern which emerged not only in Paleolithic times, but continues to emerge in myth and folklore, in modern literature and art, and in the myriads of unconscious-imaginative productions of modern men and women. We have seen, for example, from the previous discussion of the cosmic tree symbolism, that the symbol has a plurality of related possible meanings, depending upon the aspect and context of the focus. The tree is a means of access, a ladder of ascent/descent into the other world (of the collective unconscious), and it is at once a symbol of the archetypal Self, a central point of orientations (axis mundi) uniting the opposites (of lower and upper worlds), and of the feminine in its maternal and psychopompous aspects (anima). It symbolized these meanings for shamanism as it also does so for alchemy, and the underlying archetypal form is discernible the world over in myth and folklore, and in modern dreams and psychotic productions. What the shaman discovered thousands of years ago was how to tap into an underlying archetypal realm for psychological development, healing, and mystical exploration. What was discovered by the shaman has been rediscovered by other individuals in other times and places. In all probability, there has also been much dissemination, as Eliade has argued.

Part Three
SOME IMPLICATIONS
AND APPLICATIONS

Introduction to Part Three: Dissociation/Soul Loss/and Retrieval

We now turn to a consideration of areas of practical and theoretical application in the dialogue between Jung and shamanism. We have discussed the structure of shamanism in Part One, and discussed the fundamental notions of Jung's analytical psychology and compared and contrasted them with classic shamanism in Part Two. In Part Three we turn to a consideration of some major areas of practical and clinical interest. The areas of considerable convergence of interests between Jung and shamanism are the areas of psychopathology concerned with dissociation, imagination, and ritual control of chaotic and anomalous psychic functioning. Additionally the importance of the sacred and the numinous as therapeutic resources provides another area of convergent interest which shall be discussed.

Dissociation, as we discussed in Part Two (Chapter 4), is foundational to understanding Jungian psychology, especially its view of psychopathology and its therapeutic goal of integration (wholeness). Dissociation is also a bridge concept, albeit of psychological origins, for understanding the shamanic concept of soul loss, and the shamanic methods to retrieve lost souls and extract and exorcise pathogenic invasions/intrusions. In Part One and in Part Two we discussed classic shamanic ideas as they have been practiced since Paleolithic times (at least 20,000 years). In the discussion that follows we aim to show a couple of ways in which a shamanic soul loss and soul retrieval can be understood today, in modern western urbanized society. We shall take as our examples the shamanic practices adapted by two modern psychotherapists, one a psychiatrist specializing in dissociative disorders (Colin Ross), the other a mental health counselor turned

167

white shaman (Sandra Ingerman). Their adaptations of shamanic understandings and practices of soul loss and soul retrieval to modern mental health problems will be reviewed. This will be followed by some Jungian perspectives in response to their work. Next, we will turn to a special problem that emerges in dissociative disorders which resembles classic pathogenic spirit possession. We will discuss the topic of possession because it provides an example of one type of intractable and potentially dangerous disorder which is often amenable to the shamanic and Jungian understandings and treatment methods. It thus provides another bridge area of focus for shamanic and Jungian resources. In the final chapter, we shall discuss Jungian and shamanic views of the importance of the sacred as a resource in healing, and in daily living. It is here that shamanism and Jungian psychology present us with the importance of the spiritual dimension of sickness and health, and of living in general.

Dissociation, Possession, and Soul Loss: Clinical and Theoretical Applications Today

DISSOCIATIVE IDENTITY DISORDER (MULTIPLE PERSONALITY)

We will begin our discussion of the relations between dissociation and soul loss by discussing a most serious form in which these notions manifest today: as dissociative identity disorder (DID). Until recently this disorder was referred to as multiple personality disorder (MPD), and we shall use the terms interchangeably throughout our discussion. MPD was, until very recently, thought by clinicians to be a rare phenomenon. Movies like *Sybil* and the *Three Faces of Eve* popularized the disorder and made it something of an exotic interest for the public. Many scientifically biased mental health professionals from all disciplines (psychiatry, psychology, social work, pastoral counseling) were skeptical or disbelieving that such a phenomenon existed. Part of the reason for the resistance rested upon a Platonic/Cartesian assumption of the unity of the soul, that there can only be one personality or personality organization in a given body. To modern scientific ears the idea of multiple personalities smacked of magical thinking, of the supernatural, of the old spirit and demon possession beliefs. But at the beginnings of psychological research in the late nineteenth and early twentieth centuries there was considerable interest in dissociative phenomena by researchers such as Pierre Janet, Alfred Benet, C.G. Jung, Morton Prince, and many others. But with the rise of behaviorism with its focus on observable behavior, and the increasing popularity of Freudian psychoanalytic understandings with its emphasis upon repression rather than dissociation, research into dissociative disorders fell by the wayside. With this loss of interest in dissociative disorders went a bridge to understanding one of the most common of current and past forms of serious mental disorder. It was only in the 1970s with researchers like Ernst Hilgard[1] doing laboratory studies of hypnotic and dissociative states that clinical and research interest in the subject was rekindled, and this at a time when many clinicians were noticing that some victims of childhood sexual abuse, combat, stress, and rape were demonstrating chaotic behavior and symptoms of pathologic dissociation.

There is substantial evidence that pathological dissociation has been around for many millennia, although previously it was culturally shaped and labeled as spirit possession, demon possession, and the like. It is still understood as possession in many premodern and developing societies where the scientific-technological view of modernity has not redefined it. It is likely that until very recently patients going to modern psychotherapists were misdiagnosed as suffering from a variety of disorders, depending on which alternate personality (alter) was in control while being observed by the therapist. If the presenting alter was depressed, a diagnosis of depression was likely. If the presenting alter was angry, or fluctuating between neediness and anger, perhaps a diagnosis of borderline personality. If the patient heard voices from his or her other alters, he or she might have been diagnosed as schizophrenic and placed on a phenothiazine medication to reduce symptoms. In short, this disorder has been widely misdiagnosed by well-meaning mental health professionals.

In recent years the growing attention that childhood sexual abuse has received in the media, and by clinicians, has made it possible for more of the public who were sexually abused to come forward and tell therapists. If more victims (survivors) of such abuse are coming forward, and if pathologic dissociation is one possible effect of such abuse, then it is reasonable to assume that this makes it more likely that the disorder will come to the attention of more therapists and researchers. Additionally, as therapists and the public become more knowledgeable of this disorder, this too will bring more people into therapy, and better informed therapists are now recognizing what previously they would have missed. Typically, fifteen to twenty percent of my own patients suffer from a dissociative disorder and the closely related post traumatic stress disorder (PTSD), and most cases are related to sexual abuse.

Treating multiple personality disorder is a fairly complicated process which requires considerable knowledge and patience on the part of the psychotherapist. There are profound levels of distrust that have to be overcome. The complexity of the patient's internal psychological organization (or seeming lack of one) can be overwhelming to the therapist. Cases of MPD range from simple to complex, from two or three alters, to more than a hundred. One important complication is that one (and sometimes more) alter(s) may be quite hostile, even dangerous, to self and others, including the therapist (although this danger appears to be remote in most cases). There may be alters of whom the patient (i.e., the host personality) is aware, and there may be others that are hidden from him or her. There may even be those who are lost, or who have run away for protection to an inner place that is difficult to find and access. It is the shaman's knowledge of inner- and intrapsychic worlds and ritual knowledge of how to retrieve lost souls (in our culture lost alters, dissociated memories and libido, etc.) and exorcise intruding molesting spirits (hostile alters, personified pockets of rage/outrage about the trauma) that make contributions from shamanism most promising in this area of pathologic dissociation. Jung's understandings of dissociation and integration of archetypes and autonomous complexes, and of the integrating power of the archetypal Self, also have much to contribute in understanding this modern form of soul loss and retrieval.

WHAT IS MULTIPLE PERSONALITY?

Multiple personality has recently been renamed by the *Diagnostic and Statistical Manual of Mental Disorders* (DSM-IV) as dissociative identity disorder (DID). The purpose of changing the name was to classify it as a dissociative disorder and thus remove the stigma associated with what, to many in modern Western society, often seems a strange idea of having more than one personality in one body. It is hoped that this change in terminology will promote less resistance to diagnosing and researching the disorder. However, we will continue to use the term *multiple personality disorder* (MPD) throughout our discussion since it is still the more familiar term, and since it still conveys the reality of the imaginative personification of fragmented parts of the person. This personification is easier to correlate with the shamanic view of lost vital souls, and the Jungian conception of complexes and possession.

MPD is sub-classified as a dissociative disorder. Some dissociation is normal. Anytime we drive a car while listening to the radio and aren't conscious of the road or of the executive functions involved in driving the car, we have dissociated. This can come as a startling realization when we realize we've driven the last twenty miles without being aware of it. Perhaps we have had the experience of reading a book and tuning out the voice of someone calling out to us. Anytime we enter an altered state of consciousness, have prayed, or been hypnotized, we have experienced some degree of dissociation which contrasts with our so-called normal waking state of consciousness. However, a dissociative disorder involves pathological dissociation in which there is "a disruption of the usually integrative functions of consciousness, memory, identity, or perception of the environment".[2] Pathologic dissociation, while it may have been helpful in surviving a trauma, becomes a hindrance to effective living later in life.

There are several types of dissociative disorder, all related to the effects of trauma and stress as described by the DSM-IV. These include the following: 1) Dissociative amnesia is the inability to recall important personal information, usually of a traumatic or stressful nature. 2) Dissociative fugue is characterized by sudden automatic travel away from home and the assumption of a new identity. When the subject switches back to the original identity, there is typically total amnesia of the fugue state. 3) Depersonalization disorder involves a persistent feeling of being detached from one's body or mental process, but is accompanied by intact reality testing. 4) dissociative identity disorder (multiple personality) is characterized by the existence of two or more distinct identities or personality states that recurrently assume control of the individual's behavior. This is frequently accompanied by the inability to recall important personal information which is too extensive to be explained by normal forgetfulness, and it may sometimes entail a lack of reality testing making it look similar to schizophrenia or other psychoses.

ORIGINS OF MULTIPLICITY

MPD can be caused by a variety of traumatic and stressful situations including childhood abuse, rape, loss of a parent in childhood, combat stress, and so on. However, for the sake of simplicity and convenience we will focus on childhood sexual abuse as our main example of how pathological dissociation begins. We shall keep in mind that whatever the cause, the processes are essentially the same.

It is a sad fact that many children are abused by parents, relatives, and other caretakers. It is not likely that this is a new fact, but it is probably a reality that has been too unpleasant for many of us to want to believe and honestly face as an epidemic problem. So horrendous are the facts of child abuse that we prefer to think humans are more civilized and moral than they may be in fact. Children can be, and probably for a long time have been, physically abused, sexually abused, ritually abused, emotionally neglected and abandoned. Unfortunately, when children undergo such extreme treatment they are not constitutionally able to tolerate it. They do not have the developed adult cognitive capacities to evaluate the situation, to understand what is happening, to know what their options are. Often, they can't even know if what happens to them is normal or justified by some misbehavior of their own. They may thus think that they have caused or deserve the abuse, and that they are therefore ugly and bad. They often try to figure out how to stop the abuse, but they simply can't. They are too small, too powerless. Abused children are terrified, deeply sad, very lonely, and feel there is no one who can come to their aid and help them fight to survive.

Some children seem to survive the abuse without any serious degree of dissociation. Usually these children have figured out some way to numb out by placing a protective wall or defensive barrier around themselves. Their ways of coping often develop into other serious problems that later show up in promiscuity, fear of sex, addictions and eating disorders, depression, low self-esteem, inability to trust, and post-traumatic stress symptoms. Other children, perhaps because of genetic and/or neurobiological giftedness in combination with severe stress and pain, are able to develop highly elaborated ways to avoid the pain and misery of their abuse. They find ways to numb out, ignore, or forget (become amnesic) that involves the separating of dissociated or split-off parts of themselves, which become more or less personified into alternate personalities (alters). Dissociation becomes a very effective way for them to survive by enabling them to escape the pain mentally. Probably using neurobiological and psychological processes related to self-hypnotic trance states, they are able to wall off pain and anxiety from themselves, and even believe that they are not actually experiencing their abuse. They often believe or imagine that the abuse is really happening to someone else (i.e., to some other alter). While the body is being abused, a little girl may dissociatively float up to the ceiling and watch the abuse taking place to the little girl or boy down below.

Not all persons who dissociate to survive the trauma of abuse do it in the same way. One child may create alternate selves to handle various responses to the offense, for the purpose of functioning in a protected way. These alters often have symbolic-like names which indicate the aspects (i.e., functions, roles, purposes, etc.) of the total personality which they perform in dissociation from the totality (personality as a whole). One alter may house the feelings and thought reactions of helplessness (the helpless one), another may house feelings of magical-playful-creative innocence (magical thinker), another may house promiscuous parts of the self (the whore/male slut), and still another may house puritanical responses (the prude). Often there will be a figure who is characterized by anger if not intense rage (the angry one, or the evil one). Therapists working with multiples can find this part to be quite troublesome, and sometimes dangerous. Often it constitutes a potentially serious threat to treatment progress, and in a few cases it may even claim to be a demon or evil spirit. Most experienced clinicians believe it is more important to understand this part as holding the rage feelings which it

making an ally of the demon : integration

was not safe for the child to vent. It is therefore believed that it is important to gain rapport with this alter, reframe its intentions away from being an evil one to being a potentially helpful one who has understandable feelings, and who can use those angry energies for the benefit of the entire personality system. In this way the reframing gives the angry alter a constructive and purposeful outlet. However, this is not always easy to achieve and there are documented cases of severe intractable self-destructive possession, one where a psychiatrist (Ralph B. Allison) specializing in MPD turned to ritual exorcism as a last resort.[3] More will later be said about complications of this angry alter in relation to so-called demonic possession and ritual exorcism. For the moment we want to clarify its distinctive nature.

We have said that not all children suffering dissociative disorders learned to dissociate in the same way. One girl was abused by her brother and father. She learned to leave mentally and invite another older girl who was bigger and wasn't afraid to take over and receive the abuse. The therapist learned that this personality was called Angretta, and that her job was to protect her host, whom we shall call Susan. With the passage of time that part of Susan's self called Angretta became characterized by increasing hostility towards men, and fear of sexuality. When Angretta would rudely act out her rage towards any man who seemed attracted to Susan, she had another alter, named Regretta, who functioned to clean up the social mess and placate the man. Needless to say, Susan confused numerous men with this strange inconsistency in her identity, and often they would withdraw their interest in her. Susan often wondered why she could not find a heterosexual mate, why she drove men away, and had little insight into the fact that she was sending inconsistent messages simultaneously to these men.

Frequently persons suffering from pathologic dissociation create entire inner families, with each alter having a certain role and perspective, a part or fragment of the self. Often these dissociating children learn to dissociate so well that they create numerous selves, and they learn to take off, go inside, leave, or hide when under threat or stress. Dissociation does work in helping the individual channel the pain into pathways that help him or her

survive. However, once pathologic dissociation is no longer necessary because the person has grown up and is no longer in danger
of abuse, it may remain and create serious problems for the individual, as it did for Susan. Although the pain is numbed or dissociated from conscious awareness, it doesn't just go away, unless it
is consciously recalled, understood, and effectively worked
through. Among the problems that untreated MPD involves are
such phenomena as waking up and not knowing how you got
where you are, having long unexplained periods of blanked-out
memory (amnesia), having chaotic and disorganized living, and
being unable to plan and consistently achieve goals. One of the
most disturbing effects of pathologic dissociation is the fact that
dissociations may become a reflex response (like the blink reflex
when something comes toward your eye). When the individual
was a child and was threatened with abusive behavior he or she
automatically learned to go away or switch to another alter who
would take the abuse. Let's say an older brother repeatedly raped
his sister. He wore a certain aftershave that her sensory memory
system recorded. The scent of that aftershave meant danger when
she was a little girl. Now the stimulus of that aftershave may have
generalized to any man who uses that or a similar aftershave. It
may even have generalized to all aftershaves. Thus in adult life,
whenever the individual smells the aftershave, she has flashback
memories of abuse, or feels imminent danger and dissociates to
another alter. The aftershave thus serves as a trigger that provokes
flashback memories and dissociative defenses. This behavior is
often interpreted by her family, friends, and co-workers as peculiar. People come to view her as strange and avoid her. In this way,
pathologic dissociation continues to damage her life. One of the
tasks of therapy is to help the individual learn to avoid this automatic reflex switching.

THE THERAPY OF DISSOCIATIVE DISORDERS TODAY

If MPD represents a fragmentation of the self, then healing
would imply a reintegration of these fragments or splinter psyches. Reintegration of the parts into one whole self has indeed
been held out as the goal of MPD therapy. However, this notion is

not without difficulties. First of all, integration to an individual who has experienced traumatic abuse and violence tends to sound like more violence and abuse, even death to the various alters. It is not surprising, then, that so many MPD patients resist and even protest against the therapist's proposal of integration or fusion as the treatment goal. Certainly some form of integrative functioning should be the desired goal of therapy, but it should be recognized that this is not always possible and that talk of integration can slow therapy. In my experience integration should be discussed as a goal and then laid aside so that the work of recovering traumatic memories and working through affects and cognitive distortions brought about by the abuse can get under way. Typically a great deal of integration takes place as this preliminary work is in progress. Usually at a later stage of therapy, the idea of some kind of model of integration is not so threatening to the patient. There are numerous models of the treatment stages replete with various strategies. The model I employ is a three-stage model similar to the one Colin Ross describes.[4] It involves four treatment goals: 1) Recover abuse memories. 2) Come to terms with them cognitively and affectively. 3) Integrate into one person. 4) Learn how to function and live effectively without pathological dissociation. The stages of treatment are divided into three phases: a) an initial phase, b) a middle phase, and c) a post-integration phase. We will discuss these phases briefly so that the reader has a context for the shamanic and Jungian discussions of dissociation, possession, soul retrieval, and ritual which follow.

The initial phase consists of making the diagnosis and sharing it with the patient. This often involves considerable education of the patient about the nature of the disorder, its effects, and the self-destructive costs of continuing to operate in a pathologically dissociative way. Treatment goals of some sort of integrative functioning are discussed, and more specialized treatment goals are set. The treatment contract is negotiated and the limits and therapeutic frame are set. The therapist begins to explore the internal world of the patient, meet and identify as many alters as possible, and determine their positive and negative value in the personality system as a whole. This allows the therapist to make an initial map of the patient's internal world and prepares the ground work for the therapeutic challenges, recovering of memories, and the abreactions which follow in the middle phase.

In the middle phase the actual recovery of abuse memories, whether by clinical hypnosis or direct exploration, takes place (MPD patients are often in a trance-like state anyway, so formal hypnosis is often not needed). This work may entail further discovery and recovery of other alters, even a different layer of alters which only becomes accessible through one alter who knows of their existence. There may be alters who have run away or been stolen and taken to another psychic realm where they are not easily accessible. The therapist may employ various hypnotic techniques to try to draw these missing parts back. The therapist works on cognitive distortions of various alters, reframes negative intentions, and may spend considerable time working with distrustful or enraged alters, challenging their pathologic cognitive errors, reframing their intentions and behaviors. As a result of all this middle phase work the therapist's mapping of the system changes and improves. Late in this phase there is extensive negotiation aimed at some sort of integrative or cooperative personality organization. For those patients who refuse the idea of integration, the therapist may shift to a democratic metaphor, where various alters can hold internal counsels when considering situations and which actions to take. In other cases an integration ritual in which each part dissolves its separate identity and brings its unique values and perspectives into one integrated person is possible. Sometimes the integration takes place easily because so much integration work silently took place during the middle phase work.

The postintegration phase focuses on non-dissociative coping strategies, that is, on ways of dealing with fear and stress that do not employ the pathologic dissociation processes with which they are so familiar. Other defenses are taught which include sublimation and repression, but the accent is on non-defensive strategies which involve higher-level cognitive processes, self-assertiveness training, and turning to others for help when needed. In this phase the therapist watches for signs of reversion to dissociation. Often this happens during periods of stress; the dissociations are only partial, and frequently resolve after the stress is removed or effectively mastered. This phase is probably the least demanding, but it can last several years as the patient draws continuing support from the therapist, and may need to experience the mirroring, idealizing, and guiding functions of the therapist as an integrated individual before those processes are transmuted into self-functions.

Now that we have given an overview of pathologic dissociation we will turn to a discussion of some resources from shamanism and Jungian psychology for the treatment of this most disrupting disorder of the soul. We shall focus on two major problems that arise in the treatment of pathologic dissociation for which shamanism and Jungian psychology can be especially helpful: soul loss, and possession. We shall discuss soul loss and its therapy of retrieval first. Then we shall turn to pathologic possession and its traditional cure through ritual exorcism. These discussions will finally be followed by Jungian and post-Jungian understandings and clinical resources.

SHAMANIC RESOURCES FOR TREATING PATHOLOGIC DISSOCIATION TODAY I: COLIN ROSS, M.D., AND THE HYPNOTHERAPEUTIC ADAPTATIONS

One of the most perplexing problems that can arise for the modern clinician treating dissociative disorders has to do with how to access, retrieve, and integrate those parts of the self which seem to have disappeared, been dissociatively hidden for protective purposes, or which have been reportedly stolen by other intrapsychic forces (alters). One psychiatrist and researcher, Colin Ross, has found that shamanic methods of journey and retrieval can be useful adjuncts to psychotherapy with such patients. Noting that the shaman utilizes trance and image work for purposes of retrieval, and that the shaman can take journeys to locate wild game for the hunt, Ross has adapted these shamanic methods as trance-work strategies for alter location and retrieval.[5]

Shamans and persons suffering dissociative disorders have much in common. Both know how to dissociate and utilize trance states, and both have exceptionally enhanced imaginative powers. Shamans have been the great masters of psychological dissociation, and they have been able to use it for therapeutic purposes as well as for the benefit of the larger community. This is one of the reasons Ross believes that therapists treating dissociative disorders like MPD should consider the similarities and differences between shamanism and MPD, and should study the methods and techniques with an eye to clinical application.

Because there are actually numerous areas of similarity and difference between the experiences of shamans and MPD patients, it may be useful to briefly review some of the dissociative features of shamanism, and compare and contrast them with MPD. Such phenomena as trance states, meaningful hallucinations, hypnotic amnesia, symbolic dreams, ritual dismemberment, possession by spirits, possession by ancestral souls, neurological exhaustion following trance work, use of intoxicants (or hallucinogens) to stimulate dissociation, out-of-body experiences, and transformation of identity are common to the shaman and the person suffering MPD.

The shaman intentionally evokes dissociative states for the purpose of exploration of non-ordinary reality, for the purposes of making diagnosis and contacting healing potentials, and for the purpose of healing his or her patient. By contrast, the person suffering from MPD is more victimized by the incongruity and autonomy of dissociated states. The shaman as well as the MPD patient may see visions and hear voices; for the MPD patient these may be chaotic, meaningless, not understood. By contrast, for the shaman they are highly structured and meaningful. The shaman deliberately induces altered (dissociative) states in order to converse with helping spirits, make diagnosis, procure treatment. Both shaman and MPD patient employ a kind of auto-hypnosis or self-generated trance state. For the MPD patient, the self-hypnotic strategies operate largely non-consciously, outside the executive control of the ego. They are more the response to stimuli which activate them. By contrast, the shaman intentionally enters trance by ritual methods, and for intended and limited purposes. The shaman can control trance and dissociative depth, and does so for intentional purposes. Like MPD patients, the shaman can be observed talking as if he or she were another person, animal, or other spirit entity. However, the purpose is not defensive but consciously undertaken for a specific (often therapeutic) reason. Just as MPD patients report anesthesia for physical and mental pain caused by abuse or self-infliction, the shaman also is able to control pain through dissociation. They can perform fakir-like feats, swallow fire, walk on hot coal beds, withstand extreme temperatures, and undergo painful initiatory ordeals.

Shamans have also been specialists in interpreting dreams for pathological and teleological import. Dreams are often employed in a visionary way to help locate a lost soul, foretell the future, find game, and learn about and find their way around in the underworld. Dreams were considered sources of information about the real world. Shamans have intentionally navigated in their own dreams (lucid dreaming), and have interpreted their patient's own dreams diagnostically. Dreams of MPD patients frequently are revelatory. What they reveal may be symbolic, but is often not far from literal in revealing forgotten connections, abuse memories, and even diagnostic/prognostic information about the next stage of treatment. In my own work with MPD patients, I have observed dream motifs of the patient living in a house or castle with many rooms sealed off by thick walls. As therapy proceeds, and as recurrent dreams appear, the room themes reappear with thinner walls, even glass walls, or doorways, which suggests that defensive amnesiac and dissociative barriers are wearing away, and that communication between dissociated states (rooms) is either beginning, or is imminent.

Shamans typically have experienced a psychic dismemberment in their initiatory rituals, where the shaman's soul is torn apart, the bones cleaned, and the subtle body flesh put back on the bones. For the shaman this has been a visionary death/rebirth experience. The MPD patient has also undergone psychic dismemberment, but has not experienced rebirth and re-integration. Whereas the shaman intentionally undergoes psychic dismemberment, the MPD patient has fragmented and dissociated in order to defend against pain, and, in our culture, typically to survive childhood sexual abuse, rape, or other traumatic ordeals.

Possession by ancestral souls is also common to MPD and shamanism. Important ancestors, typically ancestral shamans, would speak through the mouth or body of the shaman for such purposes as providing the society with prophetic guidance or advice. In 20.6 percent of American and Canadian MPD cases, alternate personalities claiming to be dead relatives appear.[6] This is a much more common phenomenon in societies where ancestral spirit possession is broadly assumed in the assumptive world of the culture (e.g., Japan, Taiwan, Korea, Haiti, Nigeria, India, Sri Lanka).[7] MPD patients also manifest entities who claim to be helpful, some of whom claim to be spirits, angels, or other helpers from a spiritual dimension. These figures are often quite helpful to the therapist in providing valuable information and guidance in the psychotherapy of the MPD patient. Shamans also claim to have spirit helpers and to be on familiar terms with at least one, while being able to intentionally summon others. The shaman evokes these spirit helpers to help him diagnose, restore power, heal, and prognose. The egos of the MPD patients are often unaware of their spirit helpers, and, before treatment, have not utilized them with conscious intentionality to help themselves.

MPD patients and shamans also report out-of-body experiences, and sometimes use intoxicants to stimulate trance/dissociative states. Whereas the shaman uses intoxicants in limited levels so as to maintain control of the trance for therapeutic purposes, the MPD patient may use drugs in an uncontrolled manner for the purposes of defending against psychic pain. Shamans, by virtue of their journeys to the upper and lower worlds of non-ordinary reality, can be said to have out-of-body experiences. Again, these experiences are intentional, and have to do with healing, or other shamanic functions. Shamans, as we already mentioned, sometimes send their spirit helpers out to search for a lost soul or for game. By contrast, those MPD patients who have had out-of-body experiences initially had them in childhood to defend against the pain of abuse or other trauma. This use of dissociation in not unlike burn patients who have reported letting their minds float to the ceiling of their hospital rooms while undergoing the excruciating pain of debriding.[8] Ross has given the example of a little girl who would float up to the ceiling and count dots in the plaster or travel to another location to play with friends or dolls while abuse was taking place.[9] For MPD, once this capacity has been developed and habituated, it can become detached from abuse situations and be employed in a variety of contexts.

Shamans and MPD patients become exhausted from their trance work, which involves switching the psychological and neuro-physiological processes associated with flashback memories and activation of various alters. The shaman switches intentionally, and by choice; the MPD patient may not switch by conscious or intentional choice. When the shaman is possessed by a helping spirit, there is clearly a change in voice, expression, and behavior. When an MPD patient is possessed by an alternate personality, such changes are also visible. However, it is likely that the shaman understands the necessity of switching on ritual cue. The switching between alters in untreated MPD patients apparently is not ritually structured, and so can be chaotic, prolonged, and subject to the whims of inner and outer conditions. Both shamans and MPD patients exhibit neurophysiological exhaustion after ritual or psychotherapy in which trance/dissociation switching has occurred.

From this discussion of the similarities and differences between shamanism and MPD in the employment of dissociative states, it would appear that the mind has a natural capacity to dissociate. It would also appear that both shamans and persons suffering MPD utilize this capacity in different ways. It can be intentionally used to defend against pain and trauma. It can come autonomously into play in cases of MPD, and it can be intentionally and ritually controlled, as in shamanic journeys, soul retrieval methods, and dialogue with spirits. These capacities can be either pathologically generated, or generated for therapeutic, creative healing, or spiritual and communal purposes.

Colin Ross believes that since shamans are masters of intentional use of trance states and imagination for therapeutic purposes, and because there appears to be some neuropsychological linkage between abuse, dissociation, and the visual imagination, clinically adapted shamanic methods can be quite powerful and therapeutically effective. He argues that MPD patients have very intense modes of visual-thought, are very hypnotically suggestible, and some multiples are highly visually elaborated. A frightened alter may run off to hide in a faraway park, or into a safe room in an internal house, unavailable for treatment. Shamans have been masters at locating such remote intrapsychic places and in retrieving vital souls (i.e., alters, or parts of self), and Ross believes this fact demands attention from psychotherapists and clinical researchers interested in the treatment of MPD.

For the sake of those patients who will respond to shamanic-style techniques, Ross has created a shamanic-ritual-symbolic ambience in his consulting room: "My office contains a number of amulets, medicine bundles, and shamanic power objects that testify to my authority and healing power and reveal to the patients that therapy is a prolonged spiritual ritual."[10] Ross indicates that this shamanic ambience is not so obvious as to be offensive to other patients who might not understand or appreciate it. "I have magically transformed these possessions into objects consistent with the cultural expectations of my patients. Non-shamanic people who enter my office see only degrees on the wall, filing cabinets, professional books, and a computer. I, however, know that therapy is a mysterious ritual."[11]

Ross believes that the therapeutic rituals should be derived from whatever mythology or thought system the patient and therapist find congruent. Shamanic or more secular scientific methods may be used, depending upon the patient, but Ross believes that all therapeutic languages are metaphoric, and it is speaking to the client in terms of a relevant metaphor that can bring about therapeutic change. For example, in order to evoke some secular and modern image of executive control for the personality, Ross might suggest that the patient imagine an inner boardroom, replete with conference tables, a chair for each alter, and remote control video equipment for reviewing memories and monitoring other alters; he may even install an imaginal intercom device so that alters who are too scared to come to meetings can listen in on their proceedings. Intercoms are also useful for tuning out alters whom the therapist wants to exclude from the proceedings. The purpose of such a boardroom is not only to establish intrapsychic order, but to create an internal ordering device for processing and integrating the discrepant perspectives and demands of a number of alters. Such boardrooms can have chairpersons to moderate the proceedings.

Intrapsychic conferences can be used for gaining an internal consensus before an action is taken. This method may protect the whole person from a complex or part of self that might act out autonomously and in a way destructive to the whole person. For example, one young woman I worked with kept getting herself into sexual situations which she enjoyed at the moment (that is, her promiscuous alter wanted to indulge sexually), but later regretted and condemned herself for. I was unable to see her more than twice as she was preparing to go off to college. However, there was a danger that she would continue behaving self-destructively in college if some remedy for her impulsive acting out behaviors was not in place. After some mutual exploration we agreed to have her learn a self-hypnotic method, whereby she would set up a conference room with enough chairs for each alter. A moderator was chosen and a democratic process for dealing with important matters was agreed upon. No sexual action could be taken unless there was first an inner conference to decide the matter. Each alter was given a vote at such conferences. If the internal majority thought it was a good thing (i.e., not self-destructive or dangerous), then this woman could engage in the sexual activity. When I received a follow-up visit from her at the end of her first semester, she said she was using the method and it worked for her rather well. In this way, internal meetings can establish some ritual control over psychological processes and may regulate otherwise self-destructive/impulsive behaviors.

In addition to such secular metaphors as boardrooms and intercom devices, Ross also adapts shamanic methods to the intrapsychic processes of the patient. He may call out alters the way a shaman may sing a sacred song to call a spirit back from the land of the dead; or may make shamanic expeditions into a patient's dream world. But in contrast to classic shamanism where the shaman takes the journey on behalf of the patient, Ross may also have the patient taking journeys on behalf of himself/herself to locate and retrieve alters:

> When I make shamanic expeditions into a patient's dream-world, through guided imagery techniques, I can enter land-scapes reported from spontaneous nocturnal dreams. There I may meet an alter for a specific task.... Alternatively I may

stand at the edge of the dreamworld awaiting an alter's
return from a journey. This provides a sense of control,
safety, and protection. Another variation is to place a magical marker on an alter as a tracking and retrieval device.

For instance, a child personality may run away into a dark
place and not know how to get back. If a marker has been
placed on her beforehand, the therapist can give a hypnotic
suggestion that because of the marker his voice is bringing
the child back to the therapy room.[12]

Ross believes this type of therapeutic intervention is the cultural equivalent of circumpolar shamans, who send out their spirit
guides across the landscape to locate game. It is perhaps because of
the hypnotic/dissociative/imaginative virtuosity of MPD patients
that the therapist or shaman can be so effective. These kinds of
methods are most important in treating MPD because they teach
the patients how to use their own hypnotic/dissociative/imagistic
resources for recovery and improved functioning.

SHAMANIC RESOURCES FOR TREATING PATHOLOGIC DISSOCIATION TODAY II: SANDRA INGERMAN'S CLASSIC SOUL RETRIEVAL

Another example of shamanic applications to modern western psychological and spiritual problems comes from a psy-
chotherapeutically trained white shaman: Sandra Ingerman.
Ingerman, a student of anthropologist/white shaman Michael
Harner, has developed a fairly classic shamanic approach to soul
loss which is adapted to a certain segment of western culture. She
goes beyond the approach of Colin Ross who adapts shamanic
methods to hypnotherapeutic techniques for working with MPD.
Rather, she claims to practice the classic model of shamanism as
described primarily by Michael Harner, and secondarily by
Mircea Eliade. She sees dissociation as a form of soul loss at the
root of many forms of physical and mental sickness, not simply
dissociative disorders and MPD. Her approach distinguishes
between the shamanic ritual and psychotherapy sessions. One is
not a substitute for the other. After a soul retrieval, Ingerman

believes psychotherapy helps with much of the work of integrating the recovered memories, affects, and energies.

Ingerman believes that the shamanic view of soul loss speaks to the widespread experience of soul loss in modern western society. Her work moves beyond mere application to dissociative disorders to a whole variety of disorders which she claims have their underlying cause in soul loss. However, she does interpret soul loss as dissociation. In keeping with a classic shamanic view, Ingerman argues that whenever a person is traumatized or shocked, soul loss is a possibility. This viewpoint has considerable clinical ramifications.

If we take a brief survey of the clinical syndromes demanding the interest and attention of modern mental health practitioners today, we find an array of disorders as defined by the *Diagnostic and Statistical Manual of Mental Disorders* (DSM-IV), the diagnostic and nosological system of the mental health profession. It is in terms of this publicly and professionally legitimized manual that the codes and conceptions for labeling and diagnosing mental pathology in western society are derived. Clinicians are finding themselves having to specialize or gain expertise in the syndromes or disorders classified in this manual. Among the most common DSM-IV legitimized disorders being treated are mood disorders (e.g., major depression, dysthymia), addictions and eating disorders, identity disorders, adjustment disorders, and especially the trauma disorders related to combat and sexual abuse. Some of these disorders are produced by the pressures of modernity, of living in a radically secular world devoid of the sense of the sacred and failing to give support to a psyche fragmenting under the demands and restrictions of an industrial, technological, and increasingly multicultural society. But it is also likely that a traditional shaman would have much to say to these disorders of modernity, and would no doubt reinterpret them in terms of shamanic categories. Among these categories, soul loss and possession would be the ones most likely to be employed.

In a classic shamanic view, these various disorders, which are often viewed as discrete if not occasionally overlapping, are really the result primarily of an underlying loss of power or vital energy described as soul loss. The shaman today might look at eating disorders, posttraumatic stress, depression, codependency, borderline and narcissistic personality disorders, and identity and anxiety disorders as surface symptoms of an underlying loss of power and vitality, that is, as soul loss.

In her pathbreaking book *Soul Retrieval: Mending The Fragmented Self*[13] Ingerman claims that she is both a trained psychotherapist and a shaman, and is able to understand her therapeutic practice from both these frameworks. Looking at the difficulties confronted by modern clinicians within our culture, Ingerman argues that soul loss is widespread in our culture, and that it is the rule rather than the exception. Many people do not feel whole, they fill themselves up with addictions, co-dependent and abusive relationships, chronic sickness, and workaholism. Many who do not feel whole desperately seek relief in a variety of secular therapies and treatments, or in spiritualities, often going from one therapist or guru to another in the hope of finding what they are lacking. Sometimes the therapy becomes stalemated because the therapist isn't working with the whole person. Some part of the soul has wandered off or is lost.

In Ingerman's classic view of these syndromes resulting from soul loss, parts of our soul may have traveled off to other realms (non-ordinary reality) as a result of shock or trauma. These parts constitute vital power and energy, and perhaps memories and potentials, even whole aspects of psychic functioning. Without these lost soul parts we do not feel whole. We are enfeebled, weak, depressed, anxious, or empty. We feel as if something is missing. Ingerman claims that soul loss, psychologically understood, is dissociation, particularly of the soul or soul parts that have wandered off as a result of trauma or shock which often, but not necessarily, arose in childhood.

Possessing a viewpoint closely approximating current psychological understandings of pathologic dissociation, she believes that this dissociation has a purpose: to protect the rest of the organism and help it to survive trauma or loss. In this view, once the soul parts are lost, gone, or dissociated, people may suffer a variety of physical, psychological, and spiritual symptoms as an effect of the resulting loss of power. Such power loss can keep people from leading healthy, fulfilling, and creative lives. Ingerman's view of soul parts corresponds to the traditional notion of having more than one soul. However, there are apparently some differences between her view and many traditional shamanic understandings of the soul. In fact, historian of religions Ake Hultkrantz has designated what he calls two soul complexes amongst tribal peoples (especially traditional Native Americans). One soul complex is made up of the vital or body souls which rule the body and mind. These are potencies which sustain individuals when they are in lucid consciousness. These souls or soul parts rule the heart movements, pulses, emotions, and the will power of the waking individual. The other soul complex is the free soul or image soul; it is active especially during sleep. This free soul can wander in sleep and dreaming. It can also be stolen or lost as the result of trauma, shock, or sorcery. According to Hultkrantz the free soul can detach itself from the person and become the carrier of the ego.[14] It is typically the free soul which may be snatched away (stolen) by a deceased relative or other spirit entity, or by a sorcerer. Sudden shocks and sudden injuries (traumas) may dislodge the free soul and cause it to jump out of the body or go astray, usually wandering off or being drawn to the land of the dead.[15] By contrast, for Ingerman, soul parts may wander off to anywhere in the three-storied cosmology of non-ordinary reality; rarely is it the land of the dead to which she finds they have gone.

Hultkrantz's descriptions of the two different soul complexes is acknowledged by Ingerman. She is familiar with his twofold distinction. However, she speaks of the soul as a whole whose soul parts, because of shock or trauma, may wander off or be stolen, resulting in various forms of mental and physical illness as a result of the decrease in vital potency. In her understanding, it is the free soul which does the journeying to retrieve the lost soul. If the patient accompanies the shaman, it is the patient's free soul which does so. Again, it is the shaman's free soul that, along with the power animal, goes in search and recovery of the lost soul part. What Hultkrantz calls the vital souls are for Ingerman the soul parts that become dissociated because of shock, trauma, and other injury. It is the vital soul parts that await retrieval by the free soul, and subsequent integration and understanding. Her notion of soul loss as loss of vital parts of the soul or psyche is a very valuable and useful theoretical hybrid integration of the two soul complexes. Her notion of these soul parts as vital energies does have much in common with the several soul potencies of which Hultkrantz speaks. Ultimately, her view presupposes a concept of the unmolested, untraumatized soul as a wholeness which becomes fragmented, and the fragments as dissociated soul parts. This understanding apparently slightly modifies traditional shamanic understandings while making a bridge between shamanic theory and practices and modern psychological theories and practices. This is a helpful step for Ingerman to take in bridging classic shamanism with modern psychotherapy.

This understanding of soul loss can be useful in working with trauma-related disorders which are showing up in the consulting room with such frequency today. For example, in the dissociative identity disorders, formerly called multiple personality (MPD) and posttraumatic stress disorder (PTSD) it is useful to consider the pathologically dissociated part as located somewhere within the psychic or psychoid realm (or collective unconscious) where it can be therapeutically accessed, retrieved, and later reintegrated with the ego-structure and personality as a whole. In Ingerman's view the location of the lost soul part can be any of the worlds or planes of consciousness in the realms of non-ordinary reality. She employs a fairly classic shamanic method of ecstatic journey to diagnose, locate, and retrieve these lost soul parts for her patients. Ingerman describes her construction of ritual space:

> The first thing I do is light a candle in a darkened room; this act is how I request the presence of the spirit in the room. Next I get ready a blanket on the floor for my client and me to lie on together. I get out my crystal soul catcher in case I need it. I have found that sometimes in my journey I have trouble holding onto the soul parts. A crystal can actually act as a comfortable waiting room for the soul parts as I continue my journey. My crystal soul catcher acts as a vacuum cleaner to sweep up the splintered parts....Next I ask my client to lie down on the blanket, I explain that when I am ready to begin my work, I will lie next to him or her, touching shoulder, hip, and ankle.

> Before I begin my journey, I kneel next to my client. I whistle to call the helping spirits to me so we are all working in partnership, then I begin to rattle and sing my power song, a song that came to me years ago.[16]

Ingerman then goes on to describe a fairly classic entry into the shamanic state of consciousness (SSC) accompanied by the sonic driving of the drum. She says that she either has an assistant drumming for her, or she turns to modern technology and plays a drumming cassette tape. While the client remains passive, he or she may accompany Sandra in some level of trance state. It is Ingerman's task, however, to locate and retrieve the lost soul parts: "My responsibility is tracking the soul parts and returning them to my client". Ingerman typically asks her power animal for help in locating the lost soul part(s), related to the patient's problem. In contrast to the approach of Colin Ross, Ingerman's shamanic retrieval methods are not employed just for the purpose of retrieving lost alters in patients with MPD. This might be one type of patient she sees, but she also seeks those lost soul parts which lie behind a broad range of symptoms including, but not limited to, abuse, addiction, grief, depression, or trust problems.

In doing a soul retrieval, Ingerman does not know beforehand how she will receive information about the lost soul parts. Sometimes she will see an image of the trauma scene, replete with details; at other times she will just see the image of a certain aged child in non-ordinary reality. There are also times her power animal will give her the information: "Go, get the four year old".[17] She believes she can always ask for more information if she needs it. Typically she finds the lost soul part, often imaged as a child (since that is when the traumas most devastating to later development take place), returns with it, and sits up. She then blows it into the chest (heart center) and fontanel at the crown of the patient's head, just as traditional shamans have done for thousands of years, because they believe these are natural entry and exit points for the vital souls.

This is a very emotionally powerful experience for the patient. According to Ingerman her patients typically report a feeling of being energized, awake, more alive than they can ever remember being. Interestingly, many of her patients are in psychotherapy with other therapists. They may have become stuck because they were lacking the power to face something, or to move forward in their healing or development. After a soul retrieval, they frequently have the energy and vitality to courageously and creatively move forward once again. A psychotherapy process that was stagnant or stalemated becomes re-energized.

It is important to note that Ingerman believes that shamanic soul retrieval is not a substitute for psychotherapy. Soul retrieval itself is not sufficient; there is much work to be done in psychotherapy after the retrieval. The retrieval may bring back lost energies and memories, but it is the task of follow-up therapy, in her view, to do the real work of integration and of learning how to live as a more whole and integrated person. If there are other lost soul parts, the dissociative result of other traumas (as in, but not limited to, multiple personalities), they must await some time and follow-up therapeutic work and integration before another retrieval is attempted.

Ingerman's work is far more complex and rich than we can suggest here. She describes new adaptations of shamanic methods as well as a host of classic approaches to soul loss. As a novel approach she reports, for example, an underworld expedition to the "Cave of the Lost Children" where hundreds of "lost children, sad, hurt, and lonely" are quartered. More classically, she describes the heroic effort and vast experience it takes to retrieve soul parts from the land of the dead. In an area reminiscent of classic sorcery and spirit possession, she discusses the importance of being able to negotiate the release of stolen soul parts from adult individuals who depended too much on various persons when they were children (such as needy parents who were overly dependent on their children). After the needy adult dies, according to Ingerman, their souls still are attached to the persons they needed. This view has much in common with Jung's complex-possessed individual. It can be a vitality draining experience, which can be corrected with such negotiative retrieval methods. Ingerman's approach to stolen souls takes the cultural equivalents of sorcery and spirit possession and transforms them with a psychologically sensitive understanding of how one modern individual may negatively effect the health and vitality of another. This is not pure classic shamanism, but a very creative and useful adaptation to the problems of modern western people.

While we have explained that Ingerman's shamanic soul retrieval method is employable with a broad range of disorders, it is nevertheless Ingerman's understanding of soul loss as a type of dissociation which gives her work a relevance to the trauma disorders so closely related to sexual abuse today. She not only brings in another model of how the spirituality and methods of shamanism may help in the healing of dissociative disorders; she provides a conceptual bridge between the disorders of traditional societies who have employed shamans, and modern forms of psychological and spiritual distress.

SOUL LOSS AND DISSOCIATION IN JUNGIAN PERSPECTIVE

In Chapter Four we discussed Jung's views of complexes and their contribution to pathologic dissociation. Here we will apply the discussion of Jung, and of other Jungian analysts, to the contemporary western understandings of soul loss and dissociation as discussed by Ross and Ingerman above. From their work we can see that our modern psyches are not really so different from those of our archaic ancestors and our non-modernized neighbors around the world. The modern soul, Jung believed, was not really so modern as we like to think. The primitive's and modern person's psychology is rooted in the same two-million-year-old archetypally structured psyche that owes its biological and psychical origins to a much more ancient prehuman ancestry. Like the primitive, the modern person develops serious psychopathology when the psyche's age-old archetypal intent is frustrated or thwarted.

We can not deny that there is a frequent malaise in the modern psyche which corresponds with what classic shamanism has considered a symptom of soul loss. We will recall that Jung believed that the phenomenon that traditional peoples called soul loss could be psychologically understood in terms of 1) a diminution of personality, and 2) possession by a complex (i.e., pathologic dissociation). These two notions are interdependent in Jungian psychology.

We will recall that Ingerman claims that the wide variety of symptoms seen by many psychotherapists today are actually symptoms of soul loss. We will also recall Ingerman's argument that soul loss means loss of vital parts of ourselves, that is, loss of vitalities, of power. Loss of parts of ourselves correlates well with Jung's notions of complexes, of autonomous complexes which split off from their integrity with the psyche and function independently of that integrity. Loss of vital souls, vital energies, correlates well with Jung's notion of psychic libido. When Jung speaks, in the language formulated by his teacher Pierre Janet, of soul loss as a kind of "abaissement du niveau mental", he means that there is a loss or slackening in ego-consciousness. Ego-consciousness is receding from its peak and becomes attenuated as psychical energy withdraws from the executive functioning of the ego. This happens when an autonomous complex splits off (dissociates) and attracts so much energy and psychical content unto itself that it becomes "swollen" and powerful. When the complex begins to act on its own, irrespective of the intentions of the ego and its executive agendas and programs, and from the archetypal Self in its quest to regulate and balance the psyche, the natural wholeness is shattered.

Jungian analysts, when they talk about the ego, ordinarily mean the "I" that we think of ourselves as being. The ego is our image of ourselves, what we believe ourselves to be. We identify our name with it. Typically when we say, "I think this way..." or "I feel that way about...", our ego is speaking. While Jung believed the ego also to be a complex because it attracted and organized a variety of conscious and unconscious processes, the ego can be analyzed into its capacities for rational intellect, its ability to will actions, to have its own feelings and desires, and to remember the past and project future actions (planning).

Consciousness researcher Ernst Hilgard, who confirmed through laboratory studies that we in fact "do more than one thing at a time all the time",[18] has suggested that the assumed unity of consciousness is an illusion; that consciousness is always multifaceted and complex. From a Jungian perspective, the unity of consciousness can be an illusion of the ego who wants to be master in its own house.

Jungian psychology has understood from its inception the multiplicity within the pregiven unity of the psyche. Often I am neither the one thinking nor the one feeling, willing, deciding, or acting. On the contrary, often some autonomous complex is operating and temporarily possessing the ego. When a complex possesses the ego, it forces it to operate out of its (i.e., the complex's) perspective. In this way the ego's own perspectives and its own goals are bypassed. The ego tends to be pretty much unaware of the other complexes and is easily fooled into thinking that it is master in the house.

We should be clear that a Jungian view of consciousness does not limit it to the ego, where the peak of consciousness is attained. The ego is often unaware of the other complexes in the personal unconscious and of the archetypal core in the collective unconscious; but the unconscious does itself possess various levels of consciousness. The other complexes are only unconscious, we could say, from the ego's perspective. They in fact have a great degree of awareness and intentionality, and are conscious of each other and of the ego and its perspective.

The autonomous complexes often constellate in response to their awareness of the ego's perspective. This becomes most obvious in the dissociative disorders, and is most dramatically illustrated in MPD. In a Jungian view, the alternate personalities in MPD are actually highly elaborated, personified, and often emotionally and energetically charged complexes, or aspects of complexes. In MPD a complex may be personified in several alters. When activated (switched on), these personified, autonomous complex manifestations behave in ways that usurp the intentions and wishes of the ego.

We have already mentioned that the dissociative disorders found in our society are the result of trauma, often of overwhelming abuse experienced in childhood. During such trauma, bits of the psyche split off and dissociate in order to perform certain psychic functions that enable the psychophysical organism of the child to survive. In a Jungian view, all of us experience some degree of traumatic childhood disappointments, parental failures of empathy, or outright abuse. Such traumata thwart and frustrate the archetypal intent, the two-million-year-old hard-wiring of the human psyche. A certain degree of dissociation is normal, even desirable. An excessive degree of dissociation is pathologic and thwarts the wholeness and integrity of the person. In less severe forms it has been considered to be at neurotic levels. Extreme forms of pathologic dissociation are involved in psychosis and dissociative disorders. While we do not all develop dissociative identity disorders, it is important to understand that we all have complexes, some of which may become more or less autonomous and disrupt the psyche's natural strivings towards wholeness and integrity. In multiple personality there is a greater degree of pathologic dissociation than in so-called normal people. However, most of us are not so far from the experience of pathologic multiplicity as we would like to think.

In a Jungian view, we all have complexes. It is the autonomous complexes that cause serious problems, which Ross and Ingerman treat with shamanic methods. They are usually the result of traumatic childhood experience. Such traumatically induced autonomous complexes tend to cause a more serious degree of psychic disintegration than normal, with the split-off parts becoming markedly alienated from the programs, energies, and intentions of the ego, therefore reducing its power and vitality (power loss). Likewise, these sharply split-off parts can resist the integrative efforts of the archetypal Self, the deep organizing center of the total psyche.

The split-off parts, having robbed the ego of some of its vital energies, are not forever lost. They become shadow aspects of the ego, awaiting conscious acknowledgment and often awaiting reintegration. Reintegration is possible, and their retrieval is the goal of both Jungian psychoanalysis and of shamanic healing. Jungian analyst Robert L. Moore has written of the disintegrative effects of trauma, of the value of the parts which become dissociated (lost), and of their reintegrative possibilities:

> During early traumas, our emerging Egos split off and repress aspects of the psyche that parents, siblings, or society found unacceptable. These split-off aspects could be thoughts, feelings, images, or associations. Often they are

valuable and worth recall. They may carry hidden talents, intuitions, abilities, or accurate feelings that would make our personalities wiser and more complete if we could reintegrate them. Until reintegration can occur, our psyches are like pieces of a broken mirror, which hold in fragments what was once a complete reflection.[19]

It is important to note here that soul retrieval can be done by methods other than shamanic ones. Hypnosis, witchcraft, psychoanalysis, and other healing disciplines all have methods for integrating split-off or lost parts of the self.[20] The important thing is that there be a potential for retrieval and integration as well as a technology for bringing it about. Jungians have long followed Jung in trusting in the psyche's self-healing capacities, and believing that the healer only assists the natural process along. In a Jungian view, the shaman, by virtue of his or her use of trance, dissociation, imagery, and other methods and ritual skills, is not only able to access and retrieve lost parts of the self, but is able to access and mobilize the healing energies of the doctor within us all, that is, the archetypal Self.

In accessing the split-off parts, the shaman, in a Jungian view, can be understood as employing a trance device similar to active imagination for accessing at will the personal and collective unconscious of his/her patient (depending on where the split-off energies are located). A special advantage of the shaman is the map he or she has acquired through numerous ecstatic journeys. This map of the inner world serves as a navigational guide, a way of conceptualizing the various places to which these soul parts can wander or be held captive (e.g., by the numinosity of an archetype).

The potential for Jungian psychology to illuminate pathologic dissociation and soul loss today is considerable. Like Ingerman's view, Jung does have a model of the psyche as an original and undifferentiated wholeness. Jung adds a developmental perspective to this wholeness. At birth there is an unconscious and undifferentiated wholeness, which then must become differentiated through the unfolding development of the individuation process, and finally move towards a more differentiated and mature wholeness. The wholeness is always there as a potential, and it can always be fragmented through trauma. Like classic shamanism, Jung does have an understanding of the loss of vitality which arises as a result of shock or trauma and which correlates with the loss of power characteristic of soul loss. He does have a psychological model for those parts of the psyche which split off and become autonomous as a result of trauma. Like Ingerman, he held that dissociation is at the root of many modern problems. Unlike shamanism, Jungian analysis and psychotherapy (and numerous other psychotherapies) have many methods for facilitating reintegration of retrieved, formerly dissociated parts of the psyche (active imagination, dream analysis, sand tray and dance techniques, and analysis of the transference).

SOME PROBLEMS IN JUNG'S PERSPECTIVES

In addition to the strength of the correspondence between Jungian and shamanic views, there are some areas of weakness in Jung's actual views on what he called the primitive experience of soul loss. He tended to think soul loss was mainly a problem for primitives, although modern men and women experienced something similar. Jung believed, as we discussed in Chapter 4, that soul loss was closely tied to the condition of primitive consciousness, which lacks the firmness and coherence of the consciousness of modern people. Jung erroneously believed that modern individuals had more control of their will than primitive peoples, and that they were better at resisting the whims of the unconscious because they had more ego strength. Today, with the large volume of people showing up with dissociative disorders, many of whom were abused by family members who couldn't resist the whims of their unconscious, it seems Jung greatly overestimated the strength of the modern ego.

Another problem with Jung's thought concerns his belief that in multiple personality the alters are really personified autonomous complexes. While this may be the case occasionally, it does not square with much of the vast clinical data available today. In my own clinical experience, and in the experience of experts on dissociative disorders today, the multiplicity of alters are often organized into clusters. Each alter, depending on its degree of dissociation and elaboration, may have a distinct identity. Often the identity of an alter is rather stereotyped, however, because it is really only a part, a specific function within the whole self-system. In complicated MPD there may be many alters, with several or more alters being organized into layers or clusters. There may, for example, be a cluster of alters who are related like brothers and sisters. They may share feelings of powerlessness in the face of sexual approach, and they may all feel hopeless and helpless around older men (and are dominated by a father complex). Another cluster of alters within the same person may be characterized as having more power, even being aggressive and angry towards women (and is dominated by a mother complex). If relatively accurate, this view suggests that the lines of archetypal influence are to be drawn between clusters of alters, and that one or more alters may be dominated by a complex, or more than one complex. All this would suggest, contra Jung, that alters should not automatically be identified as complexes personified. It is more likely that they are bits of psyche, imaginatively elaborated parts of the total self from which they have been split off.[21] Since they are imaginatively elaborated, they fall under the same archetypal structures and influences as does all imagery, and all parts may still be conceived as potentials for reintegration under the questing influence of the archetypal Self for wholeness. The shaman and the modern psychotherapist treating pathologic dissociation enhance the natural archetypally patterned questing of this deep psychic center for healing (integration/wholeness).

NOXIOUS ALTERS, POSSESSION, AND EXORCISM

So far, the shamanic applications we have discussed have been related to soul loss as dissociation in MPD and in a variety of mental disorders and complaints. In discussing Collin Ross' and Sandra Ingerman's applications to the problem of locating and retrieving lost soul parts and alters, we argued that shamanic soul retrieval had something to offer. But there is another form of dissociative problem related to MPD that is worthy of some consideration. It is the problem of a noxious and unruly alter who refuses therapeutic assistance, and who is bent on destroy-ing its host and perhaps other persons as well. What techniques might be helpful in treating an alter that is dangerous and that refuses help? According to anthropologist and neuroscientist Felicitas Goodman, ritual exorcism deserves more scientific attention than it has been getting by researchers and clinicians interested in complicated dissociative disorders. She, along with psychiatrist Dr. Ralph B. Allison, believes that some intractable forms of dissociative disorder might be better treated with this ritual which has ancient roots in shamanism.[22]

In many traditional societies, historically and cross-culturally, a form of soul sickness is understood as spirit possession, the anthropological equivalent of possession by a complex in Jung's understanding. Most forms of destructive spirit possession involve some type of pathologic dissociation in which an alternate person-ality or part-self is culturally constructed in a demonistic or spiritis-tic idiom. Sudhir Kakar describes a variety of cases of spirit possession amongst young women in India.[23] Typically these cases resemble dual personality (multiple personality when there is more than one spirit). Often the possessing spirit is unruly, and vigor-ously protests against family norms and sacred values. Psychologi-cally understood, Kakar sees the motive for such dissociation as being a culturally sanctioned form of pathology which allows the Indian woman to vent her pent-up hostilities towards a patriarchal world that offers her little hope of fulfillment.[24] Since, in the assumptive world of the patient, it is believed to be a spirit or demon who takes over her behavior, the woman is not considered responsible for it. She can thus air her frustration and express pent-up hostility against her social world without censure, embarrass-ment, or punishment.

Indian temple healers and shamans typically diagnose and label this form of dissociation as some type of ancestral spirit or demon possession, and employ ritual exorcism to drive out the unruly spirit in the name of the local deity of the local shrine, temple, and healer. This type of possession is wide-spread and well documented cross-culturally. It is perhaps the main form of psychological illness treated by traditional heal-ers around the globe.[25] In a conceptualization similar to shamanic spirit intrusion/extraction, a great spirit is counterposed against a pathogenic, invading spirit. Typically these exorcisms follow a classic pattern: 1) There is an ecstatic diagnosis of spirit possession. 2) The healer calls out the spirit and asks its intentions. 3) There follows a period of protest and struggle as the exorcism in the name of the local deity begins. 4) And finally, at the moment of neurophysiological exhaustion, the healer commands the spirit to leave (casts it out), and it often does. 5) The patient feels exhausted, relieved, and calm. 6) Sacrifices and thanksgivings are made to the triumphant deity. 7) The healer may prescribe sacred amulets or charms to keep evil spirits away, and may request the patient come back frequently to have them recharged with numinous power (because spirits can always return).

We have a phenomenon similar to this type of spirit possession in modern western societies. In cases of severe MPD, where there is a noxious alter who acts like and believes itself to be an evil spirit, a demon, or the devil, a dangerous and life-threatening situation may arise. These cases are fairly rare, but they can quickly exhaust the healing resources of the best psychiatrists and clergy. Typically these alters will call themselves evil, and will blaspheme against everything sacred, beloved, and moral. Such spirits may exhibit unusual strength, become violent, even homicidal and suicidal. There may be paranormal-type phenomena, and inexplicable knowledge of foreign languages the victim is not supposed to know. It has dramatic effects upon the body and psyche of its victim/host, and often states its intention is to remain until it kills its host. Often there are epileptic-like seizures after which there is less of the host's identity remaining (and more of the demon/intruder's presence) after each seizure.

When they arise in a modern context, these rare but problematic cases of possession quickly exhaust the resources of the best scientifically trained and seasoned psychotherapists, and sometimes the patient dies. They are more severe than the average possession cases found in traditional societies where the invading spirits are often of lesser power and status. Those spirits are fairly easily subdued with standard exorcistic rites. But in the cases of classic demonic possession, where the invading entity has great power and seeks to destroy its host, special and lengthy exorcistic rites are the only known therapeutic in the world that has been shown to be effective. However, even ritual exorcism is not always able to stop the horrendous destruction, especially if the disorder is in advanced stages.

Examples of this life-threatening type of demonic possession can be found in a variety of sources. The most readily popular example is to be found in William Peter Blatty's novel, *The Exorcist.* While parts of Blatty's book are fictional, the phenomenology of classic demonic possession and ritual exorcism are given there. This book was based on an actual documented case of possession and exorcism of a young boy by some Jesuits in St. Louis.[26] A more scientific discussion of this phenomenon is found in Felicitas Goodman's book *How About Demons?*[27] There she seeks to identify the various types of creative and destructive possession states as they are found across cultures.

Goodman argues that many forms of possession are of a religious nature, and are ecstatic and positive. An example of a positive type of possession would be the possession by the Holy Spirit amongst charismatic Christians, or of the shaman by his helping spirits. An example of the negative type would be possession by an angry ancestral spirit, a Christian demon, an Islamic jinn, or malevolent ghost. In the positive type of possession the good spirit is ritually invoked on cue (i.e., switched on), experienced, and then ritually dismissed on cue (i.e., switched off). The religious ritual itself acts as an elaborate mechanism of regulation and control whereby sacred and profane modes of consciousness are switched on and off. The negative type of possession, by contrast, often lacks ritual regulation and control. It is a condition which often spontaneously emerges, or if intentionally triggered (as in cases of possession which emerged as a result of occult activities), is not regulated and terminated at will. Lack of ritual control of altered states of consciousness is characteristic of the autonomous activities of noxious alters and malignant possessing entities.

Both types of possession, Goodman argues, must have a neurophysiological basis, and probably involve the development of good and bad neurocognitive brain maps. In trying to distinguish demonic possession from the typical angry alters in standard MPD, she turns to psychiatrist Ralph B. Allison, a specialist in treating MPD.

Goodman draws attention to Dr. Allison's observations that what distinguishes cases of an evil alter from the typical cases of MPD with various angry, noxious alters (but not the evil or demonic alters who claim they are a demon, a ghost, or the devil himself) is that such evil entities act autonomously. Often their birth (origination) can not be pinpointed, they have or serve no specific purpose for the personality, and they frequently refer to themselves as spirits. In the several cases of this sort which Allison treated, not all of the alters could be considered absolutely evil. In distinction from those which are just bothersome, the case of Carrie, Allison's patient, stands in bold contrast. In her case,

> a truly furious possession took place suddenly and without warning, exhibiting some of the traits of demonic possession...the alter screamed obscenities, had superhuman strength, and was viciously aggressive. Before Allison could help, Carrie committed suicide. People suffering from demonic possession often report that the demon wants to kill them by forcing them into a suicidal act. In this instance, it happened.[28]

Allison thought that if these alters pretended to be spirits, or actually were, then it might not hurt to try ritual exorcism. Allison began inquiring into the nature of demonic possession and ritual exorcism. He enlisted the help of an exorcist to treat an injured man who suffered convulsive neurological seizures after an accident. Neurophysiological tests did not find enough evidence to explain the seizures in purely biological terms. Allison placed the patient under hypnosis and a voice came out that identified itself as the devil. It claimed to have entered the man years before in Japan when he had rescued a Japanese occupant from a burning house. An explosion had apparently blown him out of the house. Allison says that he contracted the services of a priest to help him with the case. The priest was able to access the devil by simply reciting his ritual formulas. The priest told Allison that he did not really believe the spirit was the devil, as known by Christian theology, but he felt the spirit was so stupid that he actually thought he was the devil.[29] According to Allison the priest carried out the exorcism with remarkable success. Allison who reported that he continued contact with the patient said the symptoms of the devil's voice and the seizures did not recur.

According to Goodman, for cases such as this, the undoing of such a negative and intractable pattern is extremely difficult. This is especially the case if the alter is evil, or, in religious terms, is demonic. Goodman argues that Western-style biomedical psychiatric treatment of multiple personality *per se* is ineffective, and is completely incapable of dealing with evil alters or demonic molesting entities.[30] To her knowledge there are not many psychiatrists treating multiple personality who would be willing to employ exorcism, like Allison, to gain ritual control over the molesting entities. Goodman claims that ritual exorcism should work regardless of whether the unruly alters claimed themselves spirits or not. She does not speculate on whether or not there actually are intelligent spiritual entities that exist, that have ontological status independent of the psyche. She does believe it is beyond the scope of science to confirm or deny such possibilities. However, Goodman does believe that, regardless of the status or source of the molesting entities, the empirical phenomenon of the more serious and life-threatening types of possession is quite real and quite refractory to treatment with modern Western psychotherapeutic methods. Ritual exorcism has been the only effective method for dealing with this more powerful form of destructive possession, even if it is not always effective.[31]

POSSESSION AND RITUAL EXORCISM IN JUNGIAN PERSPECTIVE

There are two questions we shall briefly explore here. The first question has to do with a possible Jungian explanation for demonic possession, or so-called evil alters. The second question seeks to understand how ritual exorcism can be more effective than standard biomedical and psychological models of treatment.

In response to the first question we can say that a Jungian perspective would tend to conjecture that possession by a so-called evil spirit is really a form of possession by an autonomous complex, or by an alter that is highly elaborated and whose anger and outrage is so intense that it has turned inward against the self-system. In typical cases of MPD, an angry alter often attacks the host, or other alters within the host. Such an alter often feels these other inner people were weak and permitted the abuse, and therefore deserved it. We must keep in mind that such a cognitively distorted view typically develops in a child who lacks the maturity and cognitive capacity to adequately assess her/his situation, know what the options are, and take appropriate action. Such an abused child will not have the option of expressing the outrage because it is dangerous to do so, and likewise may not be permitted to ask for help from other adults. Thus the energies of the outrage must be held within. So intense are these energies that a specific alter is often created to contain them. The psychological function of a mean or angry alter, in the libidinal economy of the MPD system, is to handle and deal with this massive rage. But even this function may overwhelm the angry alter, and others have to be created to help with the load. Sometimes the angry alter and/or its associates simply can't contain the anger well; the affective charge is too strong. It may then get retroflexively turned upon the self and its other part-selves (alters). In my own clinical practice I have known angry alters to attack, mame, and ridicule other alters. This may be viewed as an exaggerated version of the kind of self-critical monologue depressed persons use habitually to erode their self-esteem.

If the person possessing large amounts of dissociated anger and outrage should grow up in a culture (or subculture) which has a supernatural belief system that explains pathologic dissociation in terms of ancestral spirit or demon possession, the stage is set for the cultural shaping of this dissociated pocket of rage into a malevolent spirit, a demon, or the devil himself. Regardless of its traumatic cause, whether it began with abuse, taboo violation, toying with the occult, or what have you, once this enormous psychic energy is shaped into an evil supernatural being, its malevolent force becomes dangerous and life-threatening. It takes sides and identifies with the archetypal shadow aspects of the culture's respective alternate reality, and begins to blaspheme everything sacred. Because of this identification with archetypal evil, there is also an inflation that develops in such a way that the patient's ego is simply taken over by the evil intruder. Being identified with evil, the individual can no longer appeal to the sacred for help. It thus is dissociated from the healing and integrating energies of the archetypal Self. Becoming a powerful autonomous complex or alter, it continues to grow within the patient (host), attracting with the power of great affective numinosity all the contents it can unto itself. In a Jungian view, it is as if the complex or alter has become malignant, a psychic cancer which devours the psychological identity and often the body of the victim until there is nothing left but the intruder, and the patient then dies (due to neurological exhaustion and bio-systemic failures).

So strong can this evil influence become, and so intelligent, that it becomes dangerously fascinating, and seductive to others. This is why the exorcist is sometimes overcome by the demon; its evil and cunning are fascinating, and its sheer display of libido is numinous and can act like corrosive acid upon the ego-structure of the healer. Some of the libido of the complex/alter must be released in order to switch it off. Other libidinal elements must be subdued by the ego, by the development of an ego-archetype axis, and the psychic contents of the complex must be subordinated to the ordering/integrating energies of the archetypal Self. But since it is operating in hostility and defiance, and with intelligence, it automatically defeats any attempts at a talking cure. It is libido run amok. This powerful nuclear level of energy is truly chaotic and wild and will only submit to a ritual adequate to its intensity. In many traditional societies, the greater the demon or the sickness, the greater and more powerful the ritual and preparations for the ritual, to combat the evil spirit.[32] In Catholic exorcistic ritual, the positive energies of God the Father, God the Son, God the Holy Spirit, and all the saints and all the prophets and the angels are called upon to command and cast out the invading spirit in the name of Christ. These formulae can be repeated ad infinitum, the length of the rite corresponding to the power of the demon, for days, weeks, months, or even years.

Jung believed, as we discussed in Chapter 4, that it was the job of ritual to impose a restrictive form upon chaotic instinctual libidinal energies running amok. He believed that exorcistic ritual, in particular, was able to reinstate the integrity of the ego and strengthen it by reinstating the repression barrier and driving much of the unruly libido back into the unconscious.[33] The task of the healer, whether psychotherapist or shaman, is to switch off the autonomous activity of the evil entity complex by exhausting it and draining it of its affective charge. Then a subordination of that part to the greater totality under the rule of the archetypal Self must take place. In many traditional cultures this is done by the healer invoking the local deity (carrier of the projection of the archetypal Self) as the healing power that drives out the invading spirit and reinstates order. The patient is then required to pay homage and continue to worship the deity in some way, which may include becoming its devotee, or wearing sacred amulets representing its healing energies (like the Catholic crucifix to protect against evil influence).

The shaman, understood from a psychological perspective, has been the ritual master of imposing restrictive form upon chaotic instinctual and archetypal energies. Exorcism, which has roots in shamanism, is the most dramatic expression of this ritual mastery. How ritual can have the power to accomplish this task is the subject of the next chapter.

Chapter Seven

=====

The Power of Ritual, Image,
and Archetype to Bring About
Profound Psychological
and Spiritual Transformation

In this chapter we are going to consider some of the components of transformative ritual in an effort to better understand how ritual can be so effective in bringing about profound change. In traditional societies the shamans have been the ritual masters *par excellence.* Whenever there were important life crises or transitions, the shaman was often called upon to provide the proper ritual and the appropriate ritual leadership. In male rites of passage, such as the puberty rituals, for example, young boys were transformed into men through the ritual wisdom of the shamans and with the help of the tribal elders. Puberty rites have long been effective in transforming young boys and girls into mature men and women. Puberty rites are able to switch off the *puer* archetype, the young boy psychology with its irresponsibility and dependency upon the mother, and able to switch on what Robert L. Moore calls the archetypes of the mature masculine, the archetypes of king, warrior, magician, and lover.[1]

In females, the archetypal corollary of the puer is the *puella,* the girl psychology—also indicating dependency upon the maternal figure(s). We shall not go into the puberty rites of females in the following discussion for a number of reasons. There are numerous discussions of female puberty rites in the anthropological literature, and these discussions often suggest that these rituals are less intense and lengthy than male puberty rites. Proposed reasons for these differences are often said to have to do with the fact that a woman's initiation into adulthood is easier since menstruation and other bodily changes make her change of status more evident. Thus, less lengthy and less dramatic ritual efforts are required to bring about the needed transformation, or so the argument goes. This may simply be patriarchal rhetoric. It seems likely that females require the switching off of immature archetypal patterns and the turning on of mature ones just as males do. It also seems obvious that females have archetypes of the mature feminine correlating to the archetypes of the mature masculine.[2] However, because we intend to illustrate the transformative power of ritual, rather than give a full dissertation on puberty rites, because of the need to limit the length of our discussion, and because our subsequent discussion of the relation of ritual action to archetypes and their locus in the brain necessitates a discussion of Robert Moore's and Douglas Gillette's work on ritual transformation and the archetypes of the mature masculine, we shall limit our discussion of puberty rituals to the male form. We will thus proceed to discuss the prowess of male initiation and puberty rites as a demonstration of the transformative power of ritual in bringing about dramatic change and psychic transformation in ordinary living and passage through the life cycle. After discussing male puberty rites we will turn to an examination of the imagination in its power to cause and cure sickness and then to a discussion of the role of ritual in intensifying the vividness and impact of therapeutic imagery upon body, brain, and psyche. These multidisciplinary discussions will cut across psychological, anthropological, and neurobiological domains.

MASCULINE PUBERTY RITES AND RITUAL TRANSFORMATION

In tribal societies, when the young boys arrive at puberty they begin undergoing massive physical and mental changes. There is rapid growth of the central nervous system, increase in the size of muscles and bone, an increase in cognitive capacity, and an increase in general physical and mental power. All this growth means increased aggressive and sexual instinctual demands and desires, and this new power is a potential threat to the security and order of the tribe if it does not become adequately disciplined, channeled, and transformed into the mature masculine. In psycho-analytic terms, it is the job of puberty rites to install a super-ego, an internal moral authority based upon the authority and will of the ancestors or deities of the tribe.

To accomplish this task, young boys at puberty are snatched away from their mothers, for whom, as boys, they are now dead. Later they are returned to the tribe and their mothers as men, with new names designating their new status as full adult male members of the tribe, but only after the ritual transformation has taken place. From their secure dependency upon their mothers they are taken into the bush, or some remote place, for a considerable period of time (often up to several months). They are forced by the ritual elders to undergo an ordeal, a type of ritual torture in which they may be tied to red-ant hills, have teeth knocked out, have their faces permanently scarified, be circumcised, and so on. These markings not only will serve as permanent symbols of their changed condition; they recall them to humility in the face of what the tribe considers sacred and moral. Without submission to the social values of the tribe or community, the kind of social cooperation necessary for the survival of the people would be undercut. Hence, the humility necessary for mature masculine participation in tribal life is inculcated in a dramatic and forceful way.

According to anthropologist Victor Turner, these initiation rituals largely take place in a liminal space, what Robert L. Moore calls a "sacred transformative space".[3] It lies betwixt and between the normal space/time of tribal life. It is a time of heightened intensity in which familiar roles (of childhood) are put away, and in which one is stripped of one's previous profane status and identifying personae. Gods and goddesses of destruction are adored, reflecting the role of this ritual to deconstruct the former ego-identifications so that mature masculine archetypal energies can be switched on.

The candidates for adulthood are taught the sacred stories and lore of the tribe; what we call myth, religious ritual, and ethical action are amongst the most important educational agendas of the rite. Ritual performances may include the elders acting out elaborate dramas and dances in which they in effect say to the initiates, "This is what your ancestors did, and so shall you!" This is the cultural equivalent of being told the biblical story of Yahweh giving the Ten Commandments to Moses on Sinai. Taboos with respect to violence and other forms of aggression and sexuality are given.

Through dramatic enactment of sacred stories of the great ancestral warriors and hunters, the young men are also taught to be courageous warriors and hunters (activation of the archetypal warrior/hunter), learning how to protect the tribe, serve the higher purpose of the tribe, and serve the chief or king, and ultimately the will of the sacred gods and founding ancestors as embodied in stories of the tribe. In these ways, the dramatic, prolonged, and carefully structured ritual forces switch off the archetypes which control what had been phase-appropriate dependency and immaturity; and activate or switch on the now phase-appropriate archetypes of the mature masculine, which serve the life of the community.

Transformative ritual is necessary when there is a strong degree of chaos or destructive power around. Puberty rites are necessary because the young boys would not automatically decide to submit or sublimate their aggressive and sexual instinctual energies; this is a work of culture (i.e., of learning or conditioning) which ritual performs. According to Anthony Stevens, any rite of passage helps the individual to make the psychosocial transformations called for by the next step in the life cycle. The coercive power of ritual is necessary because of a natural resistance to such change. Stevens cites Whitmont's law of psychic inertia, and compares it to Newton's law of inertia in physics. Newton's law of inertia, it will be recalled, holds that a body in motion or rest tends to remain in motion or rest unless an outside force propels it to change. According to Jungian analyst E.C. Whitmont, the psyche, being a part of nature, operates on a psychic law of inertia. Psychic inertia is a tendency towards habit and obsessive clinging: "Every pattern of adaptation, outer and inner, is maintained in essentially the same unaltered form and anxiously defended against change until an equally strong or stronger impulse is able to displace it".[4] In itself this is not pathological, but is normal because it serves the needs for constancy, security, familiarity, and permanence that help to insure our survival as individuals and as a species. However, when it is time to make a phase-appropriate developmental change or transition, the psychic law of inertia may thwart the individuative needs. This happens, in a Jungian view, because of the power of complexes to seize, possess, and hold the ego in their grip. In puberty rites, the ritual seeks to pry the candidates ego-structure away from identifications with the real mother demanded by the internal mother complex. As the program of the initiation archetype proceeds under adequate leadership, the numinous energy of the mother archetype at the core of the mother complex is turned off, thus reducing the ego's investment with the external mother (i.e., the real mother), and thus freeing the initiant to activate and assume other archetypal programs. We shall turn, now, to a discussion of the relation of image and ritual as efficaciously employed in shamanic ritual and related therapeutics from neurobiological and Jungian psychological perspectives.

RITUAL AND THE BRAIN

It is important to consider images and the imagination in relation to ritual because images play such an important role in healing from Jungian and shamanic perspectives. Religious and therapeutic ritual intensifies images, making them more distinct and powerful, and thus making it easier to see the spirits, or to image the disease. In ritual trance states, images are seen for the purposes of diagnosis and treatment. Diagnosis and treatment is often conceived of in terms of images. The shaman sees a pathogenic or intruding spirit, and offers therapy with the counterposing creative spirit, which he or she also sees in non-ordinary reality. Images are also important in diagnosing and healing today. The image of the pill, whether it be a placebo or effective medicinal agent, in effect, acts as an image upon the psyche and the autoimmune system in mobilizing the body's healing energies.[5] Like the shaman showing the extracted disease-causing object to the patient, the dentist showing the patient his or her extracted and diseased tooth (or the surgeon showing a patient the extracted tonsils) has some impact upon the belief that proper action has taken place and that healing will follow. Since belief is known to enhance therapeutic effect, the role of these images should not be underestimated.

According to psychophysiologist Jean Achterberg, images interact with bodily tissues: "The imagination acts upon one's own physical being. Images communicate with tissues and organs, even cells, to effect a change."[6] They affect the functioning of the central nervous system which, in turn, affects the functioning of every aspect of bodily life. Echoing the work of oncologist Dr. Carl O. Simonton and cancer therapist Stephanie Matthews-Simonton, we can say that images are able to access pathways to health or sickness. Research done by the Simontons has shown that massive stress from which the individual believes there is no exit or forthcoming relief sets the preconditions for many kinds of sickness, especially cancer. The psychological component of this massive stress entails images of doom which are accompanied by strong affectively toned cognitions of hopelessness, helplessness, and futility.

The Simontons have provided some preliminary mappings of the neural pathways involved in sickness and healing. The impact of massive stress-related negative images, according to the Simontons, is to influence the regulatory neurophysiology of the autoimmune system. The limbic system, known as the visceral brain, is affected, for example, by depression. Since it plays an important role in the regulation of all activities important to the organism's preservation (e.g., fight/flight mechanism), and since it registers the effects of depression/stress, this registration is believed to upset the homeostatic regulatory mechanisms of the autoimmune system. The hypothalamus is an important limbic structure concerned with the mediation of such important functions as temperature control, water metabolism, control of blood pressure, hunger, maintenance of balance between sympathetic and parasympathetic divisions, and hormonal secretions, and it plays a role in emotional reactions. Because of its effects upon the pituitary gland, a very stressed or depressed individual can cause themselves to produce hormonal imbalances which result in abnormal cell growth, a precondition for cancer, and which can lead to irregular cells becoming malignant. At just the time there is an increase in irregular cells, there is a decrease in the autoimmune system's ability to destroy those irregular cells; hence, the conditions for a serious sickness are set. This is the bad news. Massive stress, plus the belief (entailing negative images) that there is no escape, can lead to depression and limbic system changes which produce sickness.

The good news is, according to the Simontons, that the same pathways that create illness can also be used to heal it, or reduce its effects. A reversal or remission of the sickness-causing processes can often be effected by reversing the cognitive component (images) which developed as a response to massive stress. This in turn utilizes the same pathways that lead to illness. If the patient will turn negative images and beliefs into positive ones, sickness can be stopped, slowed, and often healed. The positive images have the same pathways to the limbic system. There they can re-regulate the pituitary (slowing irregular cell growth), while simultaneously affecting the autoimmune system (thus promoting destruction of irregular cells). The Simontons have taught numerous cancer patients to image their disease, and to image a greater healing force destroying the disease. The patients are instructed to do this several times a day, and to believe in the efficacy of this method. Many of the Simontons' patients who employed this method actually recovered from cancer or sent it into remission. The Simontons have published their impressive results in their book, *Getting Well Again.*[7] Their methods have great affinity with shamanic methods in employing a greater counterposing image (or spirit) to attack or remove a pathological one. According to Michael Harner, the Simontons' method could be enhanced by employing a classic shamanic method along with having the patients visualize their illness and its cure. The shaman would, on the patient's behalf, shamanize and image the removal or destruction of the disease. Having the support of another caring human being work alongside the patient could enhance the therapeutic benefit.[8] In essence, what the shamanic and Simonton visualization methods do is access and mobilize the natural "doctor within," which is why, according to Dr. Albert Schweitzer, all healers are effective when they are effective.[9] Image is truly slayer or healer.

RITUAL TRANSFORMATION OF THE WORLD IMAGE (THE COGNITIVE MAP)

We have thus far argued that the shaman is the ritual master, par excellence, who through trance and ritual enhances the power of the imagination for diagnosis and healing. We have noted the highly imaginative activity of persons suffering from soul loss and dissociative disorders, and have noted some of the ways images can be causative or curative of psychological, spiritual, and bodily sickness. There is another type of image that should be noted when considering the impact of shamanic therapeutics and psychotherapy upon the sufferer: the World Image. The World Image is capitalized for emphasis because it is a special type of image. It is a very complex cognitive map of reality having numerous facets, including collective elements such as cultural assumptions and cosmological beliefs, plus the individual's idiosyncratic non-conscious assumptions and conscious beliefs based upon his or her experiences in development and living.

The World Image or Map may also be considered a heuristic device for living. It is a very complex psychical construction. Being partly conscious, and partly unconscious, it is made up of many smaller images, beliefs, rules, likes, habits, and dislikes, and is based in neurological and cultural constraints. Paul Watzlawick, who coined the term, offers a definition of the World Image and attempts to clarify the complexity of this image.

> We must think of a world image...as the most comprehensive, most complex synthesis of the myriads of experiences, convictions, and influences, of their interpretations, of the resulting ascription of value and meaning to the objects of perception which an individual can muster....It is not *the world*, but a mosaic of single images which may be interpreted in one way today and differently tomorrow; a pattern of patterns; an interpretation of interpretations; the result of incessant decisions about what may and what may not be included in these meta-interpretations which in themselves are consequences of past decisions.[10]

Although our World Image may guide us, shape us, and orient us in life, not all World Images are of equal value for healthy living. Our cognitive maps serve as metaphors or models of reality. They are not the reality itself; there is a difference between how we experience and interpret the world, and how it is in itself *(an sich)*. This is what Alfred Korzybski meant with his famous dictum that "a map is not the territory it represents, but if correct, it has a similar structure to the territory, which accounts for its usefulness".[11] All cognitive maps are incomplete representations, but some maps are too incomplete to permit health; they even generate or support a pathologic process. When the shaman removes an illness-causing spirit from his patient, something in the patient's map changes, particularly that portion of the map that deals with the belief of oneself as invaded by a disease-causing object. When the shaman extracts or exorcises the invading force, a shift in imagery and belief is effected which brings about relief in the patient. As the philosopher Paul Ricoeur said, "Change the directive image and you may change the person".[12] The shaman, who has a richer World Image, a richer cognitive mapping of ordinary and non-ordinary reality, is able to manipulate the cognitive constraints of his patient, and even expand them. The shaman can also juxtapose pieces of tribal mythology or conscious cultural belief in a way that brings about therapeutic change. I recall the story of Sudhir Kakar of an old temple healer in India who told the father of a daughter (who suffered from incest anxiety) to marry her off quickly so that the "daughter-fucker" demon wouldn't attack her.[13] Rather than directly address the collapsing barriers of the incest taboo, the healer reframes the problem as one of potential demon possession; that is, the father is given an explanation in an idiom he is familiar with (but did not think of as an explanation for his daughter's anxieties and nightmares). This hermeneutic move adds a spiritual urgency which motivates the father to take action to protect his daughter (forestalling the possibility of abuse, and at the same time, reducing the daughter's anxiety and thus her disturbing nightmares).[14] This would not be recommended treatment in our own modern Western context, as few therapists would ignore the daughter's choices and needs in such a situation. However, the case does reveal a tricksterish method of getting beyond the patient's cognitive constraints.

In modern psychotherapy, regardless of the school, some sort of change is sought. People come with some type of problem they want fixed, some type of burden they want lifted, some type of pain they want relieved. Cognitive therapists speak of "cognitive restructuring", and Freudian psychoanalysts speak of "remembering, repeating, working through", and becoming mature and adult. Humanistic therapies aim at some kind of growth or self-realization. Jungians talk of pathology as a one-sidedness in the ego's perspective and of therapy as aiming at deep psychic transformation (death/rebirth) in which the opposites are brought and held together in tension (a kind of wholeness).

The traditional shaman's method is based upon his or her own interior journeys into the non-ordinary reality. There the shaman encounters a different perspective, one which is comparatively greater than that permitted by typical social and individual constraints. Out of the experience of the non-ordinary reality, the shaman creates a much richer map of reality than the one provided by his or her society's myth (cosmology). An analogy can be drawn from Jungian psychology. The realm of non-ordinary reality would correspond to the collective unconscious. Every culture's mythology and symbolism is patterned upon archetypes. The concrete imagery of each society is like the particular clothing. The archetypes are different from the clothing, and can be experienced and expressed in a multitude of ways. The shaman's journey into non-ordinary reality is like a descent into the collective unconscious. There the shaman encounters universal structures and processes which are not culture-specific, but which transcend the culture's clothing and its local social mapping. The shaman discovers the arbitrariness of social and individual definitions (constraints of reality). The shaman draws upon his or her own richer mapping (World Image) based upon his or her experience of non-ordinary reality, for the purpose of expanding the patient's World Image. Regardless of what it is called or how it is understood, regardless of whether it is wrought by a psychotherapist, shaman, or other doctor of the soul, some kind of therapeutic change is aimed at by challenging or influencing the World Image of the patient.

The shaman, then, by virtue of his or her calling, initiation, training, and frequent journeys and mappings of non-ordinary

reality, creates, revises, and maintains a richer model of reality
than his/her patients. As an expander of the patient's World
Image, the shaman is something of a trickster–shape-shifter, able
to juxtapose meanings, elude the defensive definitions of reality
rigidly adhered to by the patient, and influence the patient's
underlying map of reality. I have written elsewhere of a Yoruban
shaman who treated a mentally ill young man, which illustrates
the shaman operating to expand the World Image.[15]

> The patient was reportedly suffering from a psychotic disor-
> der, according to my informant. The shamanic ritual
> involved the preparation of an elaborate shrine, and the
> bringing of his patient and family into the shrine. The
> shaman began by reciting the myth of the origins of the con-
> flict of Good and Evil, and of the triumph of Good, thus set-
> ting the patient's inner and interpersonal battle in a
> spiritually meaningful cosmological or mythic context. The
> shaman then reportedly induced trance in himself and the
> patient's family, and commanded the family to become psy-
> chotic, that is, to begin acting "crazy". The shaman obtained
> a diagnosis in trance from conversing with ancestral spirits.
> As the patient's family members are imitatingly convulsing
> all around him (mimicking the patient's bizarre gestures and
> behaviors), the shaman tells the patient his genealogy, and
> about his ancestors and how they had overcome evil and
> adversity. Each ancestor's admirable qualities were
> recounted before informing the patient how they overcame
> certain adversities. This instruction also included explaining
> how the patient had become wounded when he was aban-
> doned by his father, while very young. According to my
> informant, the patient came out of the "psychosis" when,
> watching his family in a crazy frenzy, and listening to the
> shaman's instruction, he suddenly realizes he has been act-
> ing strangely different from everybody else.

This "crazy" patient reportedly did not self-perceive his illness with its context-specific (consensually considered) bizarre
behavior and style of thinking as unusual to his social group. It
was, in the language of psychoanalysis, ego-syntonic. The patient's
own internal mapping (World Image) apparently did not permit
him to see that certain features of his psychological functioning

and behavior were sick. The shaman challenges this image by the combined use of elements which resemble family therapy (participation of concerned family members), psychodrama (having the family become "crazy"), and explanation of the origins of the patient's personal wounding (abandonment). All this was integrated in a narrative rooted in an ancestral genealogy, and integrated with a sacred tribal myth of the victory of good over evil. The theme that good can be victorious over evil is used by the shaman in a way which says, at the level of the World Image, that positive change or transformation is possible. The use of the family to dramatically act out the patient's craziness gave the patient a visual, kinesthetic, and emotional reflection of what strange behavior must be like. In seeing his family act radically different from the way they normally do (that is, like him), the patient was able to render his own image of his behavior into an ego-dystonic position, thus viewing it as strange (i.e., sick). In Jungian terms, the ritual helps the patient to see his own complex-driven and related behavior in bold dramatic contrast. The father complex is consciously accessed and rendered ego-dystonic, and after being consciously understood, is now an influence which the patient wants to change. The shaman, through his recitations, persuaded the patient that his condition (illustrated by his family) could be changed, for "his ancestors were victorious", as were the tribal divinities "at the beginning of time" (inspiring hope). Thus the shaman integrates a variety of elements, cosmological, cultural-ancestral, familial, and individual, into the ritual in a way which overloaded the patient's defenses of his own restrictive World Image, and allowed it to be expanded. Only after the patient recognized he had been acting crazy, according to my informant, was the patient able to switch off his craziness and become normal.

RITUAL IMAGE AND BRAIN ASSYMETRY

The Yoruban shaman's method is a classic example of the therapeutic employment of imagery intensified by the use of ritual sonic driving and explanatory narrative to challenge the patient's World Image. Through the ritual performance with its evocation of all sensory channels, through use of incense, fire, sacred space, chanting, familial and social participation, rhythm, and trance, the shaman acts dramatically upon the patient's imagination to forge a pathway into those cognitive and neurobiological correlates which drive the chaotic behavior, and turns it off. Conversely, by the same imaginal technology the shaman is able to access and turn on the appropriate ordering structures.

Psychological, spiritual, and neurological correlates are involved. Let us consider the neurobiological correlates. We have already noted that images interact and influence tissues and communicate with cells. We have even mentioned that images access various neuropathways in the brain which can lead to the development of sickness as well as to its cure. In ritual process, image acts upon image to bring about cognitive, affective, and behavioral change. In thinking about what neurobiological processes might be involved in this ritual action of image upon image to effect psychological and somatic change, we might think in terms of brain assymetry.

Paul Watzlawick guesses that the World Image has its neurological locus in the non-dominant hemisphere of the brain's neocortex (normally the right hemisphere). The dominant hemisphere appears to translate perceptions and experiences into logical-digital-analytic and semantic representations, some of which are partly conscious, some which aren't. The non-dominant hemisphere is quite different. It is specialized in holistic-representing and communicates in terms of images, relationships, patterns, structures and configurations. It operates in a more intuitive-holistic mode, and seems to be more closely wired to the phylogenetically older sections of the brain which have to do with instinct, ritual, emotion, and autonomic functioning. The *pars pro toto* principle seems to characterize the operations of the non-dominant hemisphere. That is, things can be recognized or associated on the basis of parts in relation to the whole. All sensory functions operate on the pars pro toto basis. A single chord or note of a symphony can evoke recognition of the identity of the piece because it relates that piece to the entire musical pattern. A scent can evoke recall of an event which, once recalled, is perceived internally with all sensory modes. Watzlawick notes that good caricature drawings are based upon the pars pro toto principle, requiring the strictest economy of line to evoke recognition of the personality suggested by the visual abbreviation. The non-dominant hemisphere is more accessible through the employment of visual, acoustic, olfactory, gustatory, rhythmic, tactile, and other stimuli associated with movement.

An insight into the power of ritual to effect dramatic psychological changes follows from this understanding of the World Image as having its probable locus in the non-dominant hemisphere. If the World Image has its locus there, then ritual, with its strong use of visual, acoustic, aesthetic-dramatic, symbolic, and olfactory-gustatory stimuli, aims to activate pathways of access to, and influence on, the World Image by circumventing the dominance of the dominant hemisphere, and to influence the gestalt structures and processes by which the World Image is generated and maintained (in the non-dominant hemisphere).

If the non-dominant hemisphere speaks the language of figure, symbol, gestalt, and image, if it speaks the language of dreams, fantasies, myths, fairy tales, daydreams, active imaginings, and delusions and hallucinations, why not seek to speak back to it and influence it on its own terms? This is what shamanic ritual does. It speaks to the psyche, to the World Image, to the non-dominant hemisphere in its own language, and is able to circumvent the linguistic-analytic-rational totalitarianism of the dominant hemisphere, which tends to ignore it. Ernst Rossi, a Jungian analyst and hypnotherapist, has equated the non-dominant hemisphere with the unconscious, the archetypal substrate. This is a position which we shall partially disagree with, following Anthony Steven's, Victor Turner's, Robert L. Moore's, Douglas Gillette's, and even Jung's suggestions that the collective unconscious has its roots in the phylogenetically older parts of the brain.

THE REPTILIAN BRAIN AND THE COLLECTIVE UNCONSCIOUS IN RITUAL

The World Image, and the ritual which acts upon it, involve neurological structures which are of a phylogenetically much older evolution. While psychology has been preoccupied with the study of psychological process involving the neocortex; biologists, ethologists, and other non-psychological researchers have been accumulating evidence for the importance of the phylogenetically much older portions of the brain, in human behavior. The older structures are not defunct. They are well integrated and interrelated with the higher cortical functions. The strongest research in support of the importance of the influence of the older portions of our neuroanatomy has come from Paul MacLean, former chief of the Laboratory of Brain Evolution and Behavior at the National Institute of Mental Health. MacLean describes the brain as having a triune structure, being composed of three distinguishable but related systems which are each active and influential in psychological functioning. These three systems have been named to correspond with their evolutionary ascendancy; the reptilian brain (also called the R-complex), mostly associated with the brain stem; the paleomammalian brain (associated mostly with the limbic system); and the neo-mammalian brain (the cerebral cortex). The cerebral hemispheres with their bilateral specializations, are of a phylogenetically more recent development, associated with cognition, sophisticated perceptual processes, as distinguished from affective and instinctual behavior.

Underlying the neocortex is the system of subcortical structures known as the midbrain which includes the limbic system, hypothalamus, and the hormone-regulating pituitary gland. As discussed above, the limbic system mediates and records emotional experiences which impact the hypothalamus and pituitary systems, which in turn regulate the capacity for sickness and health throughout the organism. As homeostatic mechanisms, the pituitary and hypothalamic systems maintain sensitive control of hormone levels, and balance hunger's satiation, sexual desire/gratification, thirst/fluid retention, and sleep/wakefulness. At the state of evolution in which this part of the brain developed, emotions had emerged and become important, especially fear and anger, and the associated fight/flight behavioral responses. There is some low-grade level of conscious experience, most likely in the form of awareness of vague and intuitive images, kinesthetic awareness, and other forms of preverbal language, and no doubt is an important source of imagery, and of the affective tone charging and surrounding imagery. It is apparently the role of the neocortex to consciously elaborate and process this imagery and give linguistic meaning and expression to it, if possible. Both hemispheres, not just the non-dominant one, are involved in the elaboration of meaning and expression.

As we descend deeper into the neuro-archaeological layers we come to the reptilian brain (R-complex), which includes a system of related structures known as the brain stem, shared by all vertebrates. It contains various nuclei and neuro-chemicals which control vital autonomic processes, cardiovascular and respiratory systems, as well as the ascending recticular activating system (ARAS) which is responsible for alertness and the arousal and maintenance of consciousness. It plays an important role in sleep/wake cycles. At the evolutionary stage in which the reptilian brain emerged, emotions apparently had not emerged, nor had cognitive awareness of past and future events. The behavioral functions and responses rely primarily upon the basis of instinct and are apparently automatic. What little psychic awareness there might have been was a slave to precedent, the demands of the animal body, and its instinctive attunement to environmental stimuli. Behavior associated with the R-complex includes territoriality, dominance-threat-display rituals, mating rituals, aggression, establishment of social hierarchies, and dominance behaviors.

These various levels of the brain, while having their own system of neuronal pathways and neurochemistry, interact and mutually influence the other systems. There is much ritualistic behavior mediated by the R-complex, and this fact probably suggests that rituals originate in the R-complex and are further modified by the emotional factors added by the limbic system, and by the cognitive activity of the neocortex. While the neocortex, especially the dominant hemisphere, has the greatest freedom from the lower instinctual and emotional centers, it does partially affect and direct the lower systems, as well as being partially affected by them. As Sagan has pointed out, this is observable in much political behavior. The themes of social hierarchies, dominance, aggression, and territoriality do characterize much political behavior. However, neither the R-complex nor the mammalian substructures could construct the Bill of Rights of the United States Constitution. Modern politics presupposes open communication between the higher and lower brain systems.

If the phylogenetically older brain, termed the "hot brain" by James Olds, resembles the Freudian id, in its functioning in accord with the pleasure principle, and in its impulsivity and demanding behavior, the neocortex, or "cold brain," is more rational and susceptible to social conditioning, and could be said to function on the basis of the reality principle. It appears to be responsible for mediating the passions of the hot brain with those demands of the external environment. In this way the brain seeks to achieve some type of balance between opposing systems. Insofar as they are different, there are difficulties in evoking integration. According to Jung, one of the functions of dreams, curative rituals, and psychotherapy was to reconcile the more archaic parts of our organism with the most recent, that is, to facilitate integration of oppositions and polarities.

JUNGIAN PERSPECTIVES: RECONCILING WITH THE TWO-MILLION-YEAR-OLD PERSON INSIDE

Anthony Stevens, Jungian analyst and psychiatrist, has argued that Jung's clinical and psychological intuitions anticipated much of the recent research into neuroanatomy and neurophysiology of the brain. In his book, *Archetypes: A Natural History of the Self,* Stevens attempts to show the neurobiological basis of Jung's psychology. Of particular interest to our discussion at this point is Stevens' drawing of our attention to the way Jung's psychology is congruent with the findings of both the split-brain research into the specializations of the hemispheres of the neocortex, and also with MacLean's convincing theories on the phylogenetically older portions of the brain. Unlike Ernst Rossi, who has located the archetypes in the right hemisphere, Stevens suggests that it is more likely to be the phylogenetically older brain systems which are the probable loci of the archetypes, although the process of archetypal experience in the non-dominant hemisphere is likely.[16] Stevens argues that this is more in keeping with Jung's view that if the archetypal systems could be given a biological locis, they would have to be in these phylogenetically much older parts of the brain.[17] Stevens cautions, however, that it is not really possible to limit the locus of an archetype to any one neurological site. Stevens is no doubt aware of more recent neuropsychological research showing the way various systems are interconnected with various neurobiological structures, preventing the determination of the precise locus or seat of specific perceptual processes in many cases. Theories on neuroanatomy currently stress an inter-relational pattern of brain structures in processes which seem simple. No doubt archetypal processes follow this pattern of interconnection with various systems, and various levels of phylogeny. According to Stevens:

> Inasmuch as one archetypal system can be differentiated from another, each must have a complex and widely ramifying neurological substrate involving millions of neurons in the brain stem and limbic system (the instinctive or biological pole) and both cerebral hemispheres (the psychic or spiritual pole). When one considers which of the two hemispheres is more appropriate to processing of archetypal components, one can agree with Rossi that it must be the right: Jung's concepts of the collective unconscious and symbol are more closely associated with the use of imagery, gestalt and visuospacial characteristics or right hemispheric functioning.[18]

The view of Henry and Stephens that the left (dominant) hemisphere can inhibit communication from the right, and that both hemispheres can inhibit communication from the limbic system, and thus suppress those communicational processes which are essential to psychic and physical health, sounds much like the defensive-dissociative functioning of the ego. For Jung, the ego is essential to actualization of the Self. However, Jung believed it tended to become estranged from the deeper unconscious and bodily processes, and from the archetypal Self. The aim of Jungian analysis is to bring the ego into relation with these deeper processes, that is, to integrate deep archaic process with ego-structure. Jung believed that dreams served to facilitate an integration between the ego and the unconscious, on the psychological level. According to Stevens, this translates into neurobiology as the integration of the limbic and older systems with the processes of both hemispheres of the cerebral cortex. The theory that dreams may represent information originating in the older parts of the brain, and passing via the right hemisphere during the REM sleep stage, has been suggested by researchers such as Galin and Henry and Stephens.[19] Evidence for this view is suggested by Jouvet's findings that low voltage–high frequency EEG waves characteristic of the dream state of sleep originate in the brain stem, and that they proceed upwards via neural pathways which extend through the limbic system to the surface of the neocortex. This view provides support for Jung's and other depth psychologists' view that dreams come from the archaic depths of the psyche.

Jung argued that the psyche has a teleological thrust which quests for integration and integrity, and that the psyche strives for the reconciliation and integration of opposites. For Jung, psychological wholeness means consciously striving to integrate all kinds of oppositions, masculine and feminine, conscious and unconscious, mental and physical, the phylogenetically older and more recent. The breaking up of the psyche's integrity, or the failure to achieve integration, characterizes Jung's understanding of psychopathology. While the goal of Jungian therapeutics is integration of polar oppositions (integration as conjunction of opposites rather than fusion), the psyche, whether it is in therapy or not, quests for integration; for wholeness. The unconscious is continually prompting the ego to become aware of irreconciled oppositions, and to embrace them. The prompting, largely conceptualized as the promptings of the archetypal Self, typically comes in non-verbal imagistic-symbolic forms, such as dreams, fantasies, symptoms, and pathological behaviors. The deep psyche (or Self) is constantly critiquing the ego by way of images, symbols, and symbolic impulses, in an effort to get it to come into relation with the contents represented or embodied in such imagery and symbolism. Jung's own method of therapy sought to listen and respond to the proverbial imagery emerging from the unconscious. Understood on the neurobiological level, Jung believed that the purpose of dreams was to promote integrations of lower with higher neurophysiological processes. In terms of our discussion of the triune brain, a Jungian view would argue that the purpose of dreaming is to facilitate the reconciliation of reptilian and limbic processes with those occurring in the cerebral hemispheres.

The reptilian brain, which, we have noted, is typically a slave to precedent, that is, to instinct, and which is engaged in cold-blooded processes, in social-hierarchical dominance and in ritualized behaviors, often emerges into dream and fantasy in the form of reptilian imagery. The warm-blooded animals which appear in some shamanic imagery, as well as in modern dreams, could likewise be interpreted as representations of processes and energies deriving from the limbic system.[20] Dreams put us in touch with our phylogenic past, with our reptilian and mammalian ancestry. Jung, believing his task was to put the two-million-year-old man inside us in reconciliation with the ego, believed that psychopathology could be characterized as arising from the loss of "contact with our instincts, with the age old unforgotten wisdom stored up in us. And where do we make contact with the age old unforgotten wisdom stored up in us? In our dreams."[21]

For Jung, the psyche was every bit as much a self-regulating system as the body:

> Every process that goes too far immediately and inevitably calls forth compensations, and without these there would be neither a normal metabolism nor a normal psyche. In this sense we can take the theory of compensation as a basic law of psychic behavior.[22]

Jung's therapeutic methods of writing down dreams, journaling, active imagination, and dramatic symbolic enactment in music, sculpture, and painting, with respect to dream and other imagery emerging from the unconscious, could be understood as an attempt to enhance the importance or vividness of the images, and thus enhance their compensatory effect upon consciousness. However, Jung believed the image had a beneficial effect whether it was consciously understood or not, since images can alter moods. In fact, most of what takes place in shamanic ritual is effective without much of it being consciously understood. It is image acting upon image, which in turn acts upon psyche and body through neurophysiological processes. But Jung believed the participation of consciousness to be important for persons undergoing an analytically assisted individuation process. The analytic rituals involving dream journaling, active imagination, and amplification by mythological parallel were aimed at enhancement of integration with the content embodied in such images, and they helped to facilitate, on the neurological level, integration between cerebral hemispheres. Rossi's view that ritual, prayer, mantra, and mandala act similarly by promoting bilateral hemispheric integrations, can be extended by Stevens' view that bilateral hemispheric integration also means integration with the phylogenetically older portions of the brain. Recently, the work of Robert L. Moore, Jungian analyst and psychologist of religion, and of mythologist Douglas Gillette has extended the views of Jung and Stevens on the connections between the archetypal energies accessed by the healer and their correlate neurobiological bases in the brain. We turn now to a discussion of their work.

THE MAGICIAN ARCHETYPE, RITUAL, AND NEUROBIOLOGY

If ritual has the power to activate and deactivate powerful archetypal energies, switching them on and off, the capacity to effectively and safely do this would seem to be rooted in special archetypal structures, and in the correlate neurobiology of the brain. According to Moore and Gillette, the ritual mastery and skill of the shamans presupposes the ability to access such an archetypal structure, which enables the shaman or the psychotherapist to be a healer. Moore and Gillette argue that there is no archetype of the shaman, but, rather, a more fundamental archetype of the mature masculine, and mature feminine, which they call the magician (or magus).[23] The shaman is the highest expression of this archetype.

Before we say more about the magician archetype in relation to ritual process and leadership, we shall first place the archetype in the broader context of their theory. Moore and Gillette have been seminal thinkers and major theorists in the so-called men's movement of today, and have been developing a systematic view of the mature masculine based upon a Jungian view of archetypal structures. They claim there are four archetypes of the mature masculine self: the king, warrior, magician, and lover.[24] Although we can't go into the considerable complexities of their analyses of these archetypes, we shall review their salient features.

Each archetype of the mature masculine correlates with an archetype of the mature feminine, and both sexes have both masculine and feminine archetypes, in a Jungian view. We will be concerned here only with the descriptions of the archetypes of the mature masculine because that is what Moore and Gillette focus their analyses on, and because it will help simplify a subject which is already too Byzantine. In Moore's and Gillette's view, each archetype has a high and low expression. The highest expression of the archetype is positive and creative; the lowest expression of the archetype is one of the bipolar shadow expressions of the archetype, and tends to be destructive. The archetypal king, in its highest expression, represents the center of the personality, what Jung refers to as the archetypal Self. It is an archetype of balance, order, and of fertility, nurturance, and guidance, serving its subordinates and taking pride in their accomplishments. In its lower shadow expression, it can be jealous, even murderous (Herod the King, King Saul). The archetype of the warrior, in its highest expression, is characterized by disciplined aggression, subservience to a higher principle, is goal focused, and tends to vigorously defend boundaries of king, kingdom, and people. In its lowest expression it can be wantonly aggressive, even raping (Bosnia) and murderous (Lt. Calley at My Lai). The archetype of the lover, in its highest expression, is emotionally warm, passionate, aesthetic, deeply sensual, vital, and playful. It can be a connoisseur. In its lowest expressions it becomes obsessive and addictive (Don Juanish promiscuity, substance abuse), and/or impotent. The archetypal magician is a knower and a master of technologies. In its highest expressions, this archetype is socially creative and often healing, such as we find in the activities of great ritual elders, the shamans, and also in scientists, doctors, lawyers, and others who have specialized knowledge and use it for the social good. In its lowest shadow expressions it can be self-serving and manipulative, exploiting others with its power and knowledge, and it can get others into a crazy mess (mad scientists, and the not-so-mad nuclear physicists who begged their innocence when their ingenious research was turned into a weapon of mass destruction). Taken together, the four archetypes of the mature masculine interact with and regulate each other, and although in the mature masculine personality, the warrior, magician, and lover should be subordinate to the king, they are all part of the integral wholeness of the personality.

Moore's and Gillette's reflections on the neurobiological basis for these archetypes is indebted to MacLean and Stevens. The archetypes of the mature masculine for humans (as well as for all primates), while augmenting the more basic instincts and prehuman archetypal patterns of the reptilian brain (R-complex), are rooted in the limbic structures of the paleomammalian brain. In addition to the neurological structures of the limbic system mentioned above in reference to MacLean and Stevens, Moore draws attention to MacLean's division of the limbic system into three primary subsystems:

1. the affiliative/attachment subsystem
2. the autonomy/aggression subsystem
3. the integration/inhibition subsystem[25]

The affiliative/attachment subsystem, as its name suggests, is responsible for general mammalian tendencies to form social units characterized by affection, nurture, play, and psychosocial interdependence and collaboration. It seems to arise, along with other species-specific structures of affiliation, in the area of the cingulate gyrus. The autonomy/aggression subsystem is concerned with exploration, fear, frightening and defensive strategies, and self-preservation behavior. It appears to be mediated by the amygdaloid complex, and there is evidence that in primates, hierarchically ordering behaviors arise through the mediation of the amygdala. Moore and Gillette speculate that the autonomy/aggressive impulse enables humans to form cohesive selves through adversity.[26] The integration/inhibition subsystem is apparently mediated by the septum and hippocampus that MacLean believes to be the integrative center for the entire central nervous system. The hippocampus is considered a gate mechanism and is apparently responsible for regulating, modulating, prioritizing, and arranging data from other aspects of the nervous system in an integrative way. Moore and Gillette discuss the location of the archetypes, especially of the archetypes of the mature masculine, within these three limbic subsystems distinguished by MacLean:

> It seems clear that what we call the *Lover* arises originally in the affiliative/attachment subsystem, and our *Warrior* arises in the autonomy/aggression subsystem. The *Magician* (which some other psychologies mistake for the Ego) arises in the integration/inhibition subsystem at its interface with neocortical structures. We'd locate the Ego within the neocortex proper. This maintains the Ego's status as the apparent center of waking consciousness. Here it is separate from the Magician, but more closely related to this archetype than it is to the Lover or Warrior.
>
> The King manifests as the integrated, mature functioning of all neocortical and limbic subsystems. Though it seems to arise in the septal-hippocampal subsystem, it transcends this subsystem's gate keeping functions. More than a regulator, the King embraces the Warrior, Magician, and Lover in an integrated, constitutive manner.[27]

Moore and Gillette believe that these human archetypes arise in the limbic system and are then elaborated and refined by the neocortex. In respect to cerebral assymetry, both hemispheres are believed to be involved; either the left brain's rational, logical functions, or the right brain's intuitive holistic functions, or both, are involved. The rationally strategic and emotionally detached modes of the warrior and magician suggest primary mediation by the left brain, and secondary mediation by the right brain. The aesthetic, visually oriented, sensuous, and intuitive modes of the lover suggest primary mediation through the right brain, and secondary mediation through the left brain. The king may draw upon both hemispheres equally.

Moore and Gillette suggest that the frontal lobes may be involved in giving humane form to the archetypes, since they are responsible for mediating empathic and altruistic emotions and refined cognitive processes. The ego, while more associated with the left brain processes, actually seems to draw upon both hemispheres. It may experience the archetypes as numinously other because their sources are neurologically located so much deeper than the sources of ego-consciousness.

We mentioned that Moore and Gillette claim that there is no archetype of the shaman, but only an underlying archetype of the magician. Now that we have placed that archetypal structure in the broader context of Moore's and Gillette's work on the archetypes of the mature masculine, and have discussed their views of the relation of these archetypes to brain structure, we can turn to a discussion of the nature of shamanism and ritual mastery in terms of their work. In Chapter 2 we mentioned Moore's earlier work on the ritual elder in conjunction with our discussion of anthropologist Victor Turner's views of ritual structure and process. We noted that Moore found in Van Gennep and Turner an insightful mapping of the structure of transformative ritual process involving three phases: separation, transition (liminality), and incorporation. Moore credits Turner for the special attention given to the importance of the middle phases of liminality, in which previous cognitive and psychological structures are deconstructed and reconstructed as they come into contact with the powerful transformative energies of the sacred.

Turner's theory serves as a foundation for Moore's own thought about ritual mastery. Following Eliade, Otto, and others, Moore has underscored the potential danger of sacred energies, arguing that if they are not carefully and safely accessed, they may destroy or dissolve ego-structure, leading to chaos and serious pathology, rather than to creative transformation. Moore also adds to Turner's insights by drawing our attention to the importance of how sacred-transformative space is constituted, being demarcated by strong boundaries and properly stewarded. Moore believes that only a knowledgeable ritual elder, who can effectively constitute and maintain strong boundaries around sacred space, can help facilitate deep structural change psychologically, socially, or spiritually. Moore likens the importance of strong boundaries to the *vas bene clausum,* the well-sealed vessel of alchemy, which is necessary to protect and insure deep transformation.

According to our discussion of Moore and Gillette, it is the magician archetype which is accessed by the shaman, which makes his or her ritual mastery possible. This archetype has a two-fold aspect: 1) magician as "knower of deep and mysterious things", and magician as "master of technology".[28] As a "knower," the person embodying the magician archetype is an initiant and master of secret and hidden knowledge of all kinds. Moore and Gillette do not limit this archetype to shamans, medicine men and women, *brujos,* and other healers or ecstatics, but, interestingly, include modern men and women who seek and possess special valuable knowledge: scientists, medical doctors, engineers, lawyers, and the like. The magician as an archetype is accessible to all. But it is the shaman and other ritual masters which concern us here, for their accessing of it is essential to the effectiveness of their craft. The second aspect, master of technology, is salient in the shaman's ritual knowledge and wisdom. It is the knowledge of how things work combined with the skill to make them work which characterizes the shaman as a master of ritual technology.

Moore interprets the capacity to safely employ therapeutic ritual process as involving what, in analytic parlance, is called an observing ego. Without an observing ego, the dangerous energies of the sacred, and of the numinosity of the psychic libido, can possess and melt away important ego-structure. Neurobiologically, this can be understood as a deactivation or switching off of higher neocortical centers as lower limbic and reptilian centers take over. Moore laments that although we live in an age of magicians, that is, of scientists, engineers, and other specialists, this archetype is all too often not safely and appropriately accessed by psychologists, psychotherapists, ministers, and others whose concern is for the care and transformation of the human soul:

> Ours is, we believe, the age of the Magician, because it is a technological age. It is the age of the Magician at least in his materialistic concern with having power over nature. But in terms of the nonmaterialistic, psychological, or spiritual initiatory process, the Magician energy seems to be in short supply.[29]

Moore believes the issue of the danger of sacred space has not received enough attention by persons in the helping professions. The libidinal and numinous energies of the psyche require strong protective boundaries. If they are accessed without due ritual care, psychic chaos and rebellion can result. Moore likens the sacred energies to a nuclear generating power station. The energies must be carefully approached and respected, if disastrous results are to be avoided. He draws attention to the way encounter groups of the 1960s and 1970s sometimes activated powerful energies which were not contained, leading to psychological decompensation and destruction of the group. Again he illustrates the danger of lack of containment in reference to the powerful energies which are sometimes unleashed at rock concerts, leading to pandemonium, and sometimes to violence. He also gives another amusing metaphor based upon Walt Disney's *Fantasia*, in which Mickey Mouse desires to take the easy way out of his predicament of having to mop the workroom of his master, the sorcerer. Without the knowledge and skill, Mickey performs an incantation to get the mop and bucket to do the job for him. What happens is the now familiar image of the mop and buckets getting out of hand, multiplying, and creating pandemonium. After all, Mickey is just an apprentice, not a master. When powerful energies are activated without ritual knowledge and skill, Moore argues, the destructive unleashing of energy is the result. The psychotherapist today who wishes to effect profound psychological and spiritual transformation would do well to learn from the ritual mastery of the shamans, who have always embodied the magician archetype in their practice. Proper accessing of archetypal energies to turn archetypes on or off requires firm ego-structure. This ego-structure is a by-product of considerable knowledge, experience, and discipline.

The knowledgeable ritual elder is able to access and turn on the magician archetype in its highest form, and thus activate a safe pathway between the neocortical substrate of the ego and the limbic substructures of the integration/inhibition subsystem. Although Moore and Gillette don't say so, we could add that the ritual process of the shaman facilitates a controlled trance that safely structures the access to archetypes and their related natural structures. The shaman does not only turn on the magician within, he or she also accesses the compassionate energies of the lover, the fierce focus and dedication of the warrior (who fights sickness-causing enemies on the patient's behalf), and the balance and integrative-ordering skills of the king. The shaman thus accesses all the archetypes of the mature masculine and the related neural structures in an intentional and disciplined way. The shaman's ecstatic trance allows him or her to turn on the needed archetypal resources in his or her self, and to turn off or on the needed archetypal and related neural resources in the patient.

It may well be that powerful transformative rituals activate massive amounts of neural tissues and neural pathways. In view of our discussion of the relation between archetypes and ego-structure, and their neurobiological correlates in the hemisphere of the neocortex and in the three limbic subsystems, it appears that ritual acts do intensify imagery in a way that activates these systems. Ritual, and the ritual intensification of imagery, can be so evocative because it employs a variety of stimuli to all the sensory pathways at once, thus overloading the trophotropic and argotrophic systems of both hemispheres, and activating deep limbic substructures. The visual pathways are activated by such things as fire, candlelight, costume, sacred shrine architecture and symbolism. The kinesthetic pathways are activated by dramatic enactment, dance, and rhythm. The auditory pathways are activated by sacred music, chant, and the sonic driving of drumming. The olfactory pathways are activated by the smells of smoke, incense, and herbs, and the gustatory pathways by ritual meals, medicinal substances, and the like. All this activation opens up powerful psychic and emotional pathways. Additionally, emotional pathways are stimulated by the caring presence of the shaman, by the loving presence of the extended family and sometimes the whole tribe at the ritual. All this simultaneous multisensory stimulation helps the shaman to intensify imaginal activity and to forge into pathways that access deep archetypal structures and their neurobiological correlates.

Any well-formed ritual has a clearly marked beginning and ending, and the shaman knows these clearly demarcated ritual boundaries serve as ritual cues for turning on and off the necessary energies on ritual cue. In this way order is brought out of chaos. All true ritual elders, whether shamans, witches, temple healers, or psychotherapists, whether playwrights, civil rights leaders, or priests, know how to access and turn on and off the necessary psychic and neurobiological systems for healing purposes.

====================

Chapter Eight

Implications for the Future

We have compared and contrasted significant areas of similarity and difference between shamanism and Jungian psychology throughout this book. We have argued that both shamanism and Jungian psychologies are theories of the soul, of its disorders, and its therapeutic treatment, and that both may be considered spiritual psychologies, or psycho-spiritual systems of healing. Both disciplines rest upon the direct immediate experience of non-ordinary dimensions of reality, the collective unconscious for Jung, and the non-ordinary three-storied cosmology of shamanism. The shamanic path could be considered, as Jung suggested, an early or archaic individuation process, and we have shown that Jungian psychology includes many shamanic elements. In this chapter we would like to explore a few implications of the Jung and shamanism dialogue for the developing of a post-modern therapeutic practice now and in the future.

We should be clear that it is impossible to practice shamanism in a strict classical form, as we live in a pluralistic society of western culture. In this pluralistic society its members do not share the same myth and belief system (beyond the myth of science). The sacred is not so broadly presupposed as to be included in the legitimized health care professions, and most individuals when ill or in crisis still automatically turn to the legitimized health care professionals, the physician, the psychiatrist or psychologist, or other doctor, to help them, and such professionals tend to use a strictly secular and scientific idiom to size up the problem (diagnosis) and treat it. The spiritual and psycho-spiritual dimensions are typically ignored in most legitimized forms of health care in the west. However, there are an increasing number of alternative health care professionals emerging whose viewpoints include the spiritual basis of health and illness, and there is a growing interest in spiritual practice amongst the growing New Age movement. These developments have much in them of the traditional assumptions, perspectives, and methods of traditional health care systems, and the soul and spirit are often taken into account in their theory of health and illness, and in their therapeutic techniques.

If the increasing number of books and seminars on shamanism is any indication, it seems that a revival of shamanism in western culture is under way. There are an increasing number of western urban shamans, influenced by Michael Harner and other teachers, who are practicing core shamanism, and who have private practices in which they do soul retrievals and extractions, and some also do psychopompery and are ordained in animistic churches. These private practitioner shamans tend to work alongside other alternative and legitimized health care professionals. Additionally, there is a growing number of psychotherapists who are also trained shamans, or who are interfacing shamanism and psychotherapy, and there is a professional journal dedicated to this interface: *The Shamanic Applications Review.*[1] These are hybrid forms of shamanism; that is, classic perspectives and techniques are interfaced in an integrative or complementary way with modern secular-scientific perspectives and methods. In this revival of shamanism there is much preoccupation with the soul, with soul loss and retrieval. The problem is that soul recovery depends for its long-term meaning and sustenance upon the sacred, and this is just what is lacking in discussions of shamanism and psychotherapy today. Without a retrieval of the sense of the sacred in western culture, efforts at soul recovery will always be limited, lacking in the power of traditional shamanic retrievals in which the entire society broadly presupposed the sacred.

TOWARD A POSTMODERN SHAMANISM

To say that shamanism, as it has been traditionally practiced, cannot be totally transferred into western culture, is not to say that it cannot be practiced in modified form, or that it cannot contribute to the therapeutic and spiritual disciplines of the west. Shamanism represents a vast array of psychological and spiritual insights and healing methods, techniques and rituals, which have evolved over thousands of years; perhaps over millions. Shamanism has always had to adapt to new conditions, be they geographic, political, social, climatic, or educative (learning new methods, sharing efficacious techniques with peers from other tribes, etc.). Even though few traditional shamans might want to affirm that they could learn something from western scientific methods, it seems clear that shamanism must learn, if it is to survive in developing societies, and that it must adapt and grow if it is to make a legitimate contribution to encroaching western society in the future. This adaptation has been one of the motivations behind the production of this book. Achterberg recommends that shamans become scientifically educated and articulate if they want to preserve their contribution to health care in the future.

The kind of contribution which shamanism can make could be considered a postmodern contribution. By postmodern, I mean an approach which is sympathetic to the good and effective aspects of modernity, its valuable methods, findings, and technologies, while rejecting or constructively criticizing what is deficient in modernity. By postmodern I also mean a perspective which seeks to preserve past perspectives and technologies which are valuable and effective, and which promote human dignity and ecological integrity, while at the same time being willing to benefit from the appropriate use of Western scientific, theological, and psychological methods. In this way, what was of value in the premodern world of traditional shamanism may be preserved and combined with what is of value from modernity. In this way, a precritical naiveté may pass into a post-critical naiveté (Ricoeur). Postmodern perspectives are developing in the Western healing professions. For example, recall the Simontons' methods to relieve anxiety, stress, and to cure cancer (or send it into remission) using visualization methods which have been used traditionally by shamans. Another example is the use of shamanic methods of visualization, music, amulets, and rituals by psychotherapists treating multiple personality disorder. Recall from earlier in Part Three that Colin Ross, a psychiatrist, and one of the world's foremost psychiatric specialists in dissociative disorders, claims that because DID/MPD patients are virtuosos at trance, and are continually in altered states, shamanic methods can be very helpful in treating the disorder.[2] Ross claims his office contains amulets, medicine bundles, and shamanic power objects, which he employs suggestively as resources in his work with MPD patients. Ross considers the psychotherapy of MPD to be a kind of prolonged shamanic ritual. Yet Ross also employs the latest scientific methods and conceptualities to understand and work with this very complex and ancient disorder. Among the modern western psychological and psychiatric methods which Ross also uses are pharmacological means, cognitive therapy, psychoanalytic methods, and hospitalization, informed by statistical studies into MPD, and the latest psychiatric differential diagnostics. Ross believes that MPD is so common (previously known as possession) and so complex, it requires a variety of theoretical perspectives, and the best of premodern and modern scientific methods and perspectives. Sandra Ingerman's adaptation of classic shamanism, as already discussed, could also be practiced alongside of, or adjunctively with, psychotherapy, for a variety of mental disorders. Psychotherapy can play a vital role in helping integrate the powerful effects and implications of shamanic healing rituals, especially soul retrieval and extraction. Psychotherapy can identify areas of soul loss and seek insight and therapeutic leverage from shamanism.

Since human life on the planet is increasingly encroaching upon and absorbing traditional societies, it seems evident that human life on the planet is moving towards a multi-cultural context which will yet be largely urban and westernized. In such developing societies as Taiwan, shamanism is becoming an urban shamanism, and is adapting to new social circumstances dictated by modernization and cultural diversity. Shamans practicing alongside western trained medical doctors often refer patients to such doctors, when the disorders are beyond their professional scope, or when their patients' disorders require medical supplementation. It may be that a postmodern urban shamanic profession can develop in American culture if it is at least respectful of its own limits, and works collaboratively as one healing profession in concert with others. Beyond collaboration there is also the possibility of mutually challenging dialogue between shamanism and other legitimized health care professions. Psychotherapy and shamanism may lead to a more spiritual psychotherapy and to a more psychologically sophisticated shamanism.

THE LOSS OF THE SENSE OF THE SACRED

We have mentioned that the major difference between the context in which the traditional shaman practiced, and that of the modern psychotherapist, has to do with the presupposition of the sacred as a *sui generis* reality, broadly assumed in traditional societies. In the modern West today, there has been a loss of the sacred from the assumptive world generally, and from the healing arts specifically. Individuals may be religious, may go to church or synagogue, or practice some other form of institutional or non-institutional religion, but other areas of life are typically encroached upon by the secular. In traditional and tribal societies, every substantial aspect or function of life had a sacred basis. As Eliade has noted, such substantial events in life were founded upon the paradigmatic acts of the gods. Their sacredness guaranteed their significance, and proper social ordering. Illness was viewed as a disruption of the proper ordering, and required that the shaman restore relations with the sacred order, helping to re-establish the proper order by placing the patient, the family, and the tribe in accordance with the will of the sacred (gods and ancestors). In tribal societies, hunting, love making, going to war, illness, and therapy all have a sacred aspect. By contrast, today's modern individual may be religious, but when it comes to consulting a doctor or psychotherapist (or dentist for that matter), there is no presupposition of the sacred. The healing professions have become secularized. We do not expect our healers to attempt to restore relations with God, the creator, or the earth. We do not expect our psychotherapist to invoke, call upon, or mediate the sacred in the therapy session. Sudhir Kakar has noted that there are many scientists and health professionals in the west who now lament the loss of the sacred from the assumptive world of patient and healer:

For the West, the home of modernism and now a state of
mind rather than a geographical region, the connection of
health with orders other than that of the body and mind no
longer exists....With the irresistible march of scientific natu-
ralism over the last one hundred years, the domain of the
clinical has been finally and firmly usurped by the doctor,
and the priest forced into exile. There are many in the West
today who regret the disappearance of the Sacred from the
healing sciences and its removal generally from the world of
everyday life.[3]

The situation of the loss of the sacred has been characterized by various existentialist philosophers, in their own idiom.
Nietzche's heralding of the death of God was prophetic of the
loss of the sense of the sacred from the assumptive world, and
from life generally, in the west. Heidegger described the withdrawal of Being from modern man as equivalent to a loss of a
sense of meaning, of mystery, and of dignity. He might as well
have called Being the sacred, for it possesses those numinous
(attracting/repelling, mysterious/ineffable) qualities we have
attributed to the sacred. Calculative thinking, economic thinking, the tendency to quantify everything, goes hand in hand with
a reductionistic materialistic science, which finds nothing but
physical, mechanical, or chemical causes. The world seen only
through the lenses of scientific-calculative thinking is a thin, dry,
hollow, surface world, devoid of mystery, depth, and meaning.
There is an existential nausea (Sartre) that comes with such a
nihilistic view of reality. Such a view is itself a symptom of deep
spiritual, social, and ecological pathology. Some face this
nihilism with stoic courage, others retreat into fundamentalistic
and traditional forms of security, where they may have some limited contact with the sacred, while still being touched by the
nihilism of the modern scientific worldview. Some seek a gen-
uine sense of the sacred to give their lives meaning and direction, but cannot find it in the institutional religions of the west.
Some turn to the numinous resources of the East, some to occult
interests; some are now turning to shamanism, others to psyche-
delics, to rekindle a sense of mystery and meaning characteristic
of the sacred.

SHAMANIC DIAGNOSIS OF WESTERN CULTURE: LOSS OF THE SACRED

A shamanic view of western culture would diagnose the culture and many, perhaps most, of its individual participants as suffering not simply from a breach of relations with the sacred, but from a lack of any effective relations with the sacred at all. This would be a new type of diagnostic category for shamanism, but it is one from which western psychotherapists could learn much. For in traditional societies, it is believed that the efforts of the shaman, or other healer, are greatly aided by the continuing presence and healing power of the sacred in their societies. The entire weight of the community's religion, objectified in its myths, history, and rituals, is brought to bear upon the patient, his or her family, and perhaps the entire community. This weight is sufficient to mobilize powerful psychic energies in the patient. The patient believes and is assured that proper relations with the sacred will be restored, that healing will occur, because he or she has the gods, ancestors, or other sacred beings and emissaries present in the sacred healing ritual. By contrast, today's western patient is diagnosed and treated often in isolation from the sacred, and from his or her family and the community. The diagnosis is typically a secular one. If it is a mental diagnosis, it sounds much like a disease one has, but one which is unrelated to matters of religious or spiritual import. The loss of the sacred in western society is also a loss of soul, a loss of the soul of the earth, of the cosmos, of human society. Modern men and women are truly in search of soul, and a retrieval of the sacred is essential to their finding or recovering soul.

Jung was also aware of the problem of the loss of the sacred in the west. In fact, his psychology is largely addressed to this problem. The appeal of Jung to so many thoughtful persons today, one surmises, is because his view of the psyche, and of therapy, presupposes the sacred (numen). The appeal is also probably based on the feeling that Jung's analytical psychology is as much a spirituality as a psychology, as much a religious path as a psychological process. Jung considered the real therapy to be the experience of the numen, and the individuation process to be a kind of myth to live by for those individuals who could not live the mythic patterns provided by the traditional institutional religions of western culture. The individuation process provides the individual with a sense of deep and meaningful ordering at the base of things. This deep underlying order which the psyche intrinsically quests for, and towards which it is driven, is akin to the sacred orderings hungered for in traditional societies. Within tribal society, myth reflects the implicit ordering of personal and communal life. Jung's view was that for many modern individuals, the Christian myth could no longer be lived by the whole person. Rather than turn to the East, Jung recommended turning to one's own psyche, going within to find a deep ordering mythic pattern to live by. Jung's personal myth seemed to be a heroic one, that is, one based upon the archetypal pattern of the hero. As the hero detaches from his familiar community or territory, goes into the unknown territory to make discoveries or find the treasure, and then returns with the boon (with his findings, treasure, etc.), so could Jung's life be interpreted as heroic, since his psychological discoveries seemed to involve this same process. The shaman's way also follows the same heroic pattern of separation, initiation into the sacred mysteries, and return with the boon (healing power, etc.). There is a heroic aspect to the individuation process as well, since it requires an ordered process of leaving one's normal state of ego-consciousness (separation), a going into the unknown depths of the unconscious to discover something of value (numen, self-knowledge, archetypal powers, etc.), and a return to normal consciousness to ethically integrate and appropriate what one discovered in one's daily living.

Jung believed that the Christian myth was based upon archetypal patterns, the same as any other religion, myth, or aspect of life. However, he felt there was a certain one-sidedness in the Christian myth which made it increasingly difficult for individuals to live it with their whole being. One-sidedness, for Jung, is characteristic of neurosis, psychological imbalance, and dissociation. Jung's critique of Christianity can be considered a psychological diagnostic in which Jung identifies the imbalances, dissociations, and pathology of Christianity.

Jung's critique of Christianity included the view that spirit was exalted over matter, that the masculine was exalted over the feminine, that the problem of the opposites had not been adequately dealt with, and that the exalted elements cast the inferior elements into the shadow realm, associated with evil and the devil. While he believed that Catholicism, with its rich tradition of symbol and ritual, could still mediate the sacred to its devotees, he believed that Protestantism exalted the word (the literal), but devalued and distrusted images, symbols, and rituals, thus creating an overemphasis upon dogma, creed, and belief, and making it more difficult for its adherents to have experience of the numinosum, or live the symbolic life.

Since Christianity was too one-sided, in Jung's view, it had to dissociate or split off parts of psychical reality not contained in its God-image and dogma. Jung believed that alchemy dealt with both sides of the polarities in a way which corrected the imbalances of Christianity. In alchemy the spiritual and the material, the masculine and the feminine, were each valued in a way which held the oppositions in some kind of tension (balance).

With Freud, Jung believed that Christianity tended to devalue the sexual and sensual, to prohibit mature thinking, and to carry psychological projections. Unlike Freud, however, Jung believed there was much more to religion than projection of a benevolent father image to bolster an immature existence overburdened with the tasks of adult living. For Jung, religion was a basic instinct, a psychological fact, and could not be fully explained by, or reduced to, psychological explanations. It was not, in itself, a necessarily neurotic phenomenon, although it could become one. For Jung, religion was fundamentally "an attitude peculiar to a consciousness which has been changed by experience of the numinosum".[4] This attitude was based upon an instinct to experience the numinosum. As an instinct, religion was as natural and powerful as the sexual or aggressive instincts. Jung's definition of religion is kept carefully separate from belief or devotion to any creed, dogma, or external code.

THE FUNCTION OF MYTH AND RELIGION

Jung believed that the religion of the European (western) indivudual was inadequate to his wholeness. He believed that much of European religion was based upon intellectual assent to creed and dogma, and did not engage the individual at the level of the heart, at the level of experience, and at the level of the unconscious. Jung also believed that the religious instinct was repressed by the modern culture of scientific rationality, dominated by ego-consciousness. The result was that modern man suffers various forms of distress and frustration, a sense of cosmic isolation and despair, attended by feelings of meaninglessness. By contrast, religion has been the heart and center of the culture of tribal societies. Out of the collective unconscious of those societies arose religious symbols and rituals which forged a house of meaning and being, within which the cosmos is viewed as reliably ordered and significant, and within which human and ecological relations with one another and with the earth and its creatures are established.

Jung argued that the sacred mythology of primitive peoples springs from the collective unconscious, as do dreams, folk art, and creative ideas. These tribal myths, he believed, were patterned upon numinous archetypes, which were themselves discernable beneath their veneer of cultural disguise (particular mythological clothing). Myths ordered and gave meaning to life, to individual and collective life in tribal societies. Such order and meaning constitute the structural core of native religious experience, which touches important areas of human life. Education in tribal societies is a kind of training or preparation for responsible adult behavior, and typically has been provided in the form of initiation rituals. One of the important discoveries Jung made in his psychological expedition into Africa, among the Elgonyi tribe, concerned the relation of archetype to myth, story, and educatory aspects of puberty rites. Jung obeserved the older men (ritual elders) instructing the young male initiants in the ethical and behavioral norms of the society by means of story telling (myths). The form of this instruction involved dramatically enacting stories about some tribal god or ancestor, whose actions were to be emulated or avoided if unethical. Jung said the underlying theme was to instruct the young men that "our ancestors had done such and such, and so shall you too!"[5] Jung's observation that the appropriate behavior was modeled upon archetypes is also supported by Mircea Eliade's observations that the acts of the tribal gods, ancestors, and culture heroes in the primordial time, form the paradigmatic acts which serve to guide younger generations in appropriate behavior, and thus provide the foundations of social order. Eliade's primordial time would correspond to the timelessness of the collective unconscious from which the paradigmatic archetypal forms spring. In this way, Jung believed the foundation of culture, education, and social order was laid down by numinous archetypal structures, which provided the mythic patterns teaching tribal members how to behave. An implication is that these patterns are not so much created *ex nihilo* but are donated from the primordial source of order in the collective unconscious, and discovered universally by various cultures the world over.

NAVAJO USE OF MYTHIC HERO AND RITUAL HEALING

If myth embodies the order and meaning-giving substance of the religious instinct, it is because it exemplifies and illustrates the foundations of ethical behavior as rooted in something greater than ego-centric consciousness. It comes from beyond consciousness. Jungian analyst Donald Sandner has devoted considerable energy to the study of Navajo mythology and healing rituals, drawing parallels with Jungian discoveries. The eastern Navajo system of religion is intrinsically bound up with ritual healing, aiming to bring individuals back into harmony with the tribal tradition and cosmic order.[6] The Navajo system of myth lies behind every healing ritual chant. Each chant consists of a mythic story usually patterned upon the cultural ancestor who had the same malady as the afflicted person. For example, if the individual suffered from arthritic swelling and pain, then the patient would recall the story of that particular hero or heroine (usually a female) and actively identify with her triumphant struggle to overcome that malady.[7]

Navajo healing rituals typically involve placing the patient on a sand painting, a type of mandala constructed of sand with symbols of the requested hero/heroine (or other mythic figures) drawn upon it with brightly dye-colored sand. The patient sits upon the sand painting while the medicine man performs the sacred chants. Although the myth is not recited, since the patient knows it already, the chant assists the patient in actively evoking a religious altered state of consciousness (RASC) to facilitate the process of inwardly identifying with the numinous healing energies of the image. Sandner stresses that such healing rituals require the patient to do more than believe in the efficacy of these sacred images to heal. The patient must actively identify with these images, must actively concentrate upon them, and must inwardly seek to appropriate their power.

COMPARISONS OF NAVAJO AND JUNGIAN METHODS OF WORKING WITH IMAGES

Sandner draws parallels between these Navajo healing rituals and Jungian psychology. Just as the Navajo patient must actively focus on what is going on, and must actively seek to appropriate the power of the images objectified in the sand painting, so must the Jungian psychotherapy patient (or analysand) actively participate and seek to appropriate the images and symbols arising from the collective unconscious, in dreams and active imagination. Sandner argues that the images and symbols must enter ego-consciousness and must be actively appropriated in the life and behavior of the patient. We might add that Jung did not employ sand paintings, although he was well aware of the Navajo technique, but he did encourage the spontaneous painting of mandalas and other images arising from the collective unconscious. He also encouraged his patients to evoke and actively work with images in other ways reminiscent of primitive healing rituals, especially in dance, drawing, and sculpture. His own tower at Bollingen was rich with carvings in stone and wood, representing work with his own images, and his attempts to take them seriously and give them some permanent form. The images and symbols produced by the unconscious are more than signs to be understood, interpreted, and then done away with. Like the Navajo, Sandner argues, Jung believed that images and symbols had a healing power in their own right. We can conclude that since Jung believed the experience of the numen was the real therapy, it is the numinosity of the image which donates its psychological-spiritual value and healing power.

JUNG'S ANSWER TO THE LOSS OF
THE SENSE OF THE SACRED

Jung visited the Taos Pueblo medicine man Ochwiay Biano, on a psychological expedition in New Mexico in 1925. The impact of that visit gave Jung a tremendous insight into the religious needs of modern man. Ochwiay Biano told Jung that he thought that white men are mad because they think with their head and not with their heart. Jung was disturbingly enlightened by this medicine man's psychological and spiritual penetration into the plight of western man. Biano characterized the white man as always restless and looking for something because of his refusal to trust his own heart. Translated in Jungian terms, Ochwiay Biano had an awareness of modern man's entrapment in the rational, intellectual, and inflated tendencies of his ego. The Pueblo way of thinking with the heart, rather than with the head, meant that they lived from a deeper center (the unconscious), and not from the center of conscious rationality (ego). Jung discovered that it was because the Pueblo lived by their mythology that they were able to live out of the heart, and find their lives whole and meaningful. This medicine man spoke to Jung with tremendous enthusiasm about his people's religion, and about the importance of the great Father Sun. He believed that there could not be another God than this, since all life on the planet required the sun's energy and benevolence in order to grow, live, and survive.

> We are a people who live on the roof of the world; we are the sons of Father Sun, and with our religion we daily help our father to go across the sky. We do this not only for ourselves, but for the whole world. If we were to cease practicing our religion, in ten years the sun would no longer rise. Then it would be night forever.[8]

Jung was greatly impressed by this religious philosophy, because it afforded the Pueblo a fullness of meaning and dignity, a larger sense of purpose, with a cosmological framework, than any religion or ideology white man believed and lived. The Taos Pueblo, like members of tribal societies everywhere, had an experience of life as meaningful because it allowed them to relate to something larger and more meaningful than themselves. In primitive societies the archetypal numinosity was still mediated through their mythologies. By contrast, the European Judeo-Christian myth had fallen into decay and was no longer livable by the whole person. For most members of western society, it was no longer a way of life, and the impoverished secular myth of science had taken over, leaving modern persons with an inflated or ego-centric acquisitiveness, rather than a way of relating to something bigger than themselves. It has always been the role of religions to relate its devotees to something transindividual, transpersonal, as the Taos Pueblo was able to care for the whole world by practicing his or her religion. Jung did not believe it was possible for a new religion to emerge which could order the life of modern man as Christianity had done in the past. He believed such a religion might emerge in several hundred years, but in the interim, it was incumbent upon modern man to find a way to live a religious life, a symbolic life. Jung believed this was possible. All that was necessary, he believed, was that each individual find a myth to live by, or a way of life that was committed to something bigger than oneself. Jung's own answer to the problem of the loss of the sense of the sacred, and to a loss of a religious way of life, was to persuade individuals to turn inward to re-establish contact with the numinous archetypal images, traditionally objectified in myth and religion. The same source which gave rise to traditional religions still exists within modern man, in the collective unconscious. Since modern man has become disillusioned with a concept of God as up there or out there, that is, as external to the self, the only solution is to turn inward, to the inner source of order and meaning.

One of the ways Jung's psychology can contribute to a postmodern shamanic function in western society is its effort to persuade individuals to turn to our origins in the collective unconscious, and there to come into living relation with the powers of the numen which can order our values, our lives, and our

behavior. The need to help estranged individuals in western culture recover a sense of life as meaningful is a task of shamanic
proportions. Knowledgeable ritual elders who know how to
evoke and safely maintain relations with the sacred, and who
know how to guide individuals through the depths of the inner
life, are urgently needed. Shamanism can help us to identify the
problem (loss of the sacred and loss of the soul) and offer ways to
think about solving it. By itself, however, it is insufficient and
requires adaptation to modern culture. The resources of Jungian
psychology offer a richer understanding, in western terms, of the
important factors, structures, and processes at work in shamanic
healing. This understanding can help us to transfer many
insights and techniques from shamanism into western psychotherapy and spiritual direction. Jung helps us to understand
how we may go about overcoming the loss of the sense of the
sacred, and reestablish a way of life that is meaningful and has
religious import in our time.

Notes

CHAPTER ONE. OVERVIEW OF CLASSIC SHAMANISM

[1] Cf. Mircea Eliade, *Shamanism: Archaic Techniques of Ecstasy* (Princeton: Princeton University Press, Bollingen Series LXXVI, 1964), p. 4; also cf. Joan Halifax, *Shamanic Voices: A Survey of Visionary Narratives* (New York: E. P. Dutton Paperbacks, 1979), p. 3

[2] Eliade, *Shamanism*, pp. 3–13

[3] Ibid., p. 5

[4] Ibid., p. 7. Eliade argues that while shamans do sometimes become accidentally possessed, this is not characteristic of their calling and trade. Eliade evidently means that they may become possessed through taboo violation or become a victim through sorcery just as other members of the tribe may become possessed. When this happens, that shaman is afflicted and requires the resources of another shaman. Cf. the conversation with anthropologist Michael Harner on this point in Gary Doore, "The Ancient Wisdom in Shamanic Cultures: An Interview with Michael Harner Conducted by Gary Doore," in Shirley Nicholson, editor, *Shamanism: An Expanded View of Reality* (Wheaton, Ill.: Quest Books, 1987), p. 9

[5] Roger Walsh, M.D., Ph.D., *The Spirit of Shamanism* (Los Angeles: Jeremy P. Tarcher, Inc., 1990), pp. 9–10

[6] Sudhir Kakar, *Shamans, Mystics, and Doctors: A Psychological Inquiry into India and Its Healing Traditions* (Boston: Beacon Press, 1982), pp. 106–116

[7] Mircea Eliade, "Shamanism: An Overview," in *The Encyclopedia of Religion*, vol. 13 (New York: Macmillan Publishing Co., 1987), p. 202

[8] Eliade, *Shamanism*, p. 13

[9] Ibid., p. 21

[10] For the shaman the middleworld is sometimes considered an ordinary realm of the earth, at other times it is considered an ecstatic realm of non-ordinary reality. This is especially true among the Polynesian shamans.

[11] Eliade, *Shamanism*, pp. 259–287

[12] John A. Grimm, *The Shaman: Patterns of Religious Healing Among the Ojibway Indians* (Norman: University of Oklahoma Press, 1987), pp. 78–82

[13] Cf. Doore, "Ancient Wisdom,"p. 9

[14] Ibid., p. 9

[15] Henri F. Ellenberger, *The Discovery of the Unconscious: The History and Evolution of Dynamic Psychiatry* (New York: Harper & Row, 1970), p. 5

[16] Jeanne Achterberg, *Imagery and Healing: Shamanism and Modern Medicine* (Boston: Shambala, 1985), pp. 4–10

[17] Janet Siskind, in Michael Harner, editor, *Hallucinogens and Shamanism* (London: Oxford University Press, 1973), pp. 33–34

[18] C. G. Jung, *The Collected Works of C. G. Jung*, 2nd edition. Translated by R.F.C. Hull (Princeton: Princeton University Press, Bollingen Series XX, 1966), vol. 13, par. 75, hereafter called Jung, CW

[19] These snake and fish dreams seem to be of common occurrence among the Cherokees, and the services of the shamans to banish them are in constant demand.

[20] Cited in Lewis Spence, "Cherokees", in *Hastings Encyclopedia of Religion and Ethics,* vol. 3 (New York: Charles Scribner's Sons, 1951), p. 505

[21] Ibid., p. 508

[22] Achterberg, *Imagery and Healing,* pp. 84–87 and 138–139

[23] See Doore, "Ancient Wisdom," p. 4

[24] Eliade, "Shamanism: An Overview", p. 203

[25] Ibid., p. 203

[26] Ibid., p. 203

[27] Ibid., p. 203

[28] Bruce L. Boyer, "Remarks on the Personality of Shamans: With Special Reference to the Apache and Mescalero Indian Reservation," *Psychoanalytic Study of Society,* vol. 2, 1962, pp. 233–254

[29] Eliade, "Shamanism: An Overview," p. 203 1962

[30] Eliade, *Shamanism,* p. 217

[31] Ibid., p. 298

[32] This information is based upon a conversation the author had with Michael Abrams on the Cherokee reservation in March, 1991.

[33] Sam Gill, "North American Shamanism," in *The Encyclopedia of Religion,* vol. 13, pp. 216–219, and Ake Hultkrantz, "A Definition of Shamanism," *Temenos* 9, 1983, pp. 25–37; and Hultkrantz, "Health, Religion, and Medicine in Native North American Traditions," in Lawrence E. Sullivan, ed., *Healing and Restoring: Health and Medicine in the World's Religious Traditions* (New York: Macmillan Publishing Co., 1989), pp. 327–358

[34] Gill, "North American Shamanism", p. 216

[35] Spence, "Cherokees", pp. 503–508

[36] Gill, "North American Shamanism", p. 216. Because these elements (shamanic flight, and skeletization, death/rebirth) frequently do not occur, Hultkrantz considers most forms of North American shamanism a pseudoshamanism. He notes that certain Eskimo and Northwest Coast tribes exhibit the classic Asian pattern, but Hultkrantz also argues that a distinguishing feature of North American shamanism is the "degree of ecstatic trance depth". He argues that those forms where the healer uses a light trance should not be considered shamanism. Cf. Hultkrantz, "Health, Religion, and Medicine," p. 334. I prefer, with Gill, to not make a judgement on the basis of the classic Asian form, but find Hultkrantz's notion of trance depth helpful in characterizing North American shamanism.

[37] Eliade, *Shamanism,* p. 298

[38] Hultkrantz, "Health, Religion, and Medicine", pp. 341–342

[39] Eliade, *Shamanism,* p. 300

[40] Hultkrantz, "Health, Religion, and Medicine", p. 341

[41] Cf. Felicitas D. Goodman, *How About Demons? Possession and Exorcism in the Modern World* (Bloomington: Indiana University Press, 1988), pp. 79–126. Goodman documents various cases of demonic possession in Asia, Africa, and Europe, in the past and recently, and shows how such life-threatening states require shamanic or ritual exorcism. She distinguishes these states from spirit possession, which is often religious and beneficial, and from multiple and shamanic states. Goodman, who is a medical anthropologist trained also in neuroscience, along with Ralph B. Allison, a psychiatrist who specializes in multiple personality disorders (MPD) and possession states, and others, makes an appeal for the recovery of ritual exorcism for the treatment of intractable "evil" alters in MPD and in demonic possession.

[42] Gill, "North American Shamanism," p. 216

[43] Such a positive effect of seeing an image of the destroyed pathogenic object has been demonstrated by the Simontons, for example, to be therapeutically beneficial in the treatment of cancer patients. Cf. O. Carl Simonton, M.D., and Stephanie Matthews-Simonton, with James Creighton, *Getting Well Again: A Step-By-Step, Self-Help Guide to Overcoming Cancer of Patients and Their Families* (Los Angeles: J. P. Tarcher, Inc., 1978), p. 268

[44] Hultkrantz, "Health, Religion, and Medicine", p. 342

[45] Hultkrantz, "Health, Religion, and Medicine", p. 343

[46] *Diagnostic and Statistical Manual of Mental Disorders–Fourth Edition* (Washington, DC: The American Psychiatric Association), p. 848

[47] Hultkrantz, "Health, Religion, and Medicine", p. 343

[48] Ibid., p. 346–347

[49] Gill, "North American Shamanism," p. 217

CHAPTER TWO. TECHNICIAN OF THE SACRED

[1] Rudolf Otto, *The Idea of the Holy* (London: Oxford University Press, 1976), p. 28

[2] Ibid., p. 33

[3] Ibid., p. 34

[4] Genesis 28:17

[5] Otto, *The Idea of the Holy*, p. 67

[6] Gerhardus Van der Leeuw, *Religion in Essence and Manifestation* (Princeton: Princeton University Press, Bollingen Series, 1986), p. 23

[7] Ibid., pp. 24–25

[8] Ibid., p. 37

[9] Ibid., p. 38

[10] Ibid., p. 60

[11] Ibid., p. 45

[12] Ibid., p. 46. Along these lines, a Cherokee shaman might place a very sick person under taboo, not so much to protect others, but to protect the patient, who is weak and vulnerable to having his soul stolen by "raven mockers" (sorcerers).

[13] Mircea Eliade, *The Sacred and the Profane: The Nature of Religion* (New York: Harcourt, Brace & World, Inc., 1959), p. 12

[14] Ibid., p. 12

[15] See Mircea Eliade, *The Myth of the Eternal Return: Cosmos and History,* translated by Willard R. Trask (Princeton: Princeton University Press, Bollingen Series no. 46, 1954), pp. 5–6: 1. Facts which show us that, for archaic man, reality is a function of the imitation of a celestial archetype. 2. Facts which show us how reality is conferred through participation in the 'symbolism of the Center': cities, temples, houses become real by the fact of being assimilated to the 'center of the world.' 3. Finally, rituals and significant profane gestures which acquire the meaning attributed to them, and materialize that meaning, only because they deliberately repeat such and such acts posited *ab origine* by gods, heroes, or ancestors.

[16] Exodus 25:9,40. Also Eliade, *Myth,* p. 7

[17] Ibid., p. 9

[18] Ibid., pp. 10–11

[19] Ibid., p. 18

[20] Eliade, *The Sacred and the Profane,* pp. 99–100

[21] We may appeal to Peter Berger's argument, mentioned previously in this study, that the reasons for this integration lie in the need to keep the forces of chaos at bay, and this is the task of sacred cosmology. Hence, sacred psychotherapeutics becomes a form of "world" maintenance or restoration.

[22] Eliade, *The Sacred and the Profane,* p. 20

[23] Mircea Eliade, *Patterns in Comparative Religion* (New York: Sheed & Ward, 1958), p. 369

[24] Ibid., pp. 369–371

[25] Ibid., p. 369

[26] Robert L. Moore and Frank E. Reynolds, *Anthropology and the Study of Religion* (Chicago: Center for the Scientific Study of Religion, 1984), p. 132

[27] Van Gennep; *The Rites of Passage*

[28] Moore and Reynolds, *Anthropology,* pp. 133–134

[29] Ibid., p. 136

[30] Ibid., p. 136

[31] Ibid., p. 136

[32] Ibid., p. 136

[33] Ibid., p. 137

[34] C. G. Jung used the terms *container* and alchemical *vessel* to suggest the strong boundaries needed for deep psychological transformation; cf. Jung, CW 10, pars. 253, 255

[35] Moore and Reynolds, *Anthropology,* p. 139

CHAPTER THREE. JUNG THE WOUNDED HEALER

[1] C. G. Jung, *Memories, Dreams, Reflections.* Aniela Jaffé, editor (New York: Pantheon Books, 1973). Hereafter we shall refer to this autobiographical writing as MDR.

[2] Anthony Stevens, *On Jung: A New Authoritative Introduction to Jung's Life and Thought* (London: Penguin Books, 1990) pp. 102–103. All subsequent references to Stevens in this chapter will be to this book, indicated as *On Jung,* throughout the text.

[3] Sigmund Freud, *The Interpretation of Dreams,* in *The Standard Edition of the Collected Works of Sigmund Freud* (London: The Hogarth Press, 1900).

[4] Stevens, *On Jung,* pp. 160–161

[5] Stevens suggests that Toni reminded Jung of the maid that took care of Jung when his mother was hospitalized. If this is true, it probably meant that Jung felt a certain cohesion of personality in response to

Toni's loving care of him. See *On Jung,* pp. 171–174, for Stevens' discussion of Toni's psychological importance to Jung during this time of crisis.

⁶ Stevens, *On Jung,* p. 172

CHAPTER FOUR. JUNG'S THEORY OF THE SOUL

¹ James Hillman, *Re-Visioning Psychology* (New York: Harper Colophon Books, 1975), p. 20, and pp. 30–38

² MDR, pp. 158–159

³ MDR, pp. 161

⁴ Barbara Hannah, *Jung: His Life and Work* (New York: G. P. Putnam & Sons, 1976) pp. 16–17. Hannah was a close friend and analysand of Jung. She studied under Jung, attending his lecture in Zurich, and later shared a home with Jung's right-hand assistant, Marie Louise von Franz.

⁵ Jung, CW, p. 133

⁶ See Stevens, *On Jung,* pp. 36–37, for a discussion of the applicability of natural selection to the archetypal theory.

⁷ St. Augustine and St. Thomas Aquinas believed that the forms existed as thoughts in the mind of God, hence their numinous quality as reflections of the divine life. Paul Tillich likewise equated the essences as forms created in the divine life "above" existence, and he believed Jung's archetypes to be among those essential structures. For my extended discussion of archetypes and eternal objects in the thought of C. G. Jung and Alfred North Whitehead, see my *Psychotherapy and the Sacred: Religious Experience and Religious Resources in Psychotherapy* (Chicago: Center for the Scientific Study of Religion Press, 1995).

⁸ Jolande Jacobi, *Complex, Archetype, Symbol in the Psychology of C. G. Jung* (Princeton: Bollingen Series, 1959), p. 49. Jacobi quotes Jung on this point and cites the German article "Uber den Archetypus" (1936), p. 264. She notes that this passage is not found in Jung, CW.

⁹ Jung, CW 5, p. 268

¹⁰ Jung, CW 9i, p. 173

¹¹ We do not mean to minimize the importance of female puberty rites. The girl must be transformed into a woman. Traditionally, and cross-culturally, female archetypal patterns have been determined largely by patriarchal power structures, leaving fewer archetypal patterns accessible to females. Feminist critics today have much to say about puberty rites which switch on archetypal patterns of mother and

wife and which limit female transformation to roles desired by men. It should be mentioned, however, that females do have access, today at least, to many of the archetypal patterns once designated as masculine. There is both current and historical precedent for believing that women can access the archetypes of warrior, hunter, trickster, and other archetypes once considered masculine. Our discussion here, however, follows Jung and Eliade and other anthropologists and psychologists whose focus on masculine gender for their examples is now believed to be unfair and outdated.

[12] Jung; CW 11, par. 6

[13] Jung; CW 17, p 8

[14] Otto, *The Idea of the Holy*

[15] Doore, "Ancient Wisdom," p. 4

[16] Jung, CW 13, par. 75; CW 8, par. 618

[17] MDR, p. 3

[18] Jung, CW 9i, p 275

[19] Jung, CW 7, par. 266

[20] Jung, CW 9i, pp. 122ff

[21] Jung, CW, ii, par. 509

[22] The terminology used to describe the hero pattern is borrowed from Joseph Campbell, who, influenced by Jung in his studies into comparative mythology, speaks of the archetypal hero journey as consisting of the three stages of separation, initiation, and return (with the boon). Cf. Joseph Campbell, *Myths to Live By* (New York: Bantam Books, 1970), p. 209

[23] Jung, CW 11, par. 391

[24] Cf. Jung's discussion of the archetypal Self as "source of order", Jung, CW 10, par. 805; as "organizer of personality," Jung, CW 10, par. 694; as "regulator", Jung, CW 13, par. 18; and as source of meaning, Jung, CW 10, par. 488–588

[25] Jung, CW 12, par. 44

[26] C. G. Jung, ed., *Man and His Symbols* (London: Aldus Books, 1964), p. 161

[27] Jung, CW 11, par. 59

[28] MDR, pp. 48, 57

[29] Jung, CW 8, p. 557

[30] Jung, CW 18, p. 73

[31] Jung, CW 2, pp. 601–602

[32] Jung, CW 2, pp. 1–92

[33] C. Jess Groesbeck, M.D., "Multiple Personality Disorder and C. G. Jung", an audio cassette tape.

[34] Jung, CW 8, p. 121

³⁵ Jung, CW 2, pp. 601–602

³⁶ Jung, CW 2, p. 602, par. 354

³⁷ C. G. Jung, editor, *Man and His Symbols* (Garden City, New York: Doubleday & Company, Inc., 1964), p. 161

³⁸ Lucien Lévy-Bruhl, *How Natives Think*, Lilian A. Clare, trans. (Princeton: Princeton University Press, 1985), pp. 69–104

³⁹ John R. Haule, Ph.D., Jungian Analyst (Zurich), made this observation to me during an ongoing correspondence concerning shamanism, Jungian psychology, and the New Age spirit phenomena. A number of the insights in this discussion about the reality of spirits crystalized through these conversations. Mr. Haule is an innovator in the interfacing of shamanic and Jungian theory and experience. His forthcoming book *Downloading Wisdom: Spirit, Dream, and Transcendence in the New Age* contains many illuminating and clarifying discussions on shamanic and related spirit phenomena. It is highly recommended. Also his book *Pilgrimage of the Heart: The Path of Romantic Love* (Boston: Shambala Books, 1992) is valuable in discussing the relation between psyches, the Self-Self relation in accounting for shamanic seeing, a la Castaneda. Citing the way lovers can see into each other's souls and citing the existence of shamanic societies like that which exists amongst the !Kung tribe, Haule argues that the ability to tune into another person's psyche telepathically and see is a universal psychological potential, which can be developed.

⁴⁰ Jung is anything but clear and consistent in talking of God's reality, sometimes sounding like he's talking about a god-image, or an archetype, and at other times an objective, although subjectively experienced, divine reality. He has suggested that the locus of God, or a divine reality, would be archetypal Self, both in its all-embracing totality of the psyche, and in its guiding and directing functions as *spiritus rector*.

⁴¹ See Haule, *Pilgrimage*, pp. 50–61

⁴² Ibid., p. 54

⁴³ Ibid., p. 55

CHAPTER FIVE. JUNG'S INTERPRETATION OF SHAMANISM

¹ Jung, CW 10, pars. 21–22

² Jung, CW par. 2

³ Jung, CW 10, par. 2

⁴ Jung, CW 10, par. 22

⁵ Jung, CW 13, par. 132. Jung points out that this corresponds to Eliade's observation in *Shamanism,* p. 52

⁶ Jung, CW 13, par. 126

⁷ Jung, CW 13, 340

⁸ Jung, CW 13, par. 462; of Eliade; *Shamanism,* p. 293

⁹ Jung, CW 13, par. 462

¹⁰ Jung, CW 9i, par. 115, footnote 38

¹¹ Jung, CW 13, par. 399

¹² Jung, CW 13, par. 460

¹³ Jung, CW 11, par. 448

¹⁴ Jung, CW 5, par. 251

¹⁵ Jung, CW 11, par. 346, footnote. The brackets in this quote are mine, to emphasize that Jung's use of "medicine men" would include medicine women if rephrased today.

¹⁶ Jung, CW 11, par. 411

¹⁷ Jung, CW 11, par. 411

¹⁸ Jung, CW 11, par. 448

¹⁹ Jung, CW 9i, par. 457

²⁰ I wish to acknowledge my indebtedness, for this understanding of the shaman as epistemological mediator, to anthropologist Mary Schmidt; see her essay "Crazy Wisdom: The Shaman as Mediator of Realities", in Nichols, *Shamanism,* pp. 62–75

²¹ Jung, CW 9i, par. 457

²² Jung, CW 9i, par. 213

²³ Jung, CW 9i, par. 213

²⁴ Jung, CW 6, par. 384

²⁵ Jung, CW 6, par. 384

²⁶ Jung, CW par. 384

²⁷ Jung, CW 9i, par. 213

²⁸ Jung, CW 14, par. 602

²⁹ Jung, CW 16, pars. 214–215

³⁰ Jung, CW 14, par. 603

³¹ Jung, CW 16, pars. 215–215

CHAPTER SIX. DISSOCIATION, POSSESSION, AND SOUL LOSS

¹ Ernst Hilgard, *Divided Consciousness: Multiple Controls in Human Thought and Action* (New York: Wiley & Sons, 1977).

² *Diagnostic and Statistical Manual of Mental Disorders–Fourth Edition,* p. 477

³ Ralph B. Allison, *Minds in Many Pieces* (New York: Rawsom & Wade, 1980).

⁴ Colin Ross, *Multiple Personality Disorder: Diagnosis, Clinical Features, and Treatment* (New York: John Wiley & Sons, 1989), pp. 204–246

⁵ Ibid., pp. 268–273

⁶ Ibid., p. 111

⁷ Cf. Kakar, *Shamans, Mystics, and Doctors.* Kakar describes throughout the section on shamans how ancestral spirits are the most prominent possessing entities in Indian subcultures. He also argues that dissociation is the most widespread psychotherapeutic technique in the world, especially for dealing with possession disorders (p. 105)

⁸ Achterberg, *Imagery in Healing*, pp. 108–111

⁹ Ross, *Multiple Personality Disorder*, p. 16

¹⁰ Ibid., p. 259

¹¹ Ibid., p. 269

¹² Ibid., p. 272

¹³ Sandra Ingerman, *Soul Retrieval: Mending the Fragmented Self* (San Francisco, Harper San Francisco, 1991), p. 221

¹⁴ Hultkrantz, "Health, Religion, and Medicine," p. 342

¹⁵ Ibid., p. 342–343

¹⁶ Ingerman, *Soul Retrieval*, pp. 68–69

¹⁷ Ibid., p. 71

¹⁸ Hilgard, *Divided Consciousness*, p. 1

¹⁹ Robert L. Moore and Douglas Gillette, *The Magician Within: Accessing the Shaman in the Male Psyche* (New York: William Morrow and Co., 1993), p. 34

²⁰ There are even spontaneous retrievals, according to Ingerman.

²¹ I am indebted to Geoffry Satinover for his interpretation of the relation between clusters of alters and archetypes, given in a discussion at the C. G. Jung Insititute of Chicago, February 19, 20, 1994. Tapes of this workshop on neural network theory and dissociation in Jungian perspective are available through the Insititute.

²² Goodman, *How About Demons?* pp. 79–86

²³ Kakar, *Shamans, Mystics, and Doctors*, pp. 22–52

²⁴ Feminist critics might observe that for such a woman her illness is more a sane response to an insane world than it is an actual sickness as defined by a patriarchal diagnostic system. Be that as it may, the woman's suffering is real, and her culture, like all cultures, gives rise to a therapeutic remedy for the illness caused by the contradictions engendered by the culture itself. Our point in this example is to show how a demonological idiom is employed within a culture or subculture

to shape the symptomatology—in this case, to culturally shape dissociated contents into a demon.

²⁵ Kakar, *Shamans, Mystics, and Doctors,* p. 105–106

²⁶ Thomas B. Allen, *Possessed: The True Story of an Exorcism* (New
York, Doubleday, 1993), p. 259

²⁷ Goodman, *How About Demons?* pp. 107–122

²⁸ Ibid., p. 85

²⁹ Cited ibid., pp. 85–86. For a fuller discussion of Allison's
approach, see Ralph B. Allison, *Minds in Many Pieces,* (New York: Raw-
son Wade, 1980) and "The Possession Syndrome: Myth, Magic, and
Multiplicity," paper presented to the Second Pacific Conference of Psychiatry, Manila, Phillipines, 12–15 May, 1989

³⁰ Goodman, *How About Demons?* p. 84

³¹ Goodman herself has written a couple of books documenting
and reflecting upon these more serious cases. Felicitas Goodman, *The
Exorcism of Anneliese Michel* (New York: Doubleday, 1981), discusses the
relatively recent case of Anneliese Michel, the young German university
student who died during a Catholic ritual exorcism. She discusses several cases of possession in *How About Demons?* and gives a detailed
account of the successful exorcism of Anna Maria of Uz in the 17th century by the shaman Jacob Durr.

³² Kakar, Obeysekere, Kleinman

³³ Jung, CW 6, par. 384

CHAPTER SEVEN. THE POWER OF RITUAL, IMAGE, AND ARCHETYPE

¹ Robert Moore, Douglas Gillette, *King, Warrior, Magician, and
Lover: Rediscovering the Archetypes of the Mature Masculine,* (New York:
HarperCollins, 1990).

² See Robert L. Moore and Douglas Gillette, *The King Within:
Accessing the King in the Male Psyche* (New York: William Morrow & Co.,
Inc., 1992), p. 25. Moore and Gillette propose that females can access the
archetypes of the mature feminine (queen, warrior, lover, and magician).
However, there is no extensive treatment of how these archetypes function in female maturity. Certainly there are classical mythologic images of
woman as ruler and principle of order: queen (Hera), warrior (Athena),
magician (Persephone as psychopomp), and lover (Aphrodite/Venus).
When Moore and Gillette note that puberty rites are part of tribal cultures with their "limitations" and "drawbacks", it appears that they are
cognizant of patriarchal assumptions in defining what the ideals and

norms of mature masculine and feminine behaviors are (p. 25). In spite of these "limitations" and "drawbacks", Moore and Gillette believe that puberty rituals did provide a means of transformation for girls into mature women and boys into mature men, as defined by the gender-specific norms and ideals of the local culture. For a balanced contemporary resource by gender-sensitive psychologists, analysts, and anthropologists on initiation rites for males and females, see Louise Madhi, Steven Foster, and Meredith Little, eds., *Betwixt and Between: Patterns of Initiation* (Lasalle, Ill.: Open Court Publishing Co., 1986), pp. 201–284

[3] See Robert L. Moore's discussion of Victor Turner's work on transformative ritual, and his own discussion of liminality and sacred space-time, in Robert L. Moore and Frank E. Reynolds, eds., *Anthropology and the Study of Religion* (Chicago: Center for the Scientific Study of Religion Press, 1984), pp. 126–142

[4] Cited in Anthony Stevens, *Archetypes: A Natural History of the Self* (New York: Quill, 1982), p. 262

[5] Achterberg, *Imagery in Healing*, p. 5

[6] Ibid., p. 5

[7] Simonton, Matthews-Simonton, and Creighton, *Getting Well Again*

[8] Michael Harner, editor, *The Way of the Shaman* (New York: Bantam Books, 1982), pp. 137–138

[9] Simonton, Matthews-Simonton, and Creighton, *Getting Well Again*, p. 268

[10] Paul Watzlawick, *The Language of Change: Elements of Therapeutic Communcation* (New York: Basic Books, 1978), p. 43

[11] Cited ibid., p. 43

[12] Paul Ricoeur, *History and Truth* (Evanston: Northwestern University Press, 1966), p. 127

[13] Kakar, *Shamans, Mystics, and Doctors*, pp. 20–24

[14] We can not take the time to comment upon the culturally determined problem of the father marrying off the daughter, possibly without even consulting her wishes. In Western society today, most psychotherapists would consider this also an abusive and patriarchal move, where the daughter is penalized instead of the perpetrator (potential perpetrator in this case). However, in this cultural context, the healer's intervention would be considered legitimate and helpful. Only a careful follow-up study could determine if it was helpful or further damaging.

[15] C. Michael Smith, *Psychotherapy and the Sacred: Religious Experience and Religious Resources in Psychotherapy* (Chicago: Center for the Scientific Study of Religion Press, 1995). The events of this shamanic therapy were

reported to me by Prince Forolungsha Ogundele, of the Yoruba Tribe, Nigeria, in an interview at the University of Chicago, 1988. Ogundele reported that his grandfather was the shaman. Ogundele said the patient was psychotic by Western standards, rather than possessed. Ogundele has been trained in Western psychology and sociology.

[16] Stevens, *Archetypes,* p. 262

[17] Ibid., p. 266

[18] Ibid., p. 266

[19] J. P. Henry and P. M. Stephens, *Stress, Health, and the Social Environment: A Sociobiological Approach to Medicine* (New York: Springer-Verlag, 1977), p. 111

[20] Stevens, *Archetypes,* p. 269

[21] Cited ibid., p. 270

[22] Jung, CW 16, par. 330

[23] Again, we should note that Moore and Gillette are careful to emphasize that females also have and can access the archetypes of the masculine, especially through the Jungian animus, as men can access the archetypes of the feminine through the Jungian anima. Anima and animus are the contrasexual archetypal structures, both of which reside in men and women. This is the basis for Moore and Gillette's belief that women access the king, although the queen will be primary for most women, and men access the queen, although the king will be primary for most men. Women therefore also can access the magician and all the other archetypes. In fact, according to Eliade, the feminine is powerful to the shaman, and women are often considered more powerful shamans. This is purportedly why male shamans sometimes wear dresses. This suggests that women can access the magician archetype in its highest expression.

[24] Moore and Gillette: *King, Warrior, Magician, Lover,* pp. xv-xix

[25] Moore and Gillette, *The King Within,* p. 269

[26] Moore and Gillette, *King, Warrior, Magician, Lover,* p. 270

[27] Ibid., p. 271

[28] Ibid., p. 98

[29] Ibid., p. 102

CHAPTER EIGHT. IMPLICATIONS FOR THE FUTURE

[1] *The Shamanic Applications Review* is a journal which interfaces shamanism and psychotherapy, and also shamanism and other modern health care disciplines, and also seeks to interface findings and insights from neuroscience, clinical hypnosis, dissociation theory, theology, and

philosophy. For further information: SAR, P.O. Box 0314, Niles, MI 49120

² Colin A. Ross, M.D., *Multiple Personality Disorder: Diagnosis, Clinical Features, and Treatment* (New York: Wiley & Sons, 1989), pp. 268–269. Ross is one of the world's foremost psychiatric specialists/ researchers in multiple personality disorders. He states that he has a number of shamanic amulets, medicine bundles, and shamanic power objects in his office, and that treatment of MPD often becomes a prolonged spiritual ritual. He argues that because MPD patients are continuously in altered states, their thought patterns are magical, suggestible, and can be influenced by shamanic-type interventions and suggestions.

³ Kakar, *Shamans, Mystics, and Doctors,* p. 5

⁴ Jung, CW 11, par. 9

⁵ This is a quote from a conversation recorded on the film/video *The Wisdom of the Dream: C. G. Jung, a Steven Segallier Film,* vol. 2 (Segallier Films, 1989)

⁶ Ibid., conversation with Jungian analyst Donald Sandner, on the Navajo system of myth and healing.

⁷ Ibid.

⁸ MDR, p. 252

Selected Bibliography

Achterberg, Jeanne, *Imagery in Healing: Shamanism and Modern Medicine* (Boston: Shambala Publications, Inc., 1985).

Berger, Peter L., *The Sacred Canopy: Elements of a Sociological Theory of Religion* (New York: Doubleday & Co., 1969).

Berger, Peter L. and Luckmann, Thomas, *The Social Construction of Reality: A Treatise in the Sociology of Knowledge* (New York: Anchor Books, 1967).

Bergin, Allen E. and Jansen, J.P., "Religiosity of Psychotherapists: A National Survey," *Psychotherapy*, Vol. 27, No. 1, 1990, pp. 3–7.

Bergin, Allen E., "Values and Religious Issues in Psychotherapy and Mental Health," *American Psychologist*, Vol. 46, No. 4, pp. 394–403.

Boisen, Anton, *The Exploration of the Inner World: A Study of Mental Health Disorder and Religious Experience* (Philadelphia: University of Pennsylvania Press, 1936).

Brennan, Barbara Ann, *Hands of Light: A Guide to Healing Through the Human Energy Field* (New York: Bantam Books, 1988)

Brown, Daniel and Fass, Margot L., *Creative Mastery in Hypnosis: A Festschrift for Erika Fromm* (Hillsdale, NJ: Lawrence Erlbaum Associates, Inc., 1990).

Brown, Daniel P. and Fromm, Erika, *Hypnotherapy and Hypnoanalysis* (London: Lawrence Erlbaum Associates Publishers, 1986).

Campbell, Joseph, "Schizophrenia: The Inward Journey", in *Consciousness: Brain States of Awareness and Mysticism*, Daniel Goleman and Richard J. Davidson, editors (New York: Harper & Row, 1979).

Castaneda, Carlos, *Tales of Power* (New York: Rocket Books, 1974).

Csordas, Thomas, "Medical and Sacred Realities: Between Comparative Religion and Psychiatry," *Journal of Culture, Medicine, and Psychiatry*, Vol. 9, 1985.

DeKorne, Jim, *Psychedelic Shamanism: The Cultivation, Preparation and Shamanic Use of Psychotropic Plants* (Port Townsend, WA: Loompanics Unlimited, 1994).

Doore, Gary, editor, *What Survives? Contemporary Explorations of Life After Death* (New York: G. P. Putnam & Sons, 1990).

Durkheim, Emile, *The Elementary Forms of Religious Life*, Joseph Ward Swain, translator (New York: Free Press, 1915).

Drury, Nevill, *The Elements of Shamanism* (Dorset: Element Books, Ltd., 1989).

Eigen, Michael, *The Psychotic Core* (London: Jason Aronson, 1986).

Eliade, Mircea, *Le Sacré et le Profane* (Paris: Editions Gallimard, 1965).

—— *The Myth of the Eternal Return; or, Cosmos and History* (Princeton: Princeton University Press, Bollingen Series XLVI, 1959).

—— *Images and Symbols: Studies in Religious Symbolism* (New York: Sheed & Ward, 1969).

—— *Patterns in Comparative Religion* (New York: Sheed & Ward, 1958).

—— *Shamanism: Archaic Techniques of Ecstasy* (Princeton: Princeton University Press, Bollingen Series LXXVI, 1964).

Ellenberger, Henri F., *The Discovery of the Unconscious: The History and Evolution of Dynamic Psychiatry* (New York: Harper & Row, 1970).

Foucault, Michel, *Madness and Civilization: A History of Insanity in the Age of Reason* (New York: Random House, 1965).

Frank, Jerome, *Persuasion and Healing* (New York: Schocken Books, 1969).

Freud, Sigmund, *The Major Works of Sigmund Freud*, Vol. 54, Great Books Series (Chicago: Encyclopedia Brittanica, Inc., 1947).

Geertz, Clifford, *The Interpretation of Cultures* (New York: Harper Torch-books, 1973).

Goodman, Felicitas D., *Ecstasy, Ritual, and Alternate Reality: Religion in a Pluralistic World* (Bloomington: Indiana University Press, 1988).

—— *How About Demons? Possession and Exorcism in the Modern World* (Bloomington: Indiana University Press, 1986).

Grant, Brian, *Schizophrenia: A Source of Social Insight* (Philadelphia: Westminster Press, 1975).

Griffin, David Ray, editor, *God and Religion in the Postmodern World: Essays in Postmodern Theology* (New York: State University of New York Press, 1989).

Griffin, David Ray, editor, *Archetypal Process: Self and Divine in White-head, Jung, and Hillman* (Evanston, IL: Northwestern University Press, 1989).

Grof, Stanislav, *Beyond the Brain: Birth, Death, and Transcendence in Psy-chotherapy* (Albany: State University of New York Press, 1985).

Grof, Stanislav and Grof, Christina, editors, *Spiritual Emergency: When Personal Transformation Becomes a Crisis* (New York: G. P. Putnam and Sons, 1989).

Hannah, Barbara, *Jung: His Life and Work* (New York: G. P. Putnam & Sons, 1976).

Harner, Michael, editor, *Hallucinogens and Shamanism* (London: Oxford University Press, 1973).

—— *The Way of the Shaman* (New York: Bantam Books, 1982).

Haule, John R., *Pilgrimage of the Heart: The Path of Romantic Love* (Boston: Shambala Books, 1992).

Hick, John, *God Has Many Names* (Philadelphia: Westminster Press, 1982).

Hillman, James, *Re-Visioning Psychology* (New York: Harper Colophon Books, 1975).

Hughes-Calero, Heather, *Shaman of Tibet: Milarepa–from Anger to Enlightenment* (Sedona, AZ: Higher Consciousness Books, 1987).

Ingerman, Sandra, *Soul Retrieval: Mending the Fragmented Self* (San Francisco: Harper San Francisco, 1991).

—— *Welcome Home: Life After Healing, Following Your Soul's Journey Home* (San Francisco: Harper San Francisco, 1993).

Jaffé, Aniela, *The Myth of Meaning: Jung and the Expansion of Consciousness* (New York: Penguin Books, 1975).

James, William, *The Varieties of Religious Experience* (New York: Bantam Books, 1950).

Jung, C. G., *Memories, Dreams, Reflections,* revised edition, Aniela Jaffé, editor (New York: Pantheon Books, 1962).

—— *Symbols of Transformation: An Analysis of the Prelude to a Case of Schizophrenia,* Vol. 5, *Collected Works,* 2nd edition; Sir Herbert Read, Michael Fordham, Gerhard Adler, editors; William McGuire, executive editor; R. F. C. Hull, translator (Princeton: Princeton University Press, Bollingen series 20, 1967).

—— *Two Essays on Analytical Psychology,* Vol. 7, *Collected Works,* 2nd edition (Princeton: Princeton University Press, 1972).

—— *The Structure and Dynamics of the Psyche,* Vol. 8, *Collected Works,* 2nd edition (Princeton: Princeton University Press, 1969).

—— *The Archetypes of the Collective Unconscious,* Vol. 9i, *Collected Works,* 2nd edition (Princeton: Princeton University Press, 1968).

—— *Aion: Researches into the Phenomenology of the Self,* Vol. 9ii, *Collected Works,* 2nd edition (Princeton: Princeton University Press, 1968).

—— *Psychology and Religion: East and West,* Vol. 11, *Collected Works,* 2nd edition (Princeton: Princeton University Press, 1968).

—— *The Practice of Psychotherapy: Essays on the Psychology of the Transference and Other Subjects,* Vol. 16, *Collected Works,* 2nd edition (Princeton: Princeton University Press, 1966).

—— *The Symbolic Life,* Vol. 16, *Collected Works,* 2nd edition (Princeton: Princeton University Press, 1976).

—— *Briefe,* Aniela Jaffé and Gerhard Adler, editors, 3 Vols. (Olten, Switzerland: Walter-Verlag, 1971).

—— *The Inner World: A Psycho-Analytic Study of Childhood and Society in India,* 2nd edition (Dehli: Oxford University Press, 1981).

—— *Intimate Relations: Exploring Indian Sexuality* (Chicago: University of Chicago Press, 1990).

Kalwait, Holger, *Shamans, Healers, and Medicine Men* (Boston: Shambala, 1992).

Keller, Catherine, *From a Broken Web: Separation, Sexism, and Self* (Boston: Beacon Press, 1986).

King, Noel Q., *African Cosmos: An Introduction to Religion in Africa* (Belmont, CA: Wadsworth Publishing Co., 1986).

King, Serge Kahili, *Urban Shaman, A Handbook for Personal and Planetary Transformation Based on the Hawaiian Way of the Adventurer* (New York: Fireside, 1990).

Kleinman, Arthur and Good, Byron, *Culture and Depression: Studies in Anthropology and Cross-Cultural Psychiatry of Affect Disorder* (Berkeley: University of California Press, 1985).

—— *Patients and Healers in the Context of Culture: An Exploration of the Borderland Between Anthropology, Medicine, and Psychiatry* (Berkeley: University of California Press, 1980).

Kohut, Heinz, *Self Psychology and the Humanities: Reflection on a New Psychoanalytic Approach* (New York: W. W. Norton & Co., 1985).

Kubler-Ross, Elizabeth, *On Life After Death* (Berkeley: Celestial Arts, 1995).

Lacan, Jacques, *Ecrits: A Selection,* Alan Sheridan, translator (New York: W. W. Norton & Co., 1977).

Laing, R.D., *The Voice of Experience* (New York: Pantheon Books, 1982).

Lévi-Strauss, Claude, *Structural Anthropology* (New York: Harper Torchbooks, 1983).

Lévy-Bruhl, Lucien, *How Natives Think*, Lilian Clare, translator (Princeton: Princeton University Press, 1985).

Marino, Adrian, *L'Hermeneutic de Mircea Eliade* (Paris: Gallimard, 1981).

Meland, Bernard, *Faith and Culture* (London: George Allen and Unwin Ltd., 1955).

—— *The Realities of Faith* (London: Oxford University Press, 1962).

Moore, Robert L., "Ritual Process, Initiation, and Contemporary Religion", in Murray Stein and Robert L. Moore, editors, *Jung's Challenge to Contemporary Religion* (Wilmette, IL: Chiron Publications, 1987).

—— *King, Warrior, Magician, and Lover: Rediscovering the Archetypes of the Mature Masculine* (New York: HarperCollins, 1990).

Moore, Robert L. and Gillette, Douglas, *The King Within: Accessing the King in the Male Psyche* (New York: William Morrow and Co., 1992).

—— *The Magician Within: Accessing the Shaman in the Male Psyche* (New York: William Morrow and Co., 1993).

Moore, Robert L. and Reynolds, Frank E., *Anthropology and the Study of Religion* (Chicago: Center for the Scientific Study of Religion, 1984).

Moore, Thomas, *The Care of the Soul: A Guide for Cultivating Depth and Sacredness in Everyday Life* (New York: Harper Collins Publishers, 1992).

Nicholson, Shirley, editor, *Shamanism: An Expanded View of Reality* (Wheaton, IL: Theosophical Publishing House, 1987).

Noble, Kathleen, "Psychological Health and the Experience of Transcendence", *The Counseling Psychologist*, Vol. 15, No. 4, October 1987.

Obeyesekere, Gannath, *Medusa's Hair: An Essay on Personal Symbols and Religious Experience* (Chicago: University of Chicago Press, 1981).

Perry, John Weir, "Psychosis as a Visionary State," in Ian F. Baker, editor,

Methods of Treatment in Analytical Psychology (Verlag: Adolf Bonz Publishers, 1980).

—— *The Far Side of Madness* (Englewood, NJ: Prentice-Hall, Inc., 1974).

—— *The Self in Psychotic Process: Its Symbolization in Schizophrenia* (Dallas: Spring Publications, 1953).

Putnam, Frank W., *Diagnosis and Treatment of Multiple Personality Disorder* (New York: The Guilford Press, 1989).

Ricoeur, Paul, *The Symbolism of Evil,* Emerson Buchanan, translator (New York: Harper & Row, 1967).

Ring, Kenneth, *Heading Toward Omega: In Search of the Meaning of the Near Death Experience* (New York: William Morrow, 1985).

Ross, Colin A., *Multiple Personality Disorder: Diagnosis, Clinical Features, and Treatment* (New York: John Wiley & Sons, 1989).

Russel, Robbins Hope, *The Encyclopedia of Witchcraft and Demonology* (New York: Crown Publishers, 1959).

Otto, Rudolf, *The Idea of the Holy* (London: Oxford University Press, 1976).

Samuels, Andrew, Shorter, Bani, and Plaut, Fred, *A Critical Dictionary of Jungian Analysis* (London: Routledge & Kegan Paul, 1985).

Sanchez, Victor, *The Teaching of Don Carlos: Practical Applications of the Works of Carlos Castaneda* (Santa Fe, NM: Bear & Co., 1995).

Sandner, Donald F. and Beebem, John, "Psychopathology and Analysis," in Murray Stein, editor, *Jungian Analysis* (Boulder: Shambala Publications, Inc., 1982).

Schultz, Duane, *A History of Modern Psychology,* 3rd edition (New York: Academic Press, 1981).

Schroeder, W. Widick, *Cognitive Structures and Religious Research: Essays in Sociology and Theology* (East Lansing: Michigan State University Press, 1970).

Smith, C. Michael, *Psychotherapy and the Sacred: Religious Experience and Religious Resources in Psychotherapy* (Chicago: Center for the Scientific Study of Religion Press, 1995).

Snyder, Solomon H., *Drugs and the Brain* (New York: Scientific American Library, 1986).

Spiegelberg, Herbert, *Phenomenology in Psychology and Psychiatry* (Evanston, IL: Northwestern University Press, 1972).

Star Hawk Lake, Tela, *Hawk Woman Dancing with the Moon: The Last Female Shaman* (New York: M. Evans & Company, Inc.).

Stein, Murray, *Jung's Treatment of Christianity: The Psychotherapy of a Religious Tradition* (Wilmette, IL: Chiron Publications, 1985).

Stevens, Anthony, *Archetypes: A Natural History of the Self* (New York: Quill, 1982).

—— *On Jung* (London: Penguin Group, 1990).

—— *The Two Million Year Old Self* (College Station, TX: Texas A & M University Press, 1993).

Stigler, James, Shweder, Richard A., and Herdt, Gilbert, editors, *Cultural Psychology: Essays on Comparative Human Development* (Cambridge: Cambridge University Press, 1990).

Sullivan, Lawrence E., editor, *Healing and Restoring: Health and Medicine in the World's Religious Traditions* (New York: Macmillan Publishing Co., 1990).

Tillich, Paul, *The Dynamics of Faith* (New York: Harper Torchbooks, 1957).

—— *The Meaning of Health*, Perry Lefevre, editor (Chicago: Exploration Press, 1984).

Turner, Victor, *On the Edge of the Bush: Anthropology as Experience* (Tuscon: University of Arizona Press, 1985).

—— *The Ritual Process: Structure and Anti-Structure* (Ithaca, NY: Cornell University Press, 1969).

Van der Leeuw, Gerhardus, *Religion in Essence and Manifestation* (Princeton: Princeton University Press, 1986).

Van Gennep, Arnold, *Les Rites de Passage* (Paris: E. Nourry, 1908).

Villoldo, Alberto and Jendressen, Erik, *Dance of the Four Winds: Secrets of the Inca Medicine Wheel* (Rochester, VT: Destiny Books, 1990).

—— *Island of the Sun: Mastering the Inca Medicine Wheel* (Rochester, VT: Destiny Books, 1990).

Waya, Ai Guhdi, *Soul Recovery and Extraction* (Cottonwood, AZ: Blue Turtle Publishing Co., 1996).

Wheelwright, Joseph B., *The Analytic Process: Aims, Analysis, Training* (New York: G. P. Putnam & Sons, 1971).

Whitehead, Alfred North, *Adventure of Ideas* (New York: The Free Press, 1961).

—— *Process and Reality: Corrected Edition,* David Ray Griffin and Donald W. Sherburne, editors (New York: The Free Press, 1978).

—— *Religion in the Making* (New York: MacMillan Co., 1925).

—— *Science and the Modern World* (New York: The Free Press, 1953).

—— *Symbolism: Its Meaning and Effect* (New York: Fordham University Press, 1965).

Winnicott, D. W., *Human Nature* (New York: Schocken Books, 1988).

—— *Playing and Reality* (London: Rutledge & Kegan Paul, 1986).

—— *Psychoanalytic Explorations,* Clare Winnicott, Ray Shepherd, and Madeline Davis, editors (Cambridge: Harvard University Press, 1989).

Winquist, Charles E., *Homecoming: Interpretation, Transformation, and Individuation* (Chicago: Scholars Press, 1978).

Wolf, Fred Alan, *The Eagle's Quest: A Physicist Finds Scientific Truth and the Heart of the Shamanic World* (New York: Simon and Schuster, 1991).